PAPAGENO

Emanuel Schikaneder.
After a copper engraving
by Philipp Richter.

KURT HONOLKA

PAPAGENO

EMANUEL SCHIKANEDER
Man of the Theater in Mozart's Time

Translated by Jane Mary Wilde
Reinhard G. Pauly, General Editor

AMADEUS PRESS
Portland, Oregon

ISBN 0-931340-21-7

Amadeus Press
9999 S.W. Wilshire
Portland, Oregon 97225
Printed in Singapore

Library of Congress Cataloging-in-Publication Data

Honolka, Kurt, 1913-
    [Papageno. English]
    Papageno : Emanuel Schikaneder, man of the theater in Mozart's
time / Kurt Honolka ; translated by Jane Mary Wilde ; Reinhard G.
Pauly, general editor.
        p.   cm.
    Translation of: Papageno.
    Includes bibliographical references.
    ISBN 0-931340-21-7
    1. Schikaneder, Emanuel, 1751-1812. 2. Librettists--Austria-
-Biography. 3. Dramatists--Austria--Biography. I. Pauly, Reinhard
G. II. Title.
ML423.S34GH613   1990
782.1'092--dc20
[B]   89-17574
                                                         CIP
                                                         MN

Contents

1 An Unknown Celebrity

His name is familiar to us from the program notes of one of the most widely performed operas. But what do we actually know about this man who, hiding behind the curious name of Schikaneder, had the honor of being Mozart's last librettist? Many know that he wrote the text for *The Magic Flute*, but very few realize that he was not just by chance a successful writer, not merely a dilettante who once in his lifetime had the good fortune of collaborating with a genius on a work that became a great hit. He was a figure in his own right: the author of some one hundred plays, the most successful of which were for decades box-office draws in Viennese and provincial theaters. In addition, as a theater director, producer and actor, he was the uncrowned king of the Viennese popular theater during the time of Mozart and Beethoven.

He was Mozart's close friend, and the first performance of *Fidelio* links him to Beethoven. For years he had urged Beethoven, who was no opera lover, to compose a music drama for the Theater an der Wien. He had commissioned the theater building, an ambitious project that still stands today. After a dazzling era of operetta, from Johann Strauss to Emmerich Kalman, the theater has become the home of the musical, but something of Schikaneder's spirit still lingers, and is compatible with the style of the musical. A complete "man of the theater," Schikaneder's universality and creative fantasy could be compared to Max Reinhardt's; to a certain extent he managed to achieve a thoroughly "modern" form of theater presentation. His Singspiele and comic operas with their two "standard pairs of characters" anticipate the later Viennese operetta, while his extravagant spectaculars point toward the revue and the musical. His predilection for grandiose crowd scenes outside the confines of the theater makes him one of the pioneers of open-air theater, which thrives world-wide today.

Conditions in the commercial theater of his time—there were neither subsidies nor royalties—forced Schikaneder to become a prolific writer, and his talent most certainly suffered as a result of this. A repertoire on which a provincial theater could survive, dependent as it was on the evening's revenue, had few resources at its disposal. The naive public was always on the lookout for something new. Schikaneder, although director, was, as actor, the chief attraction in his theater, and was continually obliged to produce new works off the cuff: opera librettos, magic plays, Singspiele, *Ritterstücke* (knightly pageants), comedies. He always included a part for himself which fit him like a glove, though most of these plays were of only passing interest. But even Goethe, the Privy-Councillor and Schikaneder's colleague, devoted more than two-thirds of the performances at his heavily subsidized court theater in Weimar to trifles by Kotzebue and lesser writers, rather than to the classics. The best of the scenes and characters from Schikaneder's fashionable magic theater point towards Ferdinand Raimund. The social criticism in his realistic local plays, held in check by petty censorship, occasionally remind us (from a critical distance) of Nestroy's more virulent denunciation of Viennese chauvinism.

But it is the part that Schikaneder played as a pioneer of German opera that is of prime importance in theatrical history. He was not only the librettist of *The Magic Flute*, but his own librettos and his launching of key works by others (for example, Wranitzky's *Oberon*) contributed to the advent of the German Singspiel. The well-endowed court theaters had failed in this by sacrificing works like Mozart's *Die Entführung aus dem Serail*, which promised success, for the Italian and French "hits" of the day. Yet Schikaneder, at his own expense, remained faithful to his old love. At times he had six Mozart operas in his repertoire, although he most certainly made less money from them than he would have earned from cheaper routine productions from Kotzebue to Iffland. He was often so daring as to put on performances of Shakespeare, Schiller's *Kabale und Liebe* and *Don Carlos*, and contemporary plays which were not surefire box-office successes. He knew that he was exposing the limitations of his own works, which were after all in competition, but for Schikaneder the "mummer" the great writers offered rewarding parts.

Considering everything, Schikaneder was a great man of the theater, but this was only acknowledged later, and so astonishingly little has been written about him. Authentic sources are scanty. Only a fraction of his vast dramatic output survives and can be verified; otherwise there is practically nothing left written by him—no memoirs and only a few letters. How illuminating a correspondence with Mozart would have been! But from their first meeting in Salzburg and throughout their work together on *The Magic Flute*, they were good friends and lived in such close proximity that any form of written correspondence was unnecessary. As a consequence, Schikaneder's most famous work, *The Magic Flute*, is the origin of most of the misunderstandings about him.

The disparity between the composer and the librettist was obvious: the more Mozart's genius was recognized, the more his unequal partner was disparaged. Goethe's later vindication of Schikaneder achieved little in the face of Otto Jahn's Mozart biography, a pioneer work of the mid-19th century which even denied Schikaneder's authorship of *The Magic Flute*. We have the Viennese music historian Egon Komorzynski to thank for bringing light into the jungle of legends in his, the first comprehensive biography of Schikaneder, published in 1901. His detailed and critical analysis of Schikaneder's character and work led to a re-evaluation of the man in general, but also of the literature concerning Mozart. However, in the revised edition of the work which Komorzynski completed during World War II, his critical and objective attitude softened and tended towards an "apologia." It is understandable that someone intent on making Schikaneder a pioneer and vindicating his honor should feel obliged to go on the offensive. But a new objective biography, making use of the latest research, cannot permit itself such license. It must aim at conveying a realistic, faithful portrait of Schikaneder's vigorous and contradictory personality, eschewing those romantic legends which for almost a century largely belittled him, but also avoiding putting him on a pedestal. For this man, son of a proletarian family from Straubing, who worked his way up from being the director of a minor itinerant troupe to becoming the epoch-making king of Vienna's popular theater, stands out like a late Baroque figure in the landscape of the Enlightenment. This extraordinary man, who squandered his talent by over-writing and other excesses, was and still is a figure of formidable stature, even when presented with all his failings.

He was not a genius who made an impression on his time, but was rather a child of his time. He was able to adapt to its pressures and learn a great deal from what others were doing. This volume seeks to throw light on the backdrop of Schikaneder's life and works: how actors lived then, how much they earned; how Vienna, Schikaneder's adopted home, developed; what the theaters looked like, from the "barns" of the provinces to the sumptuously built Theater an der Wien which was founded by Schikaneder and cast a shadow over both contemporary court theaters.

Because whatever Schikaneder wrote was so closely related to his circumstances, his most important works will be presented within the framework of the biography—critically, perhaps even a little ironically, for the author's point of view can only be a late-20th-century one, and therefore has a long history of skepticism behind it. If the reader feels that affectionate irony or ironic affection have guided this work, the author will not feel himself misunderstood.

There are good reasons why so much space has been devoted to *The Magic Flute*. Apart from the fact that it is the only work of Schikaneder's to have achieved immortality, there are doubts and questions which still haunt *The Magic Flute* literature. Was Schikaneder really the librettist, or could it after all have been Giesecke, a professor of mineralogy? Did Schikaneder and/or Mozart (they collaborated closely) later turn the original plot upside down, creating bad characters out of good, good out of bad? The question may seem rather absurd since Mozart research, especially that done after World War II, has thrown so much light on the obscure origins of the opera. But old legends keep surfacing in new guises. To investigate these thoroughly and objectively, according to the latest research, surely justifies such detailed chapters on *The Magic Flute*.

2 The Players Are Coming!

It was winter, the best time of year for troupes of itinerant players, for it was a time when people enjoyed going to the theater. But on this occasion the theater was in the distant town of Laibach (Ljubljana), where the culture-loving German inhabitants had expressed the desire to see "an excellent company from the Reich," and as just such a company was at present sporting itself on the boards in the neighborhood of Nuremberg, a hard winter journey lay ahead. Emanuel Schikaneder, the director of the group, was 28 years old and still fresh to the experience, but hardship left him undaunted. He was a dashing, adventurous young man, and his nephew Karl, visiting him during that year of 1779, remembered: "he was dressed like a cavalier of the time. He wore silk stockings, shoes with high heels, yellow silk breeches, a yellow silk waistcoat braided with silver, a scarlet coat, a three-cornered hat adorned with white feathers, and a steel dagger at his side."

Schikaneder had just demonstrated his versatile talents as actor, playwright and director in Augsburg and Nuremberg; otherwise he would not have been summoned to Laibach. He was showing his generosity—living beyond his means when he considerably enlarged the company's little ballet group of 14 souls, so that no less than 45 people set off on this winter journey. One of the actors, Jakob Neukäufler, at the time and again later a member of Schikaneder's troupe, has left an account of the ardurous expedition.[1]

Scene at a fair (The Tooth Extraction).
Etching by Franz Anton Maulbertsch, 1785.

As a mummer Neukäufler was of little stature, but as a chronicler
he is a mine of information. Few other sources reveal so much that is
authentic about the time, in particular the practical experiences of
the travelling theater and the living conditions of its actors. We shall
follow Neukäufler's report faithfully.

Until they reached Augsburg, he tells us, most of the 45 people
were crowded together in a single covered wagon. After that they
also hired coaches, but these were of little use; it snowed so hard in
Carinthia that everything had to be laboriously transferred to sleds.

The troupe struggled on through deep snow. Night fell with still
no sign of an inn, not even of a German village, for they were already
deep in the mountains of what today is Yugoslavia. They knocked at
the door of a rectory, but the servant slammed it shut immediately.
"He, Domine Paroche!" (Hey, Lord Host!) shouted an actor, who
had a little Latin, in despair. Finally the priest opened the door; he
spoke German. He was startled by the sight of so many people—
actors too, as it turned out. But the isolated priest was more generous

than many of his contemporaries. He invited the travellers into the rectory, and ordered his servants to fetch a barrel of wine from the cellar and with it four great loaves of bread and bowls of cream soup, eggs and fish. "As his earthenware crock was set before him, each paid immediately for his wine. Herr Schikaneder wanted this, so that no misunderstandings should arise," reports Neukäufler. "After the meal was finished, everyone drank lustily, including Herr Schikaneder, never a spoilsport. We sang choruses and songs from well-known operas, and His Reverence himself sat down and joined us and was very merry."

They slept on beds of straw, and the next day the journey continued. A sirocco had turned the snow into slush, rain poured down, and at the Wurzen Pass the sleds had to be exchanged again for peasants' carts. Most of the company climbed the highest point of the pass on foot. At last, after 14 days of travelling, they arrived at Laibach, exhausted. Yet another mishap: the baggage cart with costumes hadn't arrived! "In the town they had already started murmuring; this is going to be the usual kind of farcical acting riff-raff." But Schikaneder knew what to do; as luck would have it, they found two of the plays they had been studying in the local bookshop: *Inkle and Yariko* and *Winter Quarters in America*. The necessary costumes were obtained by the manservant to the President of the Government, and the performances went ahead, somewhat improvised but still to the satisfaction of the Laibach audiences.

A short time later, during the ballet *Orpheus and Eurydice*, the director's resolute action saved the theater from panic. The Furies appeared wearing burning headgear—Schikaneder had a great weakness for such effects—and audience members screamed, "Their hats are burning!" Many of them began to push towards the exit in fear of the theater going up in flames, but Schikaneder leapt from the wings onto the stage, tore the hat off one of the Furies and showed the public that there was nothing to fear, it was made of metal; whereupon the threatened crowd dissolved into laughter.

All went well in Laibach, but at the beginning of Lent the theaters had to close and the players' salaries were reduced by half. They managed to make ends meet in Klagenfurt in the early summer, and then Schikaneder tried his luck in Linz. "It was better here, because there were more of the aristocracy about, and the military had subscriptions for the performances," but only during the season, and not all the plays were a draw. Once Shakespeare's *Hamlet* was put on: "The lights were lit, the orchestra was ready, but not a soul was in the house." Schikaneder ordered "a roast chicken for each player" to be sent from the White Cross Inn. A table was set up on the stage, the orchestra was ordered to play, and all dined in good spirits. He threw open the theater doors with great ostentation. When the Linz townspeople peered in cautiously, they were given to understand: here's the *Hamlet* that nobody wanted to see! Two days later Schikaneder put on a performance of *The Ship from Regensburg* and the theater was full. "There's an example of public taste for you!" writes Neukäufler.

For a supporting actor such as Neukäufler, who made up most of the troupe, it was a miserable existence. The six to seven florins a week that he was paid guaranteed only a minimal existence, even by lower middle class standards. There was no protection against sickness, no old age pension. Much later, even when he was a mature, experienced actor at the ducal theater in Darmstadt, Neukäufler earned only 40 florins a month. Yet he enjoyed a certain security which no travelling company of players could offer him. The average player was happy when an especially lean theater season, during which his salary had been halved, was over; when he received a contract for more than six weeks; or free dinners were provided by a generous director. The actors in the civic theaters of the time, who Neukäufler tells us earned between 200 and 400 florins a year, seem like real proletarians; but compare their lot with the princely standards of the court theaters. It was not only the primadonnas and the castrati who were liberally compensated by the court—a prominent librettist like Metastasio collected the imperial salary of 4,000 florins a year, a sum that Mozart never dreamed of, even when he finally rose to the position of "kaiserlich-königlicher Kammerkomponist" (Imperial and Royal Composer). In civic theaters though, only very popular actors or extremely businesslike directors—both professions were often united—could become wealthy.

Even so, directors never lacked up-and-coming young actors. They poured in from all levels of society; seldom before had they been so numerous as in the 1770s and '80s, the years in which the young Schikaneder came of age in the theater.

It was a time of epoch-making changes. From itinerant bands of jugglers and jesters emerged ambitious actors, and from them the first historical figures such as Ekhof, Iffland and Schröder. The old bands of strolling players of the late Baroque era endeavored to get off the roads and find work in established town theaters. But there were few of these theaters until the latter part of the century. Indeed, a few wealthy towns would convert a ballroom now and then so that plays could be put on, or sometimes allow enterprising directors to erect wooden stages in town squares. But commercial theaters in their own buildings were only found in the North, for example at Gänsemarkt in Hamburg, where as early as 1678 wealthy citizens had built a German opera house. It was even harder for the theater. It took a long time for the large German cities to follow the example of the Viennese city council which in 1710 leased a fireproof theater to "German players." Princes from south to north, the men of influence who build theaters, were completely won over by the splendors of Italian opera.

As sumptuous residences which aped Versailles were built, dozens of Baroque tiered theaters sprang up too. To put on an opera implied rendering homage to a prince, who saw his own image reflected in the classical heroes from Achilles to Alexander and who, if he was as ambitious as Louis XIV, also acted and danced along with the company. There was no better way of celebrating coronations or royal weddings than through the magnificence and pomp of an opera performance. For these, special theaters or grandiose arenas were constructed. For instance, Giuseppe Galli Bibiena, the theater architect, in 1723 erected on the Castle Hill in Prague a gigantic open-air set depicting Rome for the festival opera *Constanza e Fortezza* by Johann Joseph Fux, composer to the imperial court.

Elsewhere the court opera scene was also gripped by a mania for the gigantic. Four hundred extras, one hundred horses and eight dromedaries were mobilized for performances of Johann Adolf Hasse's *Ezio* in Dresden, and even the more modest Duke of Brunswick could afford to build an opera house with five tiers and seats for no less than 2,500 people. In order to fill the seats he was forced to admit the "paying public," a most unusual practice in court theaters. By 1700 this seems to have paid off so well that the Duke broke even as an opera manager. In Berlin Frederick II (before he became "The Great" and was not yet such a parsimonious Prussian) commissioned Knobelsdorff to build the fine Unter den Linden opera house, where Italian primadonnas and ballerinas sang and danced for him. Seating in the theater was strictly according to rank and title, and when it was too cold (there was no heating) a company of grenadiers was assigned to provide adequate bodily warmth.

The interiors of Baroque court theaters were constructed of wood, so few survived the inevitable fires. We can, however, still admire their architectural beauty in the Cuvilliés Theater in Munich, in the Bayreuth Margrave opera house, and in the Schlosstheater in Schwetzingen. Operas by Scarlatti, Handel, Hasse and others, which once filled these theaters with artful entertainment, disappeared almost as completely as the siren voices of the primadonnas and castrati. But at the time, as end products of a highly developed theatrical culture (the Neapolitan Bel Canto opera), these operas served as the prevailing status symbols. They were extravagant in the extreme, but who dared to dictate to kings, electors or dukes about their civic duties as theater patrons?

There was no German opera and almost no German theater repertoire. The citizens of Hamburg had made some attempt to rectify this but gave up after about half a century. Players from England introduced audiences to Shakespeare and Marlowe, and generally speaking to the art of acting. The Paris of Moliére, Corneille and Racine set the trend, but considered itself too refined to send companies of actors to Germany and Austria which, as far as the theater was concerned, were still in the Dark Ages. The French spiritual emissaries of Reason and Enlightenment, however, exerted a stronger influence. The writer Johann Christoph Gottsched tried to gain acceptance for the reform of the German Baroque theater which was little more than a dissipated, bloodthirsty, half-improvised fairground spectacle performed by strolling players. "What is reasonable is natural," was his plausible motto. He loathed "witchcraft, magic and juggling," and the six volumes of his *German Theater (Deutsche Schaubühne)* made their mark before Lessing derided his dry, fanatical sophistry. But by then Gottsched's principal actress and the greatest of her time, Karoline Neuber, had deserted him.

"The Neuber woman," as she was called, made early attempts to improve the quality of plays. She allied herself with Gottsched and in

1737 from her stage on the Rossmarkt in Leipzig, in an action which made theatrical history, she ceremonially banned (not burned, as is sometimes said) Harlequin from the German stage. German rationalists regarded the Harlequins and the *Hanswurst* (Punch and Judy) shows as the dregs of the theater. "The Neuber woman" was able to pump new blood into Gottsched's model drama, *The Dying Cato*, but she had acting in her bones, and she finally broke away. She scorned Gottsched's dryness and set off with her own company, travelling great distances, as far as St. Petersburg. Finally she died, poverty-stricken and all but forgotten. *Hanswurst* survived both Gottsched and Neuber; he continued to muddle along, entirely dependent on the talent of his impersonators. He did not inspire a theatrical literature of lasting influence, like Goldoni's Arlecchino-Truffaldino plays, and the authors who were enlisted by Gottsched, *Hanswurst's* arch enemy, proved weak reeds.

Lessing's works did little to alter the lamentable state of the German theater; they were no more than oases in the desert. Neither Shakespeare nor Moliére, the two most vital forces in the European theater, were able to improve matters, as they were only known in Germany in adapted versions which were often grotesquely distorted. Even *Hamlet*, a century and a half after Shakespeare's death, was usually played with a happy ending and entitled *Fratricide Revenged*. The German itinerant actor was far too busy protecting his livelihood or keeping an eye on the box-office to pull himself up from being a lackey of the public to become an instrument of poetic expression. "Die Neuberin" had tried; her recent failure was not encouraging. But in spite of these dire circumstances, outstanding German stage figures emerged from about the middle of the century onward.

Konrad Ekhof (1720–1778) bears the honorary title of "Father of German Acting." He began as a strolling player, developed into a character actor (for which he earned Lessing's praise), and achieved much for his despised profession by establishing a "Theatrical Academy". He was also the founder of German theatrical history. His pupil, August Wilhelm Iffland (1759–1814), author of 65 success-ful "tearjerkers", continued Ekhof's realistic style of acting, and has been immortalized in theater history by the first performances of Schiller's early plays at the Mannheim National Theater. Ekhof's

Academy was also attended by his admirer Friedrich Ludwig Schröder (1744–1816), the most celebrated actor of his time. Schröder was widely acclaimed as a Shakespearean actor, and as Shakespeare's most recent translator he came relatively close to the originals. As director of the Viennese Burgtheater, and in Hamburg, he was one of the great pioneers of Goethe and Schiller.

Even these historic personalities, who rose to become acknowledged masters in court theaters or in the great civic theaters, had behind them long years of apprenticeship in the hazardous world of the itinerant player. Schröder, for example, started as a tightrope walker and jester. For the previous generation, that of actors in the "Volkstheater" (people's theater), the usual home was a cart on wheels. The players would find quarters for a couple of weeks at a time in rough-and-ready lodgings and shacks. Their social standing was as low as their artistic level, characterized by the oft-quoted cry, "Take down the wash! The mummers are coming!" Even the Neuber woman, who had been so famous in her heyday, was denied a Christian burial. Her coffin "had to be hauled over the wall as secretively as possible." A priest refused to give the last rites to a man called Uhlig in Frankfurt because he had once been an actor. Neuber wrote that she was a woman "whose station you would have to search for amongst the lowest of the low; for she is nothing more than a mummer."

The best of them made an effort to raise this lowly standing. In 1753 Konrad Ekhof laid down in the rules for his Academy: "The Duties of an Actor before God and the world" and demanded "honest, law-abiding and reasonable deportment. . . . so that the prejudices which so often bedevil this profession can be stifled."

Were they really simply prejudices? Almost 40 years later Baron Adolf von Knigge, a Mozart translator and himself a man of the theater, offered the following summary of Germany's "heroes and actors in the theater" in his famous book on manners, *Dealings with People*: "Persons without morals, without education, without principles, without knowledge: mere adventurers, persons of the lowest station! Insolent strumpets!" This sounds like puritan hypocrisy. But even the leading theater historian, actor and producer Eduard Devrient, who was both well-informed and kindly disposed towards his colleagues, expresses at best a kind of social pity for them in his

"The Viennese Hanswurst"—Josef Stranitzky.
After a colored engraving by Elias Baeck, 1706.

book *The History of the Art of Acting in Germany* (1905). "Try to imagine
the beggarly outfits of the majority of these troupes, the avaricious,
bombastic managers acting like 'barkers' at the circus; the starving
buffoons; the brawls, scraps and ear-splitting, full-lunged clamor of
the mummers, the insolence of most of the actresses, who were no

better than a crowd of bawds; the slovenly households with children, pitifully dragged about; and all this just for the sake of a miserable living!" The actor's life is described so vividly that we can almost imagine Devrient, who was the producer at the court theater in Karlsruhe, having been there, and having seen Stranitzky's *Hanswurst* travelling through the south German countryside.

These "starving buffoons, the brawls, scraps and ear-splitting, full-lunged clamor of the mummers" were indeed typical and absolutely essential for at least half a century. Neither Lessing nor Shakespeare could attract a paying audience to the booths, but the joker dressed as *Hanswurst* could. In north Germany, introduced by English itinerant players as a comic figure, *Hanswurst* was known as "Pickle-Herring". In the south, and this was to prove much more important for Schikaneder, Stranitzky recreated *Hanswurst* and dressed him in the costume of a Salzburg peasant, a traditional, independent, expressive stage character whom even the Viennese, that most critical of publics, could trust.

Anton Stranitzky (1676–1726) is a legendary figure in the theater. We know very little about his origins; the name, rather like that of Nestroy, points to Bohemian, Moravian or Silesian ancestry. It is certain that he was born in Graz, son of a lackey, that he became an actor and that his name appears in the matriculation list of Vienna University in 1707 as having "qualified as a dentist." It is certain that he practiced this profession and that he also had a business selling eyeglasses. But his greatest success was as a popular actor and theater director. The Viennese swarmed in by the hundreds to see him at the Kärntnertor Theater, built by the city and leased to him; it was located behind the present-day Staatsoper. There he staged "Haupt und Staatsaktionen" (plots dealing with political affairs, often involving intrigues) adapted from contemporary Baroque operas by Draghi, Bononcini or Caldara; terrifying spectacles *a la* Faust or Don Juan; or comical harlequinades, all in the German language. No one cared who the authors were, as long as Stranitzky and his "Lazzi" * were there to make the audiences laugh.

Italian remained the preserve of the Imperial Court Opera and the guest companies of the Commedia dell' arte, who were flourishing at

---

*The Viennese word probably comes from the Italian "Lázione" and means a stereotyped mimic response to a stock situation. Author.

that time in Vienna. The Italian extempore comedy was based on an established, successful tradition; it could rely on virtuoso actors who were also mummers and acrobats. They were more than a match for their ponderous German-speaking counterparts. The theme of these comedies was always basically the same: an old man crazed with love lies in wait for a young girl, but Arlecchino, the cunning servant, sees to it that the right couple find each other in the end.

It is a theme with variations, whose stereotyped figures—the duped Pantalone, the bombastic captain, the saucy Columbine—are part of the fixtures, and had their prototypes in the classical Roman comedies of Plautus. We recognize them again in Rossini's *Barber of Seville*, and they have made a brilliant entrance into the 20th century in Giorgio Strehler's Goldoni revival, *The Servant of Two Masters*.

Stranitzky's contribution to theater history was the creation of a kind of German Harlequin: *Hanswurst*. He was by no means as elegant as Arlecchino—Stranitzky's pot-bellied build was against him. Hanswurst wore, as already mentioned, the costume of a Salzburg peasant, who in the eyes of the Viennese was simply a country bumpkin.

Eighty years later, probably without knowing about Stranitzky, Schikaneder hit upon an equally ingenious costume, that of the "Tyrolean Wastel", his most popular character after Papageno. Stranitzky's *Hanswurst* was of course much coarser; later theater historians turned up their noses in disgust at his lavatory humor and sexual jokes. But 1720 had not yet seen the Englightenment, so Harlequin did not have to be banned from the Viennese stage, but simply recreated in German. Stranitzky, with all his mimicry and verbal obscenities, was only employing the ancient privileges of the court fools, and they could scarcely be crude enough. Combining Pickle-Herring (a descendant of Shakespeare's fools), the dancing Arlecchino and the old German jester, Stranitzky created a new role who became a stock character for generations. His *Hanswurst* is a husky, honest fellow. He gets into the most idiotic situations, is always hungry, always afraid and weeps often, an unexpected characteristic. Pickle-Herring usually gets off the hook by cheating, while *Hanswurst* remains basically moral—even his occasional resistance to his "masters" is kept within strict bounds.

Stranitzky could only slow the advancing tide of brilliant troupes of Italian extempore comedians. After his death, they once again dominated the Viennese popular theater. "Die Neuberin's" denunciation had fallen on deaf ears, and Gottfried Prehauser, named by Stranitzky himself as his successor, could only succeed in the theater by making *Hanswurst* Harlequin's equal.

Prehauser (1699–1769) was for decades the undisputed darling of the Viennese popular theater. Son of a concierge, an itinerant player from youth, he finally became a director in Vienna. The new intellectual movement of the European Enlightenment developed during his lifetime. He took over the traditions of the popular theater including the imperturbable and popular *Hanswurst*. But *Hanswurst* was changing, just as the social structure of imperial Vienna, turning into a capital city, was changing in the middle of the century. The differences between the lower classes were beginning to be noticed and theatrically portrayed.

Prehauser's *Hanswurst* is no longer the somewhat naive peasant, simple-minded odd-man-out in a sophisticated urban world, but rather a tailor, a shoemaker or a postillion—an urban dweller who observes the social ambience with the sharp eye of the actor, even if in his bones he is still a comic. His list of ancestors is remarkably varied: ancient mythological entertainers in costumes with phallic suggestions (even Pickle-Herring used these in his Baroque costumes), Shakespeare's philosophical clowns and German Renaissance court jesters with all their bawdiness, although the cultured Prehauser preserved only a few of their smutty jokes. As the height of his career was during the regency of the pious and morally straight-laced Empress Maria Theresia, *Hanswurst* became a well-behaved subject. Although he was allowed to sport his cheerful self as the voice of the people, he was bound by strict censorship.

The extempore theater, especially where performed in German, remained suspect to the authorities: for who was safe from *Hanswurst's* improvisations, his unpredictable, topical, often extremely pointed satire which was greeted everywhere with such enthusiasm? After Prehauser's death this satire was forbidden, and only "regular" plays could be performed—those from prescribed and accepted texts. Even Joseph II, an enlightened and tolerant monarch, tried to repress improvisations; at least at his Hoftheater next to the Burg: "no one is allowed to add to or to alter his role, or to introduce unseemly acting." The loss of one-eighth of a month's salary was threatened as a punishment. Joseph's mother the Empress was far more rigid—she had already reprimanded Vienna's new folk-play actor Bernadon for the "dirty words" he continually used. But Joseph, who was co-regent, kept Bernadon under his protective wing for some years.

Bernadon (so named after a youthful role which became immensely popular) was Felix von Kurz (1717–1783), Prehauser's rival and successor. His aristocratic "von" was authentic. He stood out among the crowd of actors, mostly of petty bourgeois origin, because he came from a patrician family in the Bavarian Allgäu. His father moved to Vienna, attracted by the street theaters, and Bernadon followed him along this adventurous path. Of aristocratic appearance, tall and elegant, he was a born actor; in one play he took no less than seven parts, both male and female. He is famous in theatrical history as the creator of the "Bernadoniaden": magic burlesques, full of action and spectacle, in which ghosts and devils did their worst, and against whom Bernadon, simple but with ample native wit—a true descendant of *Hanswurst*—held his own.

But "Kurz was no ordinary, vulgar entertainer," wrote Schröder, a member of his Vienna troupe for a time. Before the middle of the century Kurz-Bernadon had put on Voltaire's contemporary play *Alzire* at the rebuilt Kärntnertor Theater. Shortly thereafter, as director, he made a remarkably astute and progressive change in programming; extempore comedy, universally popular and the source of his box-office takings, was played four nights a week while fashionable "regular" plays were performed on the other two.

Kurtz was a restless man. He twice resigned his position, then returned, managing to hold the theater-loving Viennese public in the palm of his hand. Then he tried his luck further afield as a company director, risking and indeed losing his fortune in Warsaw. When he finally tried to revive his "Bernadoniaden" in Vienna, the public stayed away. He died in poverty: the times had outstripped him. However, when we read that in his best years at the Kärntnertor Theater, extra money was spent on so-called "fatigues"—appearing in flying machines and diving into water—it seems that indeed he was paving the way for the future. He anticipated not only Schikaneder, a producer and stage director of great imagination who effectively used flying machines in more than just *The Magic Flute*, but also the daredevil stuntmen of the flickering "pseudo-theater" of Hollywood.

In the meantime, Kurz-Bernadon's archrival Sonnenfels had triumphed. This worthy gentleman, Joseph, Imperial Baron von Sonnenfels, came from a Jewish family—his father was the scholar Lipmann Perlin—and represented the second generation of Jewish-German emancipation. He became a prominent Freemason, was advisor on economic policy to Joseph II, and as an enlightened lawyer he campaigned against torture and the death penalty. His involvement in literary activities earned him the title of "the Viennese Gottsched." He wrote and contended, just as untiringly as his literary idol, against the vulgar *Hanswurst*, locally against "Bernadoniaden" and the unpredictable and foolish extempore theater. He urged "regular" plays; that is, the reasonable and appropriate works put on at the Emperor's "enlightened" popular theater, and not the risky theatrical adventures produced by actors.

The youngest of the popular theater-pioneers with any stylistic influence was Philipp Hafner (1735–1764). In his own way, he took part in the dispute about *Hanswurst*. He died young, and his impact on the professional stage was only made in the last two years of his life. However, his success was so considerable that the few plays he wrote—eight to be exact—were great successes and shortly after his death earned him the title of "Father of the Viennese Popular Play". He was the son of a civil servant from Franconia and a Viennese mother. He studied law, then managed to make his way by writing casual articles and plays for private theaters. A confirmed bachelor, he threw all convention to the winds in his comedies, sometimes even dispensing with the proverbial lovers' happy ending.

He wrote burlesques, spectacles using machinery, and middle-class comedies. He did not dismiss the Commedia dell'arte completely, as he valued its unequalled tradition, but he was not content to confine himself only to its stereotyped plots and characters. He made them more complex and enriched them with Viennese local color, sometimes with tragi-comedy. He was no revolutionary—in his reforms he tried to build a bridge between the enlightened new age and the fading magic of the mummer. In his play, *Magära, die förchterliche Hexe* (Megära, The Fearful Witch), he paid homage to the spectacle with all its theatrical devices. This play became one of the greatest successes in the repertoire of the new Kärntnertor Theater, which had been rebuilt after a fire in 1763.

The framework of the story—the struggle between a noble magician and a wicked sorceress—set a precedent. The Mozart-Schikaneder *Magic Flute* is certainly the most ingenious tale in this tradition, but it is by no means the first nor the last. Schikaneder's local comedies owe much to Philipp Hafner; but the latter died too young for us to determine whether his talent would have developed further than supplying the box-office successes which the theater of that time demanded.

Hanswurst had not yet had his day; Hafner wrote him into roles for the aging Prehauser, but in the meantime the old joker had turned into a genuine Viennese petty bourgeois. In the highly successful *Megära* he appears in a variety of disguises, but is still recognizable as the gluttonous, coarse and comic lover of Columbine who like the other characters has arias and songs to sing.

Songs had already appeared in Stranitzky's plays—the old Viennese popular theater could not have survived without music. Music made the differences between the court and civic theaters in Vienna less pronounced after the middle of the 18th century. For Maria Theresia the only conceivable music in the theater was Neapolitan opera, but her son as Emperor encouraged a new genre—the German *Singspiel*.

Historically, Leipzig is usually seen as the birthplace of *Singspiele*. In about 1750, Heinrich Gottfried Koch directed a talented company there. They put on plays with music whose melodies must have been so simple that actors with untrained voices could sing them and the public was able to repeat them. Felix Christian Weisse wrote a libretto for *Der Teufel ist los* (The Devil to Pay), a comedy with folklike melodies, based on an English subject. Only later, in 1776, it became a successful *Singspiel*, recomposed by Johann Adam Hiller, with arias in the Italian style for the aristocratic lovers and strophic songs for "Hannchen and Töffelchen". The prolific Hiller, and Benda, Neefe and Schweitzer in north and central Germany; and Haydn, Schenk and Dittersdorf in Vienna were the successful composers of this genre. The main advantage in performance was that no Italian trained professional singers were needed; versatile and adaptable actors were adequate. This was the advent of a tradition which was to have an effect on generations to come. Lortzing* himself was still both actor and singer, and Nestroy sang many roles, including Sarastro, before he became the century's most brilliant writer of satirical popular plays.

Vienna, however, might well be given the title of the birthplace of the German *Singspiel*. If Hiller's successes were the breakthrough, it was Haydn who in 1752 composed *Der neue krumme Teufel* (The New Sly Devil) to a text by Kurz-Bernadon. Even earlier than this a comprehensive collection of "German Arias" was well known in Vienna. These arias became very popular because they made German numbers from dozens of current plays accessible to the public for singing and home music-making—piano scores were not available at that time.

In his standard work on old Viennese folk comedy, Otto Rommel pleads for Vienna's precedence over Leipzig. Certainly the German *Singspiel* reached its height in the Imperial capital, for it was a city hungry for entertainment and with several established theaters. Works performed ranged from Mozart's *Entführung aus dem Serail*, one of fortune's favorites, to the lesser, but at the time nevertheless successful little masterpieces that followed—Karl Ditters von Dittersdorf's *Doktor und Apotheker* (The Doctor and the Apothecary) and Johann Schenk's *Der Dorfbarbier* (The Village Barber).

In Italy, cheerful popular musical comedies had been creeping into the court *opera seria* of the primadonnas and the castrati for some time. They were the so-called "intermezzi" based on the classical figures of the Commedia dell'arte, artlessly sandwiched between two acts of serious opera. The most famous intermezzo was *La serva padrona* (The Maid as Mistress), composed in 1733 by the precocious Neapolitan, Giovanni Battista Pergolesi. The brief work has an amusing story, with only three characters and little scenery; it set a precedent throughout Europe. Only a few years later it triggered the national controversy in Paris known as "La Guerre des Bouffons", which led to the birth of "Opéra comique", a French version of the German *Singspiel*. Jean-Jacques Rousseau, the philosopher who made his

---

*Albert Lortzing (1801–1851), German composer of operas, some of which are still popular in German-speaking countries. For a short time he was active, as composer and conductor, at the Theater an der Wien. Ed.

living by copying music and who also composed, advocated naturalness, the bourgeois anti-pathos of the idyllic Singspiel. In England, as early as 1728, *The Beggar's Opera*, a cheeky parody by John Gay (with popular tunes by the Berlin-born Johann Christoph Pepusch) dealt Handel's courtly Baroque opera a mortal blow.

Why did Germany lag so far behind? Principally because Italian opera held a powerful grip on the palace theaters of the dozens of petty princedoms. The earlier German-speaking Baroque opera in Hamburg had no consequences nationally. Neither the leading German poets—from Klopstock to Gottsched to Lessing—nor the leading theater composers—Handel, Hasse and Gluck—showed any interest in German opera. One composed librettos written in Italian or French. Gluck, interested in reform, took great pains to produce a German version of *Orpheus and Eurydice*, and occupied himself with music for Klopstock's *Hermann's Schlacht* (Hermann's Battle) when he was an old man. But it was the awakening national feeling in the second half of the century which finally changed the musical theater. Wieland's change of heart was typical. He was an enlightened court poet, yet his opinion of German opera was for years as harsh as that of Frederick II of Prussia, who said he would rather "have a horse whinny an aria for me than tolerate a German primadonna in my opera house." (In fact he had one in Gertrud Elisabeth Mara, the first German star singer, even if she did sing only in Italian.) But in 1773 Wieland wrote the German librettos for *Alceste* and *Die Wahl des Herkules* (The Choice of Hercules), setting a precedent even though the music had been composed by a very mediocre, minor composer, Anton Schweitzer. For the first time a prince among poets had taken up the challenge of German opera. One even more famous was to do it following him and with even greater success. Goethe contributed no less than six librettos and several fragments to the new German Singspiel. His most beautiful lyrics, like "Erlkönig" and "Veilchen" (later set by Mozart, originally an operatic trio), first appeared in Goethe Singspiele. It must have been intolerably frustrating for the greatest German genius of the time not to have been able to find an able composer-partner; Mozart, whom he highly revered, avoided him.

The new domestic opera in German had a difficult time. It lacked outstanding voices, so singing actors had to do their best. Above all it lacked money. The orchestras were tiny; the Doebbelin company, for example, had to make do with a "musical director" and nine players at a time when courtly theaters like that of the Margrave of Brandenburg-Schwedt could afford an orchestra of 30, for many petty princes had a larger private purse at their disposal than the theater-loving but thrifty common folk. But the vitality and popularity of the new medium prevailed. For the first time in opera the performer bridged the gap between himself and the public across the orchestra pit. Respect for vocal acrobats singing in an incomprehensible language gave way to understanding—sharing the emotions and laughter displayed on the stage. The bourgeois public grew and could identify with the characters of the German Singspiel. Pastoral and provincial idyls were the norm, and occasionally patriotic themes were introduced. The German opera *Günther von Schwarzburg* by Ignaz Jakob Holzbauer, Viennese by birth and composer to the Elector of Manheim, was given at the National Theater of Mannheim in 1777.

> *Deutschland, Deutschland!*
> *Wie klein bist du zerteilt durch Zwietracht!*
> *Wie gross durch Brüdereinheit!*
> *Entnervender als Zwietracht ist Hang zu fremder Sitte—*
> *Stolz, deutsch zu sein—ist eure Grösse!*

> O Germany! O Germany!
> How petty you have become, divided by discord,
> How great you could be through brotherly unity!
> But the deference to foreign customs is more enfeebling than discord—
> Be proud to be German—there lies your greatness!

Anton Klein was the author of the text; Mozart was later to write a patriotic letter to him in the same vein. The opera met with a positive response throughout the German-speaking region, though somewhat muted in the Vienna of the Emperor despite Joseph II's active friendship for and patronage of German Singspiel. In 1776 he turned the Hofburgtheater in the Michaelerplatz, which had been converted from a ballroom 35 years before, into a "National Theater," naming it the Hof-und Nationalschaubühne (Court and

National Dramatic Stage). From then on, Italian opera which had dominated Vienna life shared the theater not only with German plays but with German Singspiel. The most glorious evening in the theater was the first performance of Mozart's *Entführung aus dem Serail* in July 1782. This opera went far beyond the bounds of Singspiel, and musically beyond the limits of lesser contemporary composers—its success in theaters throughout Central Europe was immediate. However, there was no follow-up to establish the style. The only person capable of such a follow-up was Mozart himself, but his life-style and creative circumstances sent him back to Italian opera. In Lorenzo da Ponte he found the partner for his three most important works in Italian. But Mozart did not give up his hopes for a German opera; he simply lacked a librettist with whom he could harmoniously work.

A year before *Figaro*, which he had to write in Italian, Mozart wrote about it to Klein, the Mannheim librettist: ". . . . if only there were a single patriot with me on the boards—it would have another face! Then perhaps our budding National Theater would burst into flower! And wouldn't it be something if we Germans should for once in all seriousness start to think in German—to act in German, to talk in German and even to sing in German!!!"

The three exclamation marks at the end, the aggressive irony of the letter, all point to his intense emotional involvement. Mozart, a cultural and political patriot—and at that time a fully mature composer—had not the slightest intimation that he would find a compatriot to be with him "on the boards" a few years later. Or, to be historically more accurate, the compatriot would find *him*. For it was the young theater director Emanuel Schikaneder, Mozart's friend since their Salzburg days and the creator of *The Magic Flute*, who "found" him.

3 *From Minstrel to Director*

His name was neither Emanuel nor Schikaneder. He was born Johann Joseph Schickeneder in the small town of Straubing in Lower Bavaria on September 1, 1751. He adopted the name Emanuel as a young actor, probably because it sounded more imposing, and was at any rate more unusual than his common Christian names. That the Bavarian Schickeneder later became Schikaneder had nothing to do with the choice of an artistic name, but was rather the result of the orthographic carelessness of the 18th century; at that time family names were not spelled with much exactitude.

Schikaneder himself was also less than exact in his accounts of his life; as a mature man he named Regensburg as his birthplace, failing to recall his first three years in Straubing and only remembering the years of childhood and youth spent in Regensburg.

He came from the lowest social strata. His father Joseph Schickeneder struggled along as a lackey and a sacristan. His mother Juliana, née Schiessl (1715–1789) from Wettzell in the Bavarian Forest, was a serving maid when in 1745 she married Schickeneder from Straubing "who was in service." They married in Regensburg, for the young man was about to move there. He anticipated a modest step up in the world in this larger town which had housed a so-called "Imperial Diet" since the Thirty Years War. The Diet was without political authority but harbored an enormous number of hangers-on: envoys, cavaliers and wealthy idlers. But he never rose higher than

"The Bavarian Imperial and Electoral Town of Straubing."

being lackey to a countess and a temporary servant to a canon. So he left Urban and Joseph, two of the three children who had been born in the meantime, with foster parents in Regensburg and returned to Straubing with Anna, the third child. Here he was assistant "to His Grace the Parish Priest" when his last, and later to become famous, son was born, followed after two years by a daughter, Maria. Then he again tried his luck elsewhere, this time as lackey to a count in Köfering near Regensburg. In the meantime his second son Johann Joseph had died, so this name was passed on to the fourth-born. Shortly after this last move in about 1753, father Schikaneder must have departed this life. We know nothing more about him. But we do know that his widow was a courageous woman, and although completely without means she did not admit defeat, but opened a stall near the cathedral where she sold devotional objects and cotton goods, and brought up her children decently. Urban and Johann Joseph actually studied "the humanities and dedicated themselves to music"; that much we can believe from the not always reliable biography by a nephew, Karl Schikaneder. The youngest brother

Schikaneder spent his childhood and early youth in Regensburg. In 1787 he returned for two years as director of "The German National Theater." (A view of the town c. 1780: French Peepshow engraving by Hocgart, after an engraving by Seutter.)

shone in the first class of the Jesuit Gymnasium in Regensburg—later, as a director, he relished showing off the little bits of Latin learned during his school days, especially when reproached for his lack of education. After their voices had changed, the choir boys, including the Schikaneder boys, were trained to be instrumentalists to perform in church music in Regensburg. Later, Schikaneder occasionally composed Singspiele, and it was here that he learned his craft. The Regensburg Jesuits also introduced him to the magic of the theater, for his school put on so-called "Endesdramen" (End-of-the-year plays) every year, and the pupils also performed Shrovetide plays.

The sparse, homely circumstances of this education certainly could not be described as academic training. The boys had to earn their own bread in the best way they could—by music. Urban obtained a post as hornist in the Bishop of Freising's orchestra, while Johann Joseph, who was no less musical—he played the violin and had a good baritone voice—was driven by necessity and youth's wanderlust to what was at the time the abode of all unsettled musicians with no fixed work—the road. He became a "minstrel", the name given to the wandering musicians who moved from place to place, spent their nights in cheap inns, barns, or under the open sky, and passed the hat for contributions. Some were semi-professional instrumentalists and others wandering scholars of whom Eichendorff sang, "these are the students—out they go, through the town gate."

The young minstrel Schickeneder travelled extensively along the roads of southern Germany. So it was in 1773 in Augsburg he witnessed a performance by Franz Joseph Moser's itinerant troupe. It was an hour ordained by fate: the theater cast its spell over Schikaneder, a spell in whose thrall he would be held for the rest of his life. The strolling minstrel became a strolling player. Shortly afterwards, in director Andreas Schopf's troupe, he was cast as "the lover." Tall, handsome, and with a pleasant singing voice, he was eminently well suited to this role. Although Schopf's company, travelling from town to town in southern Germany and Austria, may well have been only a superior barnstorming troupe, Johann Emanuel Schikaneder (soon to be just Emanuel Schikaneder) rapidly became a critical element in the ensemble. He was soon a producer, coping with the pressures of staging a different production virtually weekly, and then began to write plays himself. He was to write about a hundred during the course of his life. Most of them were simply utility pieces needed for the current repertoire—few have survived. They were written quickly and off the cuff so scarcely deserved a better fate.

But his first play was an unqualified success, and for good reason. *Die Lyranten oder das lustige Elend* (The Minstrels or Merry Misery), which Schikaneder had printed immediately after its first performance in Innsbruck in 1776, is one of his better works. The young playwright describes his own experiences as Schikaneder the minstrel. As a dramatist he always is at his best when he pours his own experiences and his sharp observations of life into his characters.

The piece calls itself "comic operetta", but is actually nothing more than a complete Singspiel in three acts with no fewer than 19 musical numbers. "If anyone wishes to obtain the music to the arias he should turn to the author who is also the composer," according to the foreword to the printed copy.[2] Schikaneder presents himself as a jack of all trades: poet, chief actor (young lover in the bargain) and composer as well! We do not know today how he composed, but this is not really important. The verse structure of the first finale does reveal some—if somewhat simple—skill at setting a text to music.

> *WIRTIN: Fort, fort aus meinem Haus!*
> *SCHULMEISTER: Ich bin Schulmeister.*
> *WIRTIN: Fort, fort, hinaus!*
> *JÖRGEL: Ich ein Geschworner.*
> *WIRTIN: Fort, fort, hinaus!*
> *LEICHTSINN: Ich ein Gereister.*
> *WIRTIN: Fort, fort, hinaus!*
> *STOCK: Ich ein Gebohrner—.*
> *WIRTIN: Fort, fort, hinaus!*
> *LEICHTSINN: Violinist!*
> *STOCK: Bassist!*
> *WIRTIN: Hinaus mit dem Mist!*

> HOSTESS: Get out, get out of my house!
> SCHOOLMASTER: I'm a teacher.
> HOSTESS: Out, get out!
> GEORGIE: I'm a sworn juror!
> HOSTESS: Out, get out!
> FOOLISHNESS: I'm a traveller!
> HOSTESS: Out, get out!
> STOCK: I'm of high birth!
> HOSTESS: Out, get out!
> FOOLISHNESS: Fiddler!
> STOCK: Bass!
> HOSTESS: Out, out with the rubbish!

The eighth aria became a popular song sung throughout southern Germany and in Vienna:

> *Ein Weibsbild ist ein närrisch Ding!*
> *Wenn man ihr Komplimente macht,*
> *So wird sie gleich verliebt gemacht.*
> *Ein Weibsbild ist ein närrisch Ding.*
> *Kaum bricht der frühe Morgen an,*

So bittet sie um einen Mann.
Ein Weibsbild ist ein närrisch Ding!

A female is a foolish thing!
If you compliment her she'll fall in love at once.
A female is a foolish thing!
Scarcely has the day begun
She's busy seeking out a man!
A female is a foolish thing!

If royalties had existed at the time, Schikaneder would have done nicely as a composer. But he did not view himself as one- only as an itinerant minstrel who had practiced getting the right chords to popular melodies, and by studying Hiller's current Singspiele had learned how to fit songs to pleasant plots and pleasant characters. For theatrical success depended upon presenting a pleasing plot and characters, and in his first work Schikaneder already reveals a gift for hitting the mark.

Just what the three minstrels of the title are up to, and their adventures after arriving at a village—two of them fall in love with the local belles—is not really important. Schikaneder created (and wrote for himself) a character from life in the student called Leichtsinn (Foolishness), who thinks he is irresistible. One of the characters steals a capon, a fattened chicken, from the poultry yard; all three are threatened with arrest, but everything ends happily in a double wedding.

The characters deserve more attention than the conventional Singspiel plot. Foolishness, Stick (Stock) and Bird (Vogel) are the names of the minstrel trio—it was the custom that names should point to character, right up to the time of Nestroy. Foolishness explains itself—he is the youthful lover; Stick, the indolent student, somewhat advanced in years, has already become a little stiff, and only the bottle can console him. Vogel is actually not such a jolly bird. He is a bird who has left the aristocratic family nest and is already regretting his adventures as a minstrel. Fortunately the governor, a real *deus ex machina*, turns out to be his father! The "liederliche Kleeblatt" (dissolute trio) which assured Nestroy's famous *Der böse Geist Lumpazivagabundus oder das liederliche Kleeblatt* of such success two generations later, has its model in Schikaneder, and Nestroy's "böse

Geist" (wicked spirit) who gives the piece its name, actually quotes Schikaneder's work when he names himself "Beherrscher des lustigen Elends" (Lord of Merry Misery) after Schikaneder's title.

I do not wish to compare Schikaneder with Nestroy, as different artistic values divide them more sharply than the half century separating their birth. Nestroy's puns and the breadth and depth of his sarcasm are foreign to Schikaneder. The similarities are found in theatrical typology. But as Nestroy was bound by the same typology in the construction of his works (which are nearly always borrowed and re-shaped), one may identify Schikaneder as one of Nestroy's predecessors without leading the readers to think them equals. Schikaneder's gullible, drunken philosopher Stick is poles apart from Nestroy's shoemaker Knieriem's inebriated vision of the end of time—"In any case, the world won't last much longer." But despite such differences the world of the Singspiel remains the same as when the minstrel Foolishness jests:

Ach, nur Damen, Damen nur,
Sind die Zierde der Natur!

Ah! only ladies, ladies only
Are nature's ornaments!

and again when in Romance No. 3 the peasant girl Rosina makes fun of the Rococo shepherds' verses in simpering lines:

An jener Silberquelle sang
Menalk vom sanften Triebe,
Und das entzückte Tal erklang
Von seiner heissen Liebe.

And at that silver fountain sang
Menalk, of soft desire,
And the enchanted valley rang
His love as fierce as fire.

But the young Schikaneder was not as respectful as were Weisse and Hiller of the Saxon Singspiel idyls. Foolishness is sufficiently forward to address the governor quite cheekily: "We are students, Mr. Governor; I've probably studied as hard as you have—but I was poor, and you were just a rich fathead!" Schikaneder was repeatedly to use similar expressions in subsequent plays, usually from the mouths of simple people. He was no disguised Figaro, always protesting against the establishment, but a cunning man of the theater who reckoned with applause from the simple folk in the gallery ("Whew! He's really telling him off!"), which was tolerated by the authorities as a harmless outlet.

The Minstrels became an immediate success for Schopf's company. Schikaneder introduced Mozart to it in Salzburg in 1780. A year later it was performed and held its own in the newly-built Viennese Theater in der Leopoldstadt, re-named *Die Bettelstudenten* (The Beggar Students). One is of course reminded of Millöcker's classic operetta.

Andreas Schopf moved from Innsbruck to Augsburg in 1776, taking his hardworking "lover" and poet-composer with him, as the citizens had just completed a new theater. It was a colossal building, with 1,000 seats in the orchestra, two tiers of boxes, and a double balcony. But it was a primitive wooden construction—only the stage had masonary walls—and was consequently soon looked down on as not doing justice to the ancient "Reichstadt" (Imperial City). However, it was indeed a monument to the bourgeois conception of the theater—it did not have to depend on a ruler's purse for its existence.

But the director who leased the theater had to count every kreuzer. The best orchestra seats cost 30 kreuzer, the cheaper ones and the balcony only 15—patricians paid between two and three florins for their boxes. Director Schopf enticed his public with current successes by Hafner, Brandes, Stephanie, or Weidmann, as well as Schikaneder's *Minstrels*, but he was not averse to more exalted fare. The public stayed at home for Goethe's *Clavigo*, yet Schopf included Shakespeare and modern German classics like Lessing's *Minna von Barnhelm*, *Miss Sarah Sampson* and *Emilia Galotti* in his repertoire as counterbalance to the then popular French works. He had less success with German Singspiel than with various ballets, one of which had a title requiring mention—*Der lustige Vogelfänger* (The Merry Birdcatcher) which Schikaneder must have known. One seasonal hit in Augsburg proved to be of great importance to "the lover, dandy and tyrant"—now Schikaneder's roles. This hit was the drama *Der Graf von Walltron* (The Count of Walltron) by Heinrich Ferdinand Möller.

The count draws his dagger on his superior officers and is condemned to death for insubordination. But after tense negotiations he is finally pardoned. The new play was presented with a great show of military pomp—44 Augsburg town guards crowded onto the stage as extras—and the public was delighted. Both the play and the production made a great impression on Schikaneder; we shall see later how often he was to develop this theme, both as playwright and as producer.

During his first season in Augsburg, Schikaneder made a fateful mistake by marrying on February 9, 1777, a member of the company, the actress and dancer Eleonore Arth, whose parts were the "young, gentle heroine in love, the soubrette, and the naive young girl." She came from Hermannstadt in Transylvania, where she was born on February 17, 1751, thus making her six months older than Schikaneder. Both acted in *The Minstrels* and often appeared together in other productions.

To put it mildly, the marriage was not a success. Although Madame Schikaneder was very popular with the public, younger, prettier girls were more popular with her temperamental husband, and in addition to her roles of "young women in love, mischievous girls and powerful characters of strong nature and sensibility," Eleonore was obliged to play mothers. But Schikaneder was only too happy to succumb to less maternal charms. "My uncle, as is well known, was always having other love affairs," wrote Karl Schikaneder in his biographical sketch. These affairs were not without their consequences. In 1779, less than two years after his marriage, Schikaneder became a father twice within six months: the first child, Emanuel Jakob, by Maria Anna Millerin, another member of Schopf's troupe; the second, Maria Magdalena Katharina, by the daughter of an Augsburg citizen.

Was Eleonore so lacking in charm that she drove her husband from their bed? The writer Ignaz Franz Castelli, a significant if not always reliable chronicler of Schikaneder's time, pokes fun at her in his memoirs *Aus dem Leben eines Wiener Phäaken* (From the Life of a Viennese Phaeacian): "this amazingly fat woman, slightly crosseyed." But this could well have been a description of the aging Frau Schikaneder. The Gotha *Theaterjournal für Deutschland* had nothing but praise for the 28-year-old actress. "She is small but charming, and her behavior is quite natural; she has it in her power to command both loose, roguish expressions and wicked airs as well as noble and elevated ones. . . . her dancing is proper and adroit, displaying much spirit and life—she has pretty little feet, and her overall posture is extremely good."

At any rate, she was able to maintain her hold on her younger husband for years, and this despite his initial critical impressions. "Nature has lent her great talents . . . her bosom is too narrow for tragedy, her voice too scratchy, her arm movements too stiff, her face empty of expression. . . . she would be well cast as a peasant girl. . . . there, what others must acquire by art, is here given her by nature." But her patience came to an end before his infidelities did, and she moved in with Johann Friedel, a friend of the family.

After Friedel's death the Schikaneders were reunited, and henceforth Eleonore was to share good and bad days with her husband. She outlived him by several years and died in poverty on June 22, 1822, in the small flat the Theater an der Wien had granted her.

When Director Schopf's contract in Augsburg was not renewed in the spring of 1777 he moved on to Regensburg, but the Schikaneders left his company to join that of Joseph Moser, which was playing in Nuremberg at the time. The Nuremberg theater was old-fashioned and inadequate, but Moser was a theater director of considerable artistic ambition, and his repertory suited Schikaneder. He was even more anti-French than Schopf, and favored Shakespeare—in his six months in Nuremberg Schikaneder played Hamlet, Macbeth, Iago and Richard III. Moser also set great store by the German Singspiel; *The Minstrels* proved itself anew. "Whenever an opera is performed, the house is full," Moser remarked in a letter of application to the Augsburg municipal authorities, who then engaged him for the fall of 1777. Thus within a short time Schikaneder had returned to the town of his first successes. As leading actor he had to portray "principal lovers, noble fathers, kings, heroes and peasants, roles requiring decorum and wit, and all the leading comic parts in Singspiel"— almost a theatrical universe! The young man's dramatic stature grew, and was not only recognized locally. Proof of this was his appearance as guest actor to the Royal Bavarian Court Theater in Munich, where he played Hamlet on December 19, 1777, with such overwhelming success that he was offered a contract immediately. He accepted with alacrity, and looked forward to acting at the Bavarian court when the season in Augsburg ended.

But it was not to be. Moser's wife died suddenly in January 1778. The aging director was so shattered and discouraged by her death that he did not want to continue alone, so he offered Schikaneder the directorship of his troupe for the handsome sum of 2,000 florins, which Schikaneder accepted. Moser did not have the money, but was confident he could scrape it together. As of January 27, 1778, the Augsburg municipal authorities entered into a contract with Schikaneder as "Director of a Company of German Actors," and put the newly rebuilt theater at his disposal for an unusually long period; that is, until Shrovetide, 1779. Schikaneder gave notice to Count Seeau, the manager of the court theater in Munich, so bringing to naught the plan to be a royal Bavarian court actor. The career of Emanuel Schikaneder, man of the theater, had begun.

He started his first season with his *Hamlet*, which was already highly regarded. The audience was not disturbed by the fact that the play was given in the bowdlerized "happy ending" version by the successful theater secretary and dramatist Franz von Heufeld. Shakespeare was treated very freely, without any literary scruples, and naively regarded in Germany as merely a source of exciting stories and good roles. *Othello* was also played as *The Handkerchief or Othello, the Moor of Venice*, adapted by a certain J. J. Steffens. Even later translations by the great actor and Shakespeare pioneer Friedrich Ludwig Schröder were fairly arbitrary versions of the original English texts.

As chief actor, producer, director and also author of the successful *Minstrels*, Schikaneder was now absolute master in his own house. He lived in the inn "At the Three Kings" and enjoyed the generous good will of the municipal authorities, as well as the good will of the new "first lady and heroine" Mademoiselle Miller—already mentioned as the mother of his illegitimate child. He was bursting with enterprise. He carried out his promise to Moser to put on German Singspiel, so the public in Augsburg was introduced to Mozart's *Bastien and Bastienne*. Though the paths of Mozart and Schikaneder crossed—when in October 1777 Mozart broke his journey to Paris and stayed with relatives in Augsburg, where he went to the theater once—they did not meet.

Between theater seasons, Schikaneder and his company went on tour. They often had to put up with small places like Ulm, although capital cities were their greatest financial draw—Stuttgart, the capital of Swabia, for example. In the early summer of 1778 Schikaneder scored a new triumph there with his *Hamlet*; and his company, enlarged to 29 actors and a ballet corps of 22, played Goethe and Lessing together with their usual repertoire, with enormous success. The critics were hardly less enthusiastic than the public in the balcony. It is difficult for us today to imagine Papageno as Hamlet: the "nature boy" as a tragic hero. And yet for many years Schikaneder was considered an outstanding Shakespearean actor in southern Germany in the court theaters of Munich and Stuttgart which were respected institutions. The first Schikaneder critique to survive is from the Viennese *Journal von auswärtigen und deutschen Theatern* (The Journal of Foreign and German Theaters). The review reports the 1778 success of *Hamlet* in Stuttgart which had created a great stir. "On July 4 Herr Schikaneder, director of a company of German actors of the same name played the part of Hamlet in such a masterly fashion that he was called back and compelled to repeat the last scene (the same honor was recently paid to him in Munich)." We learn something more about his method a year later in the Gotha *Theaterjournal für Deutschland*:

> The director Schikaneder has such natural stature and character that he cannot spoil any part. Added to this, he has magnificent eyes and is particularly strong in the art of gesture. For this reason he pleased me most in the role of Hamlet . . .; and I don't believe that in this play anyone could have more expressive eyes and gestures than Schikaneder. In other tragic parts he has been criticized for exaggerated emotion. It could be that in isolated instances there is some truth to this criticism. . . . in lower comic roles he is without comparison—even his critics have to admit this."

This is not very specific criticism as is the notice of the young Schikaneder, four years later, in the *Gallerie von Teutschen Schauspielern und Schauspielerinnen der ältern und neuern Zeit* (Vienna, 1783). "His features and his build are naturally attractive and handsome; he is tall, has a good figure and pleasing presence. He plays all main parts: lovers, comical fathers, tyrants and heroes. His manner, his pure, manly voice, his gestures which he has so well under control, all show him to be a good actor. In Singspiel he mostly plays comic parts, but succumbs occasionally to vulgar comedy and exaggerates." The first review quoted also praised him as a "charming singer" which the account in the *Gallerie* confirms: "his voice is pure and melodious; he sings with insight and taste."

Castelli's description of Schikaneder as a "miserable singer" conflicts with these assessments, but his memoirs reflect a man half a century later, and it is quite possible that Schikaneder's voice had changed as markedly during the course of the years, as had his appearance and his stage presence ("Schikaneder was tall and fat, had a rolling gait but very lively, expressive eyes," writes Castelli). Castelli could "never laugh wholeheartedly" at the 42-year-old character actor Schikaneder. "He wanted to be taken for a fine comedian, and consequently his humor was so 'super fine' that nobody noticed it."

While a personal impression, it at any rate testifies to the mature character of Schikaneder the actor. Earlier critics would never have used the adjective "super fine"—"exaggerated", on the other hand, was frequently used. Johann Friedel, a member of the company and therefore a close observer, defends his director against the accusation that he was a monotonous actor. "I have not seen another actor who had such an all-embracing range of voice and such rich inflection in his speech. . . . Schikaneder has eliminated all accentuation from his speech except in cases where passion demands it . . . his voice supports him in all required ways. One can understand every word, from pianissimo to fortissimo . . . He has made it his principle that it is inappropriate to overact . . . he does not deal in subtle nuances, but sacrifices these small points to the beauty of the whole."

The writer and traveler Johann Gottfried Seume visited Vienna and described Schikaneder as a "baroque personality," which certainly, even if in a somewhat stereotyped way, gets to the core of Schikaneder's acting qualities. The style of performance in southern Germany was governed by dictates other than those of the cooler north. *Hanswurst* had never been banned in the south, and the public's curiosity and need for laughter could not be extinguished. The response to plays was more sensuous, more emotional. The gap between popular theater and Shakespeare (who was regarded more as a rival to thrillers like *Count Walltron* than as a classical dramatist) was more easily bridged by the travelling theater companies: there the actors had to serve them both.

Lessing's *Hamburgische Dramaturgie* of 1767/68 first offered a German theory of the art of acting together with a theory of drama. It emphasized the ability to learn, to be conscious, disciplined, and master of controlled moderation. According to Lessing, the actor who was conscious of what he was doing "notwithstanding his indifference and coldness was far more useful in the theater" than the actor who simply lived out his parts. Young Schikaneder was unlikely to have been familiar with this, the third part of the *Hamburgische Dramaturgie*, and if so, one need only recall his style of acting to know that he would not have found anything useful in it. As an aging man perhaps; but there is scarcely any reliable criticism of Schikaneder the mature actor—he was overshadowed by Schikaneder the director and dramatist.

During his time in Vienna, Iffland and Schröder set the stylistic direction of acting. Both were well regarded throughout Germany, both were thoughtful actors who also wrote. In his *Fragmenten zur Menschendarstellung* (Fragments on the Dramatic Representation of Man) Iffland advocated complete identification. "The surest way to appear to be a noble man is to make an effort to be one. Each great condition of the soul is painted upon the face and informs the body with strengthened expression." Schröder espoused an opposing view: "The truth of the statement that an actor must only 'seem' to be what he is presenting if he will remain true to the dramatist, has been demonstrated by Ekhof. Never have I seen tears in the eyes of this extraordinary speaker, while his public could hardly dry its eyes."

Schröder's style, with his famous realistic gestures which were conscious, controlled and moderate, more nearly approached Lessing's theory. In comparing Schikaneder, a "people's actor," to other great players we can imagine that Iffland's call for the identification of "being" and "seeming" would have been foreign to a man of his temperament. He often appeared on the stage with Schröder at Vienna's Burgtheater. To what degree Schikaneder had managed to tame the "Sturm und Drang" of his youthful extravagant style by this time—and how much his "super finesse" was learned from Schröder's ideal of moderation—we don't know, for too few accounts have come down to us to allow us to form any clear opinion of Schikaneder as a mature actor.

But to return to the newly fledged theater director. After the Augsburg contract had expired, he applied to the Nuremberg municipal authorities, who willingly leased him the Baroque opera house; the town's memories of him as the actor who had recently shone as a principal hero and comedian were still fresh. And so Schikaneder, after a short spell as guest actor in Neuburg on the Danube, returned to Nuremberg for a period of six months, from Easter to the end of September 1779. This time he was at the head of his own company composed of 22 people and a corps de ballet of 14 dancers.

Together with the current theater repertoire he offered operas by Benda and Piccini, the highly successful new Singspiel *Das Milchmädchen* (The Milk Maid) by Johann Heinrich Faber and Egidio Duni, and many plays. The latter included *Hamlet* and *King Lear* (with Schikaneder playing Edgar this time), *Minna von Barnhelm*, *Emilia Galotti* and *Die Juden* by Lessing, *Clavigo*, and a sensational new play *Götz von Berlichingen*, performed on two evenings. Schikaneder also contributed as a dramatist. The bestseller of the time was the "tearjerker" novel of life in a cloister, *Siegwart*, by the young Swabian Johann Martin Miller, a poem from which, "Was frag, ich viel nach Geld und Gold" (What do I care for money or gold?) almost became a folk song. Something told Schikaneder that the novel was potentially good theater, so he concocted a dramatic version of the novel in two parts called *Der junge Siegwart*. While it met with great public applause the Catholic clergy was much aggrieved. Johann Friedel reported that "the cassocks in the house made a great noise and screamed murder," because the sentimental combination of secular love and Catholic monastic life obviously displeased them. Schikaneder withdrew it, foregoing the box office success he had hoped for from part two.

It is difficult to say whether this incident contributed to his taking to the road again once his contract expired. He had enjoyed unqualified success in Nuremberg to such an extent that he could afford a coach and team and dressed as an elegant gentleman. Whatever the

During his theater season in Salzburg, in the fall and winter of 1780–81, Schikaneder was a frequent guest of the Mozarts. They lived not far from the theater, in what is the Makartplatz today.

cause of this departure, the journey to Kärnten and then to Linz has already been described. The six-month stay in Salzburg that followed is of greater importance, for it was there that Mozart and Schikaneder met and the personal and artistic foundations of their later collaboration were laid.

The town on the river Salzach was ruled at the time by Archbishop Hieronymus Count Colloredo—an enlightened but most unpopular and harsh man—but it could boast of an active if somewhat provincial theater life. Performances were staged in no fewer than eight places, from the Residenz and monastery to the vulgar *Hanswurst* shows in the town's taverns. Colloredo was a lover of music and theater, but presentations were expected to conform to his despotic will. Five years earlier he had had the old ballroom in the Hannibal garden, not far from the present-day Landestheater, pulled down to be replaced by his own theater. In keeping with the custom of the times, he leased it to travelling companies—immediately before Schikaneder to Johann Böhm, a well-established director in

Munich and Vienna, who was particularly interested in promoting German Singspiel and had much to do with the Mozart family.

In September 1780 Schikaneder opened his season with two well-established favorites, the play *Die Gunst der Fürsten* (The Favor of Princes) and his own *Die Lyranten* (Minstrels), now entitled *Das lustige Elend oder: Die drei Bettelstudenten* (The Merry Misery or: The Three Beggar Students). He and his wife played the main roles in both pieces, and immediately captured the Salzburg audience. New works were added to the repertoire: *Hamlet*, now played in the six-act Schröder version; Schikaneder's new play *Das Regenspurger Schiff* (The Regensburg Ship); and the sensational new work from the National Theater in Mannheim, the tragedy *Agnes Bernauerin* by Joseph August Graf von Törring. The premiere in January 1781 tells us something about Schikaneder's production style and the naive delight of audiences deep in the provinces.

The director promoted the sensational project heavily and aroused people's curiosity, particularly as crowd scenes with 60 real soldiers clad in armor from the Archbishop's armory were on the menu. Audiences streamed in from far and wide, especially from Upper Bavaria. They were entranced by Emanuel and Eleonore Schikaneder, who acted the noble Bavarian duke and his beloved, the unfortunate daughter of a citizen from Augsburg. Some audience members, filled with passionate indignation, intervened in the action when Agnes Bernauerin was thrown into the Danube. Herr Waller-schenk, playing the wicked "Vizedom" who ordered her death, was so hated even off stage that theater fans insulted him in his inn and once went so far as to threaten him with a dagger. Schikaneder, ever the efficient director, capitalized on this episode. He announced: "Today Vizedom will be pushed off the bridge!" And so he was, to the jubilation of a full house. Four performances brought in 616 florins, but even better the last night of the season, late in February 1781, brought in 206 florins alone.

Schikaneder's own new work *The Regensburg Ship, A Comedy in Three Acts* was also a success. Its language was unsophisticated for it was probably written in a hurry. Its plot follows proven models; even *Minna von Barnhelm* seems to be included. In the end the heroine and the chambermaid find their true loves (a captain and a sergeant in the Hussars) despite the heroine's father, Kupferkopf (Copperhead), a miser who wishes to marry his daughter off richly. The good-humored, greedy servant Budel—"I prefer a good hunk of beef to the most beautiful bit of skirt"—adds to the fun. *Hanswurst* is obviously alive and well though now dressed in a domestic's costume. The success of the play, as was the case with *The Minstrels*, lies in its closeness to the audience's personal experiences. The setting is a ship of the kind that regularly sailed the Danube between Regensburg and Vienna. As a child Schikaneder had often sniffed the harbor air which smelled of adventure and far-off shores, and now he conjured up a time-tested love story on just such a large, wooden ship. In addition to the principals he peopled her with "various characters": musicians, bears, monkeys, gypsies, and thunder and lightning, all enlisted to provide vivid effects.

What is most characteristic of this forerunner of Schikaneder's later "local farces" is not contained in the spoken text but in the author's precise scenic instructions. As he wrote, he was mentally visualizing stage directions and set construction. For example, he noted down the final tableau for Act 2 in this way: "The market women scream amongst themselves just as they please. Budel hustles them about like dogs, running around them; Kupferkopf loses his wig, the women throw apples at his hump back; Budel runs to the ship, Kupferkopf follows him. . . . the monkeys pick up the apples, the musicians on the ship strike up a march. The bears' music commences at the same time while the women continue to scream, and so the act ends."

Archbishop Colloredo was apparently satisfied with the tenant of his theater and his 34-strong company of actors and dancers, for he extended the lease—which expired at the end of 1780—for a further two months. He attended some of the performances, but the Mozart family certainly attended even more as Schikaneder, after becoming acquainted with them, had presented them with three complimentary tickets for the entire season. For Wolfgang, thoroughly bored in the service of the tyrannical archbishop, the theater was a welcome diversion. The 24-year-old composer and the theater director, who was barely four and a half years older, met often. Schikaneder was in and out of the Mozarts' house (nearby on today's Makart-Platz). A particularly popular pastime among members of the Mozart family was "Bölzelschiessen" (air gun shooting). A light air gun was used to

Copy of a target used for the popular game "Bölzelschiessen" in Mozart's home. On the left Schikaneder is portrayed as an incorrigible Don Juan.

shoot at targets representing amusing, often obscene scenes. The ladies who participated, including Mozart's sister Nannerl and Madame Maresquelle of Schikaneder's company, took no offense with such targets, and Mozart most certainly not—one only has to remember his famous "Bäsle" letters!

One of these targets, of which a later reproduction exists, alludes to the young director's reputation as an incorrigible Don Juan. He is pictured flirting with a girl on the Linz bridge over the Danube, and from his mouth come the words "I promise each that which I never keep." The picture on the other side is of a girl holding a wine glass and waiting, comforting herself with the words "He will come soon." This caricature accords well with the fact that Schikaneder had once again fathered an illegitimate child by the actress Juliana Moll or Werner. The boy was born in 1780, but died a year later in

Salzburg after having been legitimized by the mother's betrothal to the actor Jakob Neukäufler, a name already known to the reader.

The budding friendship between Schikaneder and Mozart was nourished by their common interest in the theater. The German Singspiel was close to Schikaneder's heart, and Mozart had recently started to occupy himself with it, producing two works in quick succession. Six years previously he had begun to compose the music (two choruses) for Tobias Philipp Baron of Gebler's play *Thamos, König in Ägypten* (Thamos, King of Egypt) for Böhm's company. He extended these beginnings with a further chorus and five entr'acte interludes. Böhm tempted him with a performance, as did Schikaneder, but nothing came of either project. Apart from these efforts, Mozart set the Singspiel *Das Serail oder Die unvermutete Zusammenkunft in der Sklaverei zwischen Vater, Tochter und Sohn* (The Seraglio or The Unexpected Meeting in Slavery of Father, Daughter and Son). Under the title *Zaide*, which was given to it much later by a publisher, with a text written by the Salzburg court trumpeter Johann Andreas Schachtner, an old friend of Mozart's, the work was a kind of forerunner to *Die Entführung aus dem Serail*.

Thamos is particularly important as it throws some light on Mozart's and Schikaneder's later collaboration. Both the characters and location of this play, combined with Mozart's music, point to *The Magic Flute*. Prince Thamos—the similarity with Tamino is obvious—must undertake a variety of adventures in mythical ancient Egypt in order both to succeed the banished king, who has become the wise high priest Sethos, and to free the latter's daughter Sais. Even though the motif of fatherhood, plus one or two others, was obviously borrowed from Shakespeare's character of "the noble Prospero" in *The Tempest*, Gebler's play anticipates Sarastro's loftier features. It is quite possible that Mozart and Schikaneder occupied themselves with the *Thamos* theme during their Salzburg days, and that they may even have had a production in mind. Komorzynski thinks it was "highly probable" that "the two friends had already planned to create Prince Tamino out of Prince Thamos," but this argument is contravened by several historical facts. Whatever enthusiasms the two may have shared, they had little more than a month's time to devote to it. Mozart left for Munich by November 5 to complete and rehearse *Idomeneo*, his most important Italian opera seria. It is hard to believe that the few previous weeks could have been burdened with plans for a work in an entirely different genre, as the Singspiel then was. Certainly, while in Munich Mozart often inquired about Salzburg theater life, but his thoughts were occupied by matters other than their common interest in the German Singspiel. Further, by the time Mozart returned to his hated birthplace after the success of *Idomeneo* in Munich, Schikaneder had set out on a new tour.

Schikaneder had a between-season engagement in Laibach—he had to take what was offered—and two summer seasons in 1781 and 1782 in Graz. He had never in his life been at a loss for sensational works that might bring good box office receipts, and in Graz he succeeded not only in enticing the public into the theater, but out into the countryside, where he produced the highly successful *Der Graf von Walltron* as a military spectacle under an open sky. He had military tents erected, an encampment of some 200 of them, riders rode in on "real" horses, and the countess came on in a coach. The public flocked in as well. An element in Schikaneder's historical importance is undoubtedly his pioneering of the open-air festival theater.

His theatrical family grew in Laibach when his brother Urban joined the troupe having become bored with the episcopal chapel in Freising. In Graz they were joined by Urban's son Karl, but he did not get on with his uncle and soon left. Schikaneder moved on to Pressburg (a Hungarian city at the time), presenting a full season from the fall of 1782 through the spring of 1783. It was here that he became acquainted with a fellow actor of about his own age who was to profoundly influence both his personal and artistic fortunes.

Johann Friedel (born in 1751 or 1752 in Hungarian Temésvár, died in Vienna 1789) quickly became Schikaneder's admirer and friend, later his wife's companion and, towards the end of his short life, a key figure in Schikaneder's great theatrical fame. Friedel, himself an officer's son and destined for a military career, quickly left the army, being drawn to a literary life. As a young liberal he went to Berlin, where he fell out with the authoritarian Friedrich Nicolai, became an actor, returned to Austria and made his way as an "enlightened" critical journalist and novelist. He was lively, alert, and capable of great enthusiasms. Whether due to Schikaneder's presentations in

Pressburg or the attraction of his wife Eleonore, Friedel joined the company. From that moment on he became the director's close friend, an intimate friend of Eleonore (a fact which apparently did not disturb her husband) and, through his writings, an avowed champion of Schikaneder. Later he wrote the satirical *Letters from Vienna*, comedies which castigated aristocratic arrogance and false jesuitical piety; and a novel *Heinrich von Wallheim* which is counted a forerunner to the Viennese novel of manners. Friedel was a good-natured, charitable man who relentlessly strove to realize the high ideals of Josephinism—a man of some genius, an intellectual "Jacobin" in Austria. He accompanied Schikaneder to Vienna, where the troupe, reduced by adverse financial circumstances, acted a successful *Hamlet* among other plays, in the Kärntnertor Theater, and then to Pressburg for the fall of 1783 where Schikaneder was forced to seek the financial support of a certain Herr Kumpf—without much success.

In the meantime Schikaneder had enlarged the company's repertoire with several plays, both serious and comedic. As was customary at the time, he was more than generous with the intellectual property of others—as indeed Berthold Brecht was to be a century and a half later. The finer points of literature did not interest him—and when indeed could he have found time for them in his harried life as director, actor and dramatist? His main objective was that the plays, whether tragedies or comedies, should have parts that would project across the footlights and particularly that the principal roles best fitted himself. The two "historical plays", *Philippine Welserin, die schöne Herzogin von Tyrol* (Philippine Welser, the Beautiful Duchess of the Tyrol) and *Herzog Ludwig von Steiermark oder Sarmät's Feuerbär* (Duke Ludwig of Styria or Sarmät's Firebear), may have appeared as early as 1780 or 1781.

It is difficult to understand why Schikaneder included them in his *Collected Works*, printed in 1792, as they are among the weakest of his output. *Philippine Welserin* is a variation of the Agnes Bernauerin tragedy, transplanted to the Tyrolean castle of Ambras, this time with a happy ending and romantic episodes of robbers, ghosts and mountain trolls. The villain, a rascally old courtier, is given long monologues full of revenge motifs, interspersed with frequent exclamations of "Ha!" There is little to laugh about—today we would describe it as unintentional comedy. The *Herzog Ludwig*, on the other hand, with its naive, rustic pair of lovers, Matthies and Trautel, does contain some cheerful theater "business" in the midst of its courtly plot. The theme turns on the struggle for power in Styria, a province in Austria, during post-Carolingian times. The rightful duke, banished by his ambitious cousin, is aided by a noble magician named Sarmät (who sends the fire bear mentioned in the subtitle into the struggle and enlists thunder and lightning). "Do not tremble! Sarmät loves every little worm in nature; all the more does he love mankind." Sarmät reveals himself as an enlightened humanist of Josephinism, perhaps even a forefather of Sarastro. A dialogue with the rustic Matthies does in fact remind us of one of the trial scenes between Papageno and his priestly escort:

> MATTHIES: Tell me how I can escape the hangman's rope.
> SARMÄT: You must use your own reason here . . . I cannot do it! (*The Magic Flute*, Act 2. Sc.7, Second Priest to Papageno: "Your reason can best answer this question for you.")

Schikaneder published two works in Salzburg in 1783, largely examples of his vanity and self confidence, for neither is of any distinction. *Die Raubvögel* (The Birds of Prey), a drama in five acts, came impudently in the wake of Lessing's triumphant *Minna von Barnhelm*. Lessing's character Tellheim here becomes Hauptmann von Rechthold and is just as fussy about his reputation. He is obsessed by the gambling demon for which reason his wife has left him. Before a reconciliation is reached, Lessing's complete list of characters has been mobilized under different names, and the innkeeper has been redrawn in the style of popular comedy. He beats his wife, hides timidly behind furniture, and obsequiously flatters the powers that be. He is a kind of *Hanswurst*, and Schikaneder certainly wrote the part for himself. The boisterous basically honest colonel has his part too, as *deus ex machina*. Schikaneder often evinced his theatrical fondness for such swashbucklers in uniform, probably for the same reason as did his petty-bourgeois public who held the military in high esteem.

Das Laster kömmt an Tage (Vice Comes to Light) owes its inspiration to Lessing as well, this time to *Emilia Galotti*, but with a happy ending. The theme is a primitively constructed court intrigue: an aristocratic lady seeks to expose her rival in love as a brewer of poisons. "The whole play gives the impression of unintentional parody," was Kormorzynski's judgment in his first Schikaneder monograph. In the enlarged second edition of 1951, however, he has only words of the highest praise, arguing that even the great Lope de Vega was forced to write a prodigious number of mediocre plays to meet public demand. This is not to disparage either and surely not Schikaneder, who, as a playwright, was quite inferior to Lope de Vega.

His tragedy performed in Pressburg in 1784, *Kinder, reizet eure Eltern, und Eltern, reizet eure Kinder nicht* (Children, Do Not Provoke Your Parents; Parents, Do Not Provoke Your Children), curious but typical for the times, raises two matters worth noting. First, the author's instinct for a promising theme of topical interest: he deftly turned the true story of the double murder of two lovers, who had come to grief by virtue of social barriers, into a drama—such an event having occured a few weeks previously in Pressburg. Secondly, the effect this play had on a prominent theatergoer, the Emperor Joseph II. He was so impressed by this variation on the *Cabal and Love* theme that he invited Schikaneder from provincial Pressburg to Vienna.

Another tragedy in four acts written at roughly the same time—at least before 1785—*Der Grandprofoss* (The Grand Provost) proved to be a great public draw, though it was basically only a variation of another theatrical success of his company, Möller's *Count Walltron*. In Möller's play an officer awaits his death sentence, condemned for insubordination towards his superior, but in the end he is pardoned. Schikaneder intensified the inherent tension of this theme to a tearjerker, so that no eye in the house remained dry. While the military is involved, it is now a woman with whom we must identify. Her husband is an honorable but impoverished sergeant. Following Schiller's established model in *Die Räuber*, Schikaneder has this character play opposite a villainous, almost sadistic cadet sergeant. To appease the hunger of her children, the wife steals a turkey from peasants, and as a punishment and deterrent she is sentenced to be beheaded. Audiences clearly felt the ruling of the pitiless Grand Provost, the regimental judge, inhuman, and Schikaneder does his utmost to stretch his compassionate public on the rack, even

Schikaneder in the title role of the comedy *Der Fremde* (The Stranger) by Johann Friedel. Copper engraving by Hieronymus Löschenkohl, 1785.

including a scene in which an innocent child pleads for the condemned woman. Will the poor soul be beheaded or not? She is, off stage, of course. But her husband, the sergeant, takes his revenge by shooting the cruel, lustful and self-gratifying Grand Provost. Minutes before, the brave sergeant had saved the life of the king, who was threatened with death in the heat of battle. Now he gives himself up to cold justice with touching words, stolen from Schiller: ". . . I have been avenged: now I am your prisoner." In a final and to some extent enlightened speech, the upright colonel refers to the sad events—another example of Schikaneder's conforming to the public glorification of the military: "O people! O people! If only you had compassion for the right thing, if only lust for revenge never possessed you!"

Pious sentiments. But in restless times, when people sought greater humanity and justice, these sentiments touched the nerve of the public, that scarcely definable mass of people in their boxes which cost florins, together with those in the balcony, whose seats only cost kreuzers. Schikaneder's tearjerkers were virtually absent of artistic merit, but their cleverly contrived spectacular qualities met the needs of the public—the poor and the rich, the little man and the great could weep together.

The "general harvest of tears collected at this play is proof and satisfaction for my work," wrote Schikaneder in the "Preface" with which he introduced the publication of this, his most successful play to date. "I don't write for readers, I write for the theater, to which I invite my friend the critic. He may laugh about it afterwards . . . My main aim is to promote the box office and to provide what is most effective on the stage, in order to have a full house and good takings." While not very literate, these words are honest and thoroughly realistic. Schikaneder was subsidized by no prince, but rather an itinerant manager dependent on box office takings and a full house. The public only bought tickets when it could expect something from a performance, and it expected more from comedians like Schikaneder than from dramatists like Goethe or Lessing.

In the summer of 1784 Schikaneder and his troupe made their way to Pest. At that time the German theater set the tone in the Hungarian capital as it did in all the cities of the Empire. It was only to be a short between-season stay. "Here he made many enemies due to a love affair and some extemporaneous speeches, and so we were forced to leave quite soon," reports his nephew Karl Schikaneder, who was with him as an actor. Nevertheless, Schikaneder made a name for himself in the annals of Budapest theater: he performed the first opera in the German language there, *Die Schule der Eifersüchtigen* (School of Jealousy), at the little wooden theater next to the Ofen bridge. In the fall he returned with his company to the more modest conditions of Pressburg. I have already mentioned that fate ordained that Emperor Joseph II should attend two of the performances on his way through Pressburg which pleased him so much that he honored Schikaneder with a private audience and took him to Vienna.

The Emperor wished to enlist Schikaneder's assistance in his cultural-political effort to establish a German Singspiel tradition. A short time before Mozart's *Die Entführung* had had a resounding success in the Hoftheater next to the Burg. But as no other works of similar genius materialized to follow this success, the Italian opera supporters had their way yet again in the Burgtheater, and even the Emperor could offer nothing more than the lease of the second court theater at the Kärntnertor. The director of the "Schikaneder—Kumpf Company", Schikaneder knew exactly what he was doing when he chose *Die Entführung* for his opening performance on November 5, 1784. A month later he followed this with the comedy *Der Fremde* by Johann Friedel. He then presented a "fantastic comedy" which had been quite successful in Pressburg, but we do not even know its exact title. According to information that has come down to us, it must have been a work which would make Schikaneder appear as the forefather of the modern, satirical, surrealistic theater. When we read of chickens and geese cackling and honking about the stage, we can imagine a renaissance of Aristophanes's comedy *The Birds*. But are we not also reminded of Ionesco's *Rhinoceros*? Members of a society at the end of the world are to recognize themselves in Ionesco's monster animal just as the citizens of Pressburg were expected to see themselves in the geese. But the Viennese did not find "the bird comedy" at all funny and booed it off the stage.

Schikaneder, however, took his revenge: assured of the Emperor's favor he could afford to ridicule citizens who visited his theater too rarely to keep it solvent. With *Der Bucentaurus oder: Die Vermählung mit dem Meere in Venedig* (The Bucentaurus or: The Marriage with the

Sea in Venice), first performed in Pressburg as well, Schikaneder had had more serious intentions. It turns on a noble Doge who is to be overthrown by aristocratic rivals aided by a sorceress; at the same time the parade ship "Bucentaurus" is to be blown up. When these plots misfire, the Venetian ruler is as generous in his pardons as Selim Bassa in Mozart's *Entführung* and as Emperor Joseph in his enlightened Utopian reforms. Typical opera themes of love, hate and lust for power are interspersed with monologues that deserve our attention, for in them Schikaneder assumes the voice of the little man in order to give a piece of his mind to his aristocratic audience. Thus a servant philosophizes with this common touch:

> On close inspection, all these gentlemen with their riches are only poor devils in this world! Unrest—boredom—persecution—and false ambition are their closest relatives. I would rather praise the working man who eats the bread he has earned with happy cheer, and whose honest work during the day leads him to sleep well at night.

Schikaneder's directorship of the Kärntnertor Theater lasted from only November 1784 until the beginning of 1785. He succeeded only partially in fulfilling the Emperor's hopes for a flourishing German Singspiel. As the lead actor he received great applause in the new comedy *Der Fremde* in which he played the part of a count on a secret diplomatic mission. Friedel played Baron Seltenreich (Seldom-Rich), a caricature of a scheming windbag of the Viennese aristocracy. We have to ask ourselves whether the applause for such audacity contributed to the Emperor's last-minute cancellation of a performance of Schikaneder's version of Beaumarchais's famous comedy *The Marriage of Figaro*. The censors had passed the play which, robbed of its incendiary remarks had been rendered suitable for the court theater. Rehearsals were due to begin, at the Burgtheater! Perhaps Schikaneder had not drawn the play's fangs quite so thoroughly as Lorenzo da Ponte was to do a year later in his libretto for Mozart. At any rate, the Emperor finally permitted the Figaro opera to be performed, though against strong opposition.

Other questions remain unanswered, for Schikaneder's version has disappeared, along with dozens of other works from his pen. Nor do we have any knowledge of whether the honor of acquainting

Mozart with the Figaro material can be attributed to Schikaneder. Komorzynski attributes it to him without reservations. We only know that Mozart and Schikaneder met socially, that Schikaneder visited the composer in his lodgings behind St. Stephen's Cathedral, and that Mozart attended his productions.

The Emperor also attended Schikaneder's first nights at the Kärntnertor theater, but there were fewer in the audience than had been hoped for. The Kumpf-Schikaneder company was dissolved at the beginning of 1785 for reasons of personal incompatibility. The director simply could not give up his amorous, extramarital escapades, and Eleonore finally had enough. She took her revenge by breaking up the conjugal household, going off to live with Friedel and forming her own theater company with him. They tried their luck first in Wiener Neustadt and Klagenfurt. It says much for Schikaneder's reputation as an actor and for the tolerant generosity of the Emperor that the latter immediately engaged him to join the ensemble of the National Theater "next to the Burgtheater." At the time the great actor Friedrich Ludwig Schröder was director there and Schikaneder could learn much from him. However, he was engaged to sing, not to play his usual heroic roles, which were already taken. As a baritone he had great success in Gluck's *Die Pilgrimen von Mecca* and in the German Singspiel repertoire requested by the Emperor. But he had been widely acclaimed as a Shakespearean actor, and now had to be content with supporting roles in the Burgtheater, playing opposite the well-established "first hero", Johann Franz Hieronymus Brockmann. When he pushed himself into the limelight too far, Brockmann's supporters tended to boo him off the stage. Schikaneder was certainly not fulfilled as an actor at the Burgtheater.

Thus it is not surprising that in December 1785 he applied to the powerful Regent of Regensburg, Prince Carl Anselm von Thurn und Taxis, for the directorship of a "German Acting Company." When the application was rejected in a letter of three lines, he applied again four weeks later to the Emperor, whose affection he still retained. This time his aim was higher: permission to build his own theater "in a suburb," where he promised he would put on "German moral plays." The Emperor quickly granted him this privilege in February 1786. In the meantime Italian opera, although occasionally played in

German, had reconquered both court theaters, the Kärntnertor Theater (which had been rebuilt the previous summer) and the National Theater in the Michaelerplatz. In spite of *Die Entführung*, German Singspiel had no home of its own in which it could grow. Might it be able to find one outside the "Glacis" (today's Ringstrasse) in one of the suburbs which already boasted a new and extremely popular theater?

In 1781 the actor and director Karl Marinelli (1744–1803) had opened a theater in Leopoldstadt, east of the branch of the Danube that is today encased in concrete and called the Donau Kanal. The building was set inconspicuously in a crowded street, lower than the neighboring houses, small in its proportions, with an orchestra pit only 2 meters deep. The manager of such a theater had to husband his money. The theater's exterior lighting was so bad that sarcastic reports went about that the director had adapted himself to the district on purpose, because it was the prostitutes' quarter.

But Marinelli, son of a sub-cantor of St. Stephen's Cathedral, proved himself to be an extremely efficient theater director. As a dramatist his output was the usual sentimental and comic fare. Some recognition is due to him for his introduction of the character of the sympathetic, comic Hungarian, pointing toward Strauss' *Gypsy Baron*. But he soon gave up writing dramas, putting his trust in the popular "Kasperliaden" [tr. note: the German equivalent of the Punch and Judy show] with which his star Johann Laroche, the celebrated new Kasperl, could fill the house. Marinelli, who was cautious and calculating by nature, always managed to put on whatever would please at the moment; when demand for German operas and Singspiel increased he added them. And so, without any high cultural or political ambition, he later became a serious rival to Schikaneder. He died a rich man, finally raised to the rank of nobleman.

Joseph II would most certainly not have awarded Marinelli a title. He saw no future in the crude Leopoldstadt Volkstheater; his dreams of an enlightened German music theater were better founded in the younger Schikaneder and explain the rapidly granted privilege to build a theater. However, it remained a project for 15 years since Schikaneder lacked the money to build, and even the Holy Roman Emperor at that time felt less cultural and political responsibility when it was a question of money than many a small-town mayor today.

Two more comedies by Schikaneder have been preserved from this time because he thought them worth including in his *Collected Works* seven years later. They are somewhat better than his highly aristocratic pseudo-histories for they contain real parts for himself. *Die Postknechte oder die Hochzeit ohne Braut* (The Postboys, or The Wedding Without a Bride) extends the story of an honest post-master, taken from Iffland's popular comedy *Die Jäger* (The Huntsmen), into five acts. The postman is forced to defend himself against the intrigues of the powerful governor bent on revenge because the postmaster's daughter Viktorl has given him the brush-off. Before she can win her "Franz", a *deus ex machina* must intervene in the form of Count Billenhof who, Emperor-Joseph-like, has been mixing among the common people incognito. The following incident occurs five minutes before the final curtain:

> BILLENHOF: (tears off his coat which has concealed his medals and star) Lieutenant! Read these!
> LIEUTENANT: (bowing) The new Governor!

The tearing-off of the coat must have produced such cries of delighted astonishment that Schikaneder was to use the effect again later, in *Das Abgebrannte Haus* (The Burnt-down House). Now and again stock characters are refined to become sharply drawn human beings. The postmaster's wife, for example, addicted to dancing and with a childish penchant for fine things and townish styles, has had her imitators throughout the ages. The chief clerk, who considers himself somewhat better than his rustic fellow-villagers, is also exposed to ridicule because his speech continually reverts from stilted High German to his native dialect: "I shall inform her, if you will most graciously allow it—as a precaution I shall also bring a light, or t'pair of us'll go ass-over-tip down t'steps." It is perhaps too much to claim that one has a premonition of Nestroy here. At any rate, no slapstick or coarse jokes are used, but rather jokes with lan-guage. Certainly the chief clerk has something of Nestroy's black humor in the scene in which, acting as a guide for some strangers, he introduces them to the "curiosities" of the village and sings the praises of the gallows hill. "We've got such a grand show of 'eads—it 'ud be a reet pleasure to be up thar along-side of 'em!"

Die getreuen Unterthanen oder Der ehrliche Bandit (The Trusty Subjects or The Honest Bandit) is titled a comedy, but does not offer much to laugh about. And how could it, when it concerns a villainous young man who, unwilling to await the death of his uncle the worthy general for his inheritance, engages an impoverished captain to kill him? Naturally the latter does not cooperate, and turns out to be the general's son who was thought to be dead. We have already mentioned that Schikaneder always regarded the military as honorable men, and seemingly so did his public. Were it not for a pseudo-creepy midnight scene of ghosts who find the villain guilty, one could consider this so-called comedy, whose comic elements are restricted to inserted rustic scenes, as being close to the "tearful comedies" of Marivaux. Certainly Schikaneder did not have the same subtleties at his fingertips; he was more cynical, for example, when he has the legacy hunter's cheeky servant dicker with his "fine" master: "You listen! I've lied so much to the old dog that tears were brimming in his eyes . . . If you don't give me at least three ducats this time, you can do your own dirty work next time!"

After a few guest performances at the Burgtheater, Schikaneder gathered a small company together (without his wife and Friedel) and set off on tour through southern Germany. In 1786 he again made a stop in Salzburg, called on Leopold Mozart, and engaged a young tenor named Benedikt Schack, who was to go down in history five years later as the first Tamino in *The Magic Flute*. The municipal authorities in Augsburg had happy memories of Schikaneder, so leased him the town theater for the summer of 1786. He repeated his past successes including Mozart's *Entführung*, but since its source, the spoken comedy *Das Räuschchen* (The Tipsy One) by Christian Friedrich Bretzner, was again all the rage, he put it on as well. He would only too gladly have repeated his open-air sensation *Count Walltron*, but this time he had to be satisfied with a performance of it in a small theater: "Today we intend to perform *Walltron* exactly as if we were playing it in the open air"—that is, "with real tents . . . newly made uniforms . . . drum and pipes . . . Turkish music."

However, another sensational "open-air" spectacle in Augsburg inspired him to jump on the bandwagon, using his good business sense and his slick hand at writing. Baron Joseph Maximilian von

Lütgendorf, a member of the household of the Regensburg Prince Thurn und Taxis, announced a "balloon ascent" planned to take place outside the gates of Augsburg on August 24, 1786. Since Montgolfier's pioneer flight from Versailles in 1783, several attempts had been made in Germany—Goethe had sent off balloons from Weimar a year later. The city fathers of Augsburg, obviously adept at the tourist business, organized a huge public celebration to mark the ascent. They built a wooden amphitheater in a field which could seat 4,320 people. Tens of thousands of visitors streamed into the city from all over southern Germany, but all had to disperse shortly in deep disappointment, for the undertaking ended miserably: postponed many times because of bad weather, it was finally called off. Baron von Lütgendorf was forced to take to his heels one dark night. Thus neither Schikaneder's open-air spectacle *Count Walltron* nor a performance of the operetta *The Air Balloon*, written especially for the occasion, took place. All that remains of the latter are texts to the arias, but from these we can learn something about the plot. The beautiful Sophie is pursued by a rich, old sea captain, who is himself pursued by the marriage-crazed hostess of an inn. An ambitious young man named Le Blanc and yet another swain are courting Sophie. In the end Le Blanc wins her heart and hand, thanks to his bravery in ascending in a balloon, a test of courage which the young pair undergo together in the balloon basket. Sophie extols her luck on landing:

> *Geld zeigt die wahre Liebe nie*
> *Ihr Quell ist Seelenharmonie.*

> Gold never shows true love her course,
> But harmony of souls is her one source.

Then together they sing a song praising the enlightened monarchy:

> *Heil dem Staat! der sich zum Ruhme*
> *Edle Künste schützt and nährt*
> *Und im Menschenheiligthume*
> *Ihnen süssen Lohn gewährt.*

> Hail to the state, which in its glory
> Perfects and nourishes the noblest arts,

And in human sanctuary
Offers them their sweet rewards.

Schikaneder's biographer Komorzynski believes there are links to *The Magic Flute* in these verses, which relate to some of the Freemasonry ideals; and also in the layout of the work—two lovers together overcome a great danger. He finds these facts furnishing proof that Schikaneder was indeed the librettist of *The Magic Flute*. But lovers undergoing hazardous tests together are typical of a whole genre which flourished at the time in novels and plays. Sources like the *Contes des fées* of about 1700 from France, Terrasson's novel *Sethos* and Ignaz von Born's Egyptian essay (we shall come back to these in more detail when examining *The Magic Flute*), together with dozens of magic and fairy plays for the theater confirm the popularity of this theme. Schikaneder was certainly familiar with some of them. It speaks for his quick ability to cash in on a sensational event and turn it into good theater that he was able to substitute an air balloon for traditional magic with its attendant dragons, abysses and volcanoes. Komorzynski also suggests that Schikaneder here took to composing again, 10 years after his first musical work, *The Minstrels*, but recent sources point to Benedikt Schack (or Schak), the composer-tenor of Schikaneder's company, as the writer of the missing "air balloon" songs.

Another member of the troupe was the composer of a "serious, heroic Singspiel" titled *Balders Tod* (Balder's Death) which Schikaneder subsequently produced in Augsburg at the time. It was set apart from the usual run of repertoire, being a Germanic mythological theme based on a play by the Dane Johannes Ewald. Schikaneder adapted it to the German Singspiel stage, and sang its praises at great length in the program notes. He did this partly for publicity's sake, referring to the eagerly awaited spectacles of "heroes' combats" and "Valkyries' rides through the air," but partly for instruction's sake, when he explains "mythological words which occur," like Asgaard and Valhalla. Two generations before Wagner this was daring but also necessary. Finally his program notes come down in a sober fashion: "Tickets for boxes can be bought at my apartment on the third floor of 'The Three Kings.'"

In October 1786 Schikaneder extended his contract with the municipal authorities in Augsburg but meanwhile gave frequent guest performances in towns in Upper Swabia and kept a close eye on the south German theater scene. An application to the Prince of Thurn und Taxis in Regensburg had been turned down the year before, but conditions in the theater there had changed. In 1786 the Prince disbanded the Italian opera, partly because it had become too expensive, but also because theater-loving "legations" in Regensburg prefered to see German works. Schikaneder's reputation as a successful director and actor was so secure that the Prince leased him his "Comedy Theater" in the Aegidienplatz. On May 29, 1787, with a company of 20 actresses and actors, later to be enlarged by five, Schikaneder began his two-year directorship of the so-called "German National Theater" in his former home town. The poor servant's son had returned as a celebrated man of the theater.

This was indeed a promotion, even from Augsburg. Not that the two towns were of such different status—or if so, only from a theatrical point of view. Augsburg's patrician municipal authorities were well disposed towards Schikaneder, but they were miserly about every florin. When he tried to get his lease reduced from 16 florins a day to 12, they would only come down to 14. Princes certainly had no need to be so parsimonious; Carl Anselm von Thurn und Taxis had inherited a huge fortune which increased daily through the Taxis' lucrative postal service, operating throughout the entire Empire. He could afford to offer his youngest theater director— Schikaneder's former director Andreas Schopf has preceded him—a contractual guaranty of 3,552 florins a year in subscriptions from the princely household alone. Added to this were other subscriptions and the box office takings. Moreover, in Schikaneder's last year in Regensburg the guarantee, which was in effect a subsidy (by no means usual at the time), increased to almost 5,000 florins, a figure that must have made Schikaneder dizzy, but not the Prince who had recently spent 25,000 florins a year on that fashionable luxury, the Italian opera.

A comparison of these figures reflects just how low German actors of the time ranked in the aristocratic set of values, in comparison to Italian singers. Similarly Schikaneder encountered personal problems because he paid his mistress, the supporting singer Jagdstein, 56 florins a month, which other members considered excessive. The primadonna of the previous Italian company had earned about 170 florins a month, though the Kapellmeister only earned 120. The Prince may indeed have paid homage for years to the status symbol of Italian opera, as was in accordance with the times and his rank, but he had no wish to let German actors vegetate in the smoky chambers of inns like 'The Blue Pike' in Regensburg's oldtown. He was a despotic ruler, but he was also a theater lover. This is not at all obvious when one reads his correspondence relative to Schikaneder's appointment; the Prince had no intention of concerning himself "further with the theater, neither directly nor indirectly," that is, "his Highness is totally indifferent as to whether Peter or Paul be director." And yet Schikaneder was obliged to place enough tickets (usually about a hundred) at the disposal of the Prince's family and his complete household for every performance.

The princely household was enormous: it included 238 persons and 155 court pensioners. Prince Carl Anselm was a great lord holding not only the postal service monopoly but also systematically extending his estates throughout southern Germany. He was also imperial "Principal Commissioner" to the perpetual "Imperial Diet." Both were shadow titles as the "Imperial Diet" had had no authority for quite some time. The representatives of the electors, the princes of the realm and the towns of the realm dealt with trivial matters, rather like the envoys in the legations of foreign sovereigns. At any rate, Prince Carl Anselm's family, multiplied a hundred times by other aristocratic households, added up to a community bored by the old-fashioned bourgeois town, especially when the Prince left for Trugenhofen, his summer residence near Nördlingen. They were grateful for any amusement the community could offer—especially the theater.

One can imagine the exotic intrigues that this hothouse atmosphere of boredom produced. A solid, settled theater director of Schikanader's ability could have taken his ease indefinitely on the soft bed of princely subsidies, but Schikaneder had not settled down, nor did he want to take his ease indefinitely. For some reason the Prince's courtier, Baron von Lilien, who chose the plays, was not Schikaneder's friend, but this fact was balanced by the theater's achievements, which were considerable. However, Schikaneder was an incorrigible Don Juan: he embarked on affairs with his principal actresses and was finally forced to cut the Gordian knot by dismissing

The old ballroom of the Thurn und Taxis family in Regensburg, in which the court theater played from 1760–1786. After 1786 the town leased it to theater directors, among them Schikaneder, who managed it out of his own pocket. The picture shows Prince Carl Anselm's masquerade ball in 1771.

Madame Seve ("leading romantic roles in Singspiel") and Madame Engst ("leading romantic roles, ladies of quality"). He secured some internal peace—as it happened, too late, for he had alienated himself from the Freemasons of Regensburg, who were sworn to protect morality.

He had just applied for admission to their lodge "Die Wachsende zu den drei Schlüsseln," having been a "welcome but irregular visitor," when he was suspended from further visits for six months. This episode is of some importance in light of *The Magic Flute*. Its Masonic components certainly hark back to Schikaneder who was possibly a more committed Mason than Mozart. Schikaneder's humble letter of reply to his "most highly esteemed brothers," in which he protested his reverence for the "honorable position" of the Freemasons, may have been the work of a clever rhetorician. We cannot be certain whether "the incident which caused such a sensation" mentioned by the Masonic lodge refers to Schikaneder's 'amours' within his company, or to the rumors that he was having an affair with Frau von Train, the morganatic wife of the Prince. If true, the affair says much about Schikaneder's powers of attraction as a lover, and for the susceptibility of the lady, who was born into a bourgeois family and raised to the aristocracy by the Prince. It also speaks for the generosity of the ruler, who remained favorably disposed towards Schikaneder—or does it simply speak for the aristocracy's morals of the time? After all, Schikaneder was only an actor. Be that as it may, his first biographer, his nephew Carl, was not entirely incorrect when he wrote that his uncle had ruined himself yet again through his love affairs. This judgment may be appropriate to Schikaneder's character and nature, but is by no means crucial to the artistic characteristics of his career.

He was entirely successful in Regensburg as far as the theater was concerned. He had brought his established plays with him, some of which enjoyed an even greater success with splendid open-air performances. *Count Walltron* had never failed; now he produced it in high summer, advertising it in sensational and glowing terms and undoubtedly living up to them: "with all possible pomp and splendor." The claims he made for his own *The Grand Provost* were aimed at arousing curiosity: "the camp is pitched quite differently from Walltron!"

Schikaneder produced his greatest open-air triumphs on the Oberwehre, as the island in the Danube near the old bridge was then called. These were *Balders Tod* and Schiller's *Die Räuber*, with added battle scenes of his invention. But his tour de force was his one new production from his Regensburg days, the drama *Hanns Dollinger oder dase heimliche Blutgericht* (Hanns Dollinger or The Secret Blood Tribunal). Three thousand people attended a single performance on July 20, 1788, and the evening's takings reached the immense sum of 1,500 florins, which is entirely believable as the boxes cost up to 11 florins, twice as much as in Viennese suburban theaters. The best seats cost 1 florin 24 kreuzer (in the Freihaustheater such seats cost about 17 kreuzer), while the cheapest seats cost 12 kreuzer (9 in the Freihaus).

But the public's expectations were certainly fulfilled; there were duels and knightly processions with hundreds of extras, battle music with kettledrums and trumpets—Schikaneder never performed anything without music—and gruesome scenes of blood tribunals with masked vehmic courts, effects which Kleist had used in his *Kätchen von Heilbronn.*

In *Hanns Dollinger* Schikaneder appealed to the patriotic feelings of his public. His hero was a Bavarian knight in Ottonian times who had often figured in historical chronicles, and broadsheets about him were still in circulation. Schikaneder was the first to put on the stage the history of brave Dollinger, who defeated the invader Krako the Hun in knightly combat. It was an original drama, despite frequent borrowings from established theatrical situations and characters, particularly from Goethe's *Götz von Berlichingen*. Schikaneder took the plot of the wicked, poison-dealing adversaries of the noble knights surrounding the hero from that drama and borrowed the hero's character and personality in addition. However, he coarsened Goethe's enlightened and upright man into an old blustering, wooden, pompous German prig with a penchant for talking about himself in the third person. Today the yellowed old print strikes one as being unintentionally funny, like a parody of a play about knights. But the dramatic conventions of laughter and pity change, and the fact that Schikaneder wrote the part of Dollinger for himself and had great success with it both here and later in Vienna indicates, as today's readers must concede, that at least as actor and dramatist he knew how to touch the heroic chords of his time.

He borrowed from Schiller's *Die Räuber* the moving scene in which a prisoner in a dungeon is secretly brought food by compassionate and noble people. He had thoroughly absorbed the pathos of "Sturm und Drang," as witnessed by Dollinger's sister Anna who, driven half-mad by the news of their parents' death, says: "Tell me, brother, where the carpenter lives; he must come and take the measurements of my bed! Ha! ha! ha! what a resting place it will be! So many guests come daily to table—such hungry guests that they will greedily feed on my entrails." But the hero, Hanns Dollinger, is in no way afflicted by these Schiller-like, macabre lines. Schikaneder prepares us for his duel with the fearsome Krako with an almost Homerian battle of words:

> KRAKO: Kämpfer habt ihr keinen, denn ich habe keinen gefunden.
> DOLLINGER: Sollst ihn finden! Hier steht einer!
> KRAKO: Du?—Wer hat dich gebohren?

DOLLINGER: Deutschland!

KRAKO: Ins Mauseloch mit dir!

DOLLINGER: In die Hölle mit dir, du heidnischer Satan!

KRAKO: Thou hast no warriors because I have found none!

DOLLINGER: Thou hast found one! Here he stands!

KRAKO: Thou? Who hast borne thee?

DOLLINGER: Germany!

KRAKO: Into a mousehole with thee!

DOLLINGER: And to Hell with thee, thou heathen Satan!

In the end the German Emperor also joins in the patriotic sentiments when in a final tableau he raises the victorious hero, "Come to my bosom, thou upright, honest man! Come, brave German!"

How false and embarrassing this sounds to 20th-century ears! But it came straight from the hearts of most of the citizens of Schikaneder's time. It was directed against the abusive, petty princelings who exploited and sold their subjects like slaves and was in tune with the fervently desired social harmony of an enlightened ruler like Joseph II. Even Mozart, worlds away from any kind of chauvinism, always used the word "German" rather than "Austrian." Schikaneder was clearly a man of his times. *Hanns Dollinger* was a drama about knights; though of no literary substance, it held the stage in southern Germany until 1830 and beyond.

Regensburg's open-air theater gave Schikaneder a great opportunity to develop his remarkably original talent. We might today describe him as simply the champion of "Grand Spectacle." But his reputation in Regensburg was also equivocal—critics, especially those not of Regensburg, were aware of the gulf between the great success his plays enjoyed with the public and their lack of literary worth. *The Grand Provost* appeared in print in 1787, so that apart from the visual impression it had created, it now had to stand the test of critical reading. We have already quoted from Schikaneder's forthright introduction to this edition: "My main purpose lies in promoting the director's box office," etc. This remark could only lead to a lambasting by critics oriented towards pedagogy and literature. The *Allgemeine deutsche Bibliothek* wrote ironically that *The Grand Provost* would be "eligible to win a prize for the worst drama." Yet it had to be Schikaneder's most successful work—such is the way of the world! The more grandiose Schikaneder's spectacles became, the more they fed the newly-coined and derisive word "Schikanederei".

But despite criticism he continued along his path at the Comedy Theater unperturbed. Mozart's *Entführung* was often played, although the public's interest was turning from the Singspiel to other theater. The classics, Shakespeare, Lessing, Goethe and Schiller, could be seen along with current popular plays and several dramas by Schikaneder, since lost. The industry of Schikaneder and his company astonishes today's observers. It strikes us as almost superhuman when we discover that no fewer than 81 different plays were performed during the eight months from January to the end of August 1788, on only 96 evenings. The actors and singers were compelled to learn new parts constantly, for the public was avid for one novelty after another. Schikaneder's theater was full of vitality—it had to be.

Whether it was his amours or court intrigues that finally undermined his position, or whether, ambitious as he was, he looked on Regensburg simply as a springboard, at all events in May 1789 Schikaneder gave notice to the wealthy Prince. He recommended the actor Jakob Rechenmacher as his successor and in June went to Vienna with a part of his company. Attractive possibilities had opened in the imperial city for a director who already carried in his pocket the imperial privilege for the building of an independent theater.

In March 1789 Johann Friedel, leaseholder of the Theater im Freihaus auf der Wieden, had died and made Eleonore Schikaneder his sole beneficiary. She did not trust herself to run the theater alone. She contacted her legitimate husband with an offer of reconciliation and partnership. Schikaneder hardly hesitated in agreeing. A new— and the most important—chapter of his career had begun.

4 The Freihaus Theater Auf Der Wieden I

Schikaneder became the director in Vienna at precisely the right moment. German popular theater—which had previously eked out a meager existence playing in shacks or as an occasional, more tolerated than welcome guest in Czernin's Garden in the Leopoldstadt—had finally been given the opportunity to expand and perform on a regular basis in established houses. It took over several theaters—competition being good for business. The Leopoldstadt Theater had been playing in that eastern suburb since 1781 and was flourishing, thanks to the popularity of its star comedian, Laroche. Now it was joined by two new theaters: in 1787 by the Starhemberg Freihaus auf der Wieden, and a year later by the Theater in der Josefstadt. This house, frequently rebuilt and enlarged, still stands today, but at the time, and indeed during the whole of the Schikaneder period, was considered third-best. An inkeeper had it built in 1788 and leased it to his son-in-law, the *Hanswurst* actor Karl Mayr. It was the smallest of the three new suburban theaters, and survived for decades on a repertoire of Kasperl farces, seldom rising above the level of low comedy. The Freihaus auf der Wieden was from the start to be far more ambitious.

The theater was built by Christian Rossbach (1755–1793) who came to Vienna from Fulda. He had acted in a stall in Vienna's Neuer Markt, one of many similar theater booths established in the courtyards of the Freihaus. Rossbach's application to build a perma-

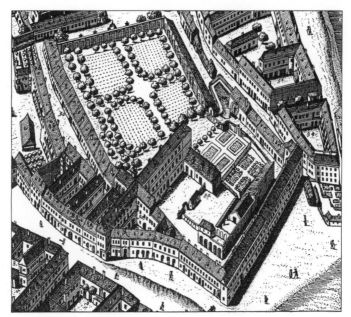

Bird's-eye view of the Freihaus auf der Wieden.

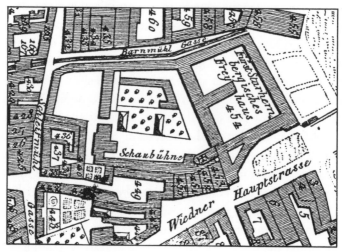

Plan of the Freihaus.

nent theater was granted in 1787. Andreas Zach, architect to the government, drew the plans. The theater was opened on October 14, 1787, and was to go down in music history as the site of the first performance of the Mozart-Schikaneder *Magic Flute*. It was in no way such a "miserable shack" as we have been led, until recently, to believe. The loss of prestige which Schikaneder suffered at the end of the 19th century also extended to "his" theater. Of course, its simple structure could not measure up to the palatial court or civic "New Renaissance" buildings then being built. But it was of solid stone, with a tiled roof. The interior was made of wood, as was usual at the time.

It was not a small theater. There were places for 800 people on the main floor and two tiers of boxes. Schikaneder later added a balcony and enlarged the seating capacity to about 1000. The ground plan of the theater is of a rectangle of 30 × 15 meters, and it is worth noting that the stage, which had a depth of 12 meters, required almost half of this area, having been planned from the beginning for opulent scenic design. The Freihaus Theater was about the same size as the Leopoldstadt Theater, but its technical equipment was far superior. The decor was simple; there was no decoration of the proscenium arch until after Schikaneder's remodeling when two life-size figures were added: a knight with a dagger on one side and a masked lady on the other. The orchestra seats were benches. Prices were similar to those of the Leopoldstadt Theater. The large boxes which seated eight cost 5 florins, smaller boxes seating half the number cost 2 florins 30 kreuzer, the *parterre noble* and balcony seats cost 34 kreuzer, rear parterre 17, and those who only had 7 kreuzer to spare had to content themselves with standing room in the balcony. Performances began at 6:30 in the winter, in summer at 7:00 p.m.

Schikaneder's choice of the Freihaus Theater was to prove fortunate later. Basically the Freihaus was a little town of its own, but it was scarcely a kilometer south of the Kärntnertor—easily reached by Viennese theater lovers.

We search in vain today for traces of *The Magic Flute*. The Operngasse south of the former Kärntnertor is a congery of anonymous modern apartment blocks. Demolition of the Freihaus began shortly before World War I and continued for several decades. Photographs taken in the 19th century give us an impression of

Vienna's once largest residential complex: a maze of tracts of land and courtyards, frequently rebuilt, including a chapel, an inn, an oil press with mill wheel, wells, ornamental gardens—and a theater! This residential quarter with 225 apartments housed over 1,100 tenants in Vienna's period of flourishing growth around the middle of the 19th century, and as many as 800 during Schikaneder's time. Tenants were craftsmen, hawkers, servants, a few artists; all were of the petty bourgeoisie. These were the people who attended suburban theater, along with other citizens of this little town within the city known as *Die Wieden*, today the 4th district. The whole complex was called "Freihaus," because its owner Prince Georg Adam von Starhemberg had been able to obtain freedom from taxation through his services to the crown.

The "Wiedner Theater," as it was generally called, stood in the middle courtyard, the sixth, in the wing which separated it from the first courtyard facing the Schleifmühlgasse. No stone remains of it. Its founder, the director Rossbach, had to give up after half a year. He was an unfortunate man. His next refuge, an old shack of a theater on the Glacis, the ramparts around the inner city, went up in flames soon afterwards. Rossbach took to the roads again with the rest of his troupe, but died a short time later in Vienna, impoverished and in debt. His successor Johann Friedel did not fare much better. With his partner Eleonore Schikaneder he opened on Easter Monday, 1788. His program was ambitious; it included comic opera, *Kabale und Liebe* and *Emilia Galotti*.

Friedel improved the building, and in order to make the journey to the suburb easier for the Viennese erected 21 lamps along the sidewalk to the Kärntnertor. But the public deserted him, even though he tried to arouse its interest with a positive flood of new plays. He once produced no less than nine new works within a fortnight; naturally they can scarcely have been properly rehearsed. "The public has begun to grumble more and more about Herr Friedel," reported the Viennese *Theater-Journal*. By then this man, a talented writer but no theater director, was mortally ill.

Schikaneder gave himself three months before he reopened the theater as its new director, or, more accurately, as co-director. He was forced to look for a wealthy backer before he could engage a better company and stand firmly and permanently on his own financial feet. He found such backing in Joseph von Bauernfeld, a wealthy officer and a Freemason. The name is well known in Austria— Eduard von Bauernfeld, writer of comic verses and Schubert's friend, was a relative, probably his illegitimate son. Until he went bankrupt three years later he was Schikaneder's co-director. (Eleonore was simply a silent partner and chief actress). After a year's activity both partners obtained from Emperor Leopold II a "privilege similar to that granted to Marinelli in the Leopoldstadt Theater," which allowed them to use the title "K.k.priv.Wiedner Theater" (Imperial and Royal Licensed Wiedner Theater). Their posters were adorned with two eagles carrying the imperial coat of arms.

For the premiere on July 12, 1789, Schikaneder had written a new work: *Der dumme Gärtner aus dem Gebirge oder Die zween Anton* (The Silly Gardener from the Hills or The Two Antons). It was called a comic opera, but with its simple song numbers it is really a farce with music. Typically enough, it was not considered necessary to mention the composers' names on the first night programs; they were Benedikt Schack and Franz Xaver Gerl, singers from the company who often worked for Schikaneder on musical settings and were joined by others when there was a need. Musical numbers of this kind were of secondary importance and not taken too seriously. The principal roles were of primary importance to the box office, and as these had been created by Schikaneder, a proven dramatist who played the main character himself, success was already halfway insured. As director he always relied on the appeal of his own works. He was to launch 19 productions before *The Magic Flute*, eight of them quite new, including several of his own plays ranging from the early *Raubvögel* (Birds of Prey) to the Regensburg *Hanns Dollinger*, as well as spoken plays. But now that he was in the Theater auf der Wieden, supported by a company which could boast several capable singers, and with a well equipped and roomy stage, he could turn his attention more often to his favorite genre, German opera. This meant that high-quality spoken drama took a back seat during the first few years. Schiller's *Don Carlos* was a notable exception among dozens of tragedies, comedies and farces, whose level at best was that of works by Iffland. But there were many Singspiele, some of them hastily put together to meet the needs of the day, but also worthwhile pieces like

Emanuel Schikaneder in the title role of the comic opera *Der dumme Gärtner aus dem Gebirge oder die zween Anton* (The Silly Gardener from the Hills or The Two Antons), for which he wrote the text. After an engraving by Ignaz Albrecht, 1790.

the romantic comic opera *Oberon, König der Elfen* (Oberon, King of the Elves) by the Viennese Czech Paul Wranitzky. Karl Ludwig Gieseke, a member of the company, wrote the text, or more correctly, plagiarized the libretto by Friederike Sophie Seyler-Hensel, based on Wieland's famous epic poem. Schikaneder also presented the well-known melodrama *Ariadne auf Naxos* by another exiled Czech, Georg Benda, and the Singspiel *Der Gutsherr* (The Lord of the Manor) by Karl Ditters von Dittersdorf, a highly respected composer who also conducted.

With his business instinct for the theater Schikaneder realized that, particularly during these first years when his immediate concern was to win an audience, he could neither fill the house with the classics nor with *Hanswurst* shows. Competition from the popular comedian Johann Laroche (1745–1806) as the "Viennese Kasperl" was too fierce. Laroche was born in Pressburg, like Stranitzky the son of a lackey. In the eyes of the Leopoldstadt suburban public Laroche had been the undisputed successor to Prehauser since the latter's death in 1769. An ugly, pockmarked, stocky, later fat man, he played Kasperl in peasant's clothes but with a Viennese dialect. He was coarse, clumsy, grimacing, graphic and obscene. Occasionally he used topical innuendos but was without satirical wit—that would have been too much to expect either from the good-natured Kasperl or from Laroche's temperament. Yet in 160 roles he never failed to succeed with the public. His greatest reputation developed during the first five years of the Leopoldstadt Theater, when the post-Baroque Kasperl burlesques, descendants of extempore theater, were still flourishing. Karl Friedrich Hensler, who joined the Leopoldstadt company in 1786 as theater poet, wrote several successful plays for Laroche, among them *Kasperl der Besenbinder* (Kasperl the Broommaker) or in 1789 *Kasperl der Schornsteinfeger* (Kasperl the Chimneysweep). Hensler (1759–1825), who came from Tübingen and had been a candidate for Holy Orders in the famous abbey there, was to become one of Schikaneder's most serious rivals; first as the author and initiator of fairytale plays (*Das Donauweibchen* The Little Woman of the Danube), tearjerking and pathetic dramas of chivalry, and popular socio-critical plays relating to Vienna (80 in all!); and later as director, when he took over the Leopoldstadt Theater after Marinelli's death in 1803.

But Laroche's great attraction as a comedian had begun to wane by the late '80s when Marinelli also started to cultivate the Singspiel. The comedian had no voice at all, not even enough to croak out couplets effectively. Now lavish and exotic operas were the rage, like *Das Sonnenfest der Brahminen* (The Sun Festival of the Brahmins) by Hensler (after Kotzebue) with music by Wenzel Müller. It was such a success with the public in 1790 that an astonishing 91 performances were given. Just before this Dittersdorf's *Doktor und Apotheker* had been equally well received, and Vincent Martin y Soler's comic opera *Una cosa rara*, produced in German at the Leopoldstadt, was performed 118 times during the course of the years. In its Hauskapellmeister Wenzel Müller (1767-1835), who came from Slovakian Hungary, the theater also had the best Viennese hack theater composer at its disposal. His productivity was absolutely astonishing; he wrote the music to no fewer than 235 plays. For some this only involved a few individual numbers, but 40 of his works were labeled "opera." With some of his later songs ("So leb denn wohl, du stilles Haus"—Farewell, You Quiet House), he has gone down into theater history as an equal of Raimund. Joachim Perinet (1765-1816), the theater's second writer, was responsible for increasing the repertoire of magic plays, Kasperl shows and plays of local interest. He was a good-natured Viennese, not very original, but extremely deft and productive in his adaptations of sources that promised to be a success, whether fairytales, old romances or popular plays by Hafner. He had special ties to Schikaneder, as the text author of *Die Zauberzither* by Wenzel Müller. During the five years when he was a member of Schikaneder's company he was one of the latter's eloquent defenders.

The theater in the Leopoldstadt, older and more firmly established, offerred fierce competition for the ambitious Schikaneder. To counter this competition, he presented musical theater on a long-term basis; but it was clear from the start that for reasons of cost alone this strategy would have to be supplemented by plays which were cheaper to produce. He relied above all on his forceful stage presence as leading actor. The opening of his musical farce *The Silly Gardener from the Hills or The Two Antons*, whether intentional or not, had a certain programmatic significance. The pompous description of the work as "comic opera" promised that this theater would cultivate

German opera. Further, the subject promised much amusement. So far as we can gather from the few musical numbers which have survived, its subject is the humorous confrontation of a nature boy, full of peasant cunning, with the civilized world. Of course Schikaneder played the wily Anton himself; one can scent a Papageno precursor. The theme was entirely typical of the theater at this time; a dozen years earlier Heufeld, the successful *Hamlet* adaptor, had already written a showy role for Prehauser in his *Bauer aus dem Gebirge* (Peasant from the Hills). Schikaneder's scheme to appear in a role similar to Laroche's popular Viennese Kasperl, rather than to try to push him out of the limelight with a direct comparison, worked perfectly. Thanks to Schikaneder's sense of comedy, which Mozart also enjoyed, *The Silly Gardener* proved to be a brilliant start for the Freihaustheater and was repeated 32 times before the end of the year. One song became particularly popular, *Ein Weib ist das herrlichste Ding auf der Welt* (A Woman is the Most Wonderful Thing in the World) with its refrain "Wer's leugnet, den schlag, ich, dass d' Goschen ihm schwellt" (he who denies it, I'll beat him 'til his teeth fall out). Obviously the Bavarian from Straubing had quickly mastered the Viennese dialect closest to the people. Interestingly, Mozart's Piano Variations K 613 are based on this melody.

Schikaneder was quick to exploit his success with the public. Out of just two Antons he reproduced more Antons: two months later they appeared in *Die verdeckten Sachen* (Hidden Things) while the sixth and last Anton was seen in 1795. By then Anton had had his day, for taste had changed, but not before the Antons had done their duty by the box office, despite being routine potboilers. By the autumn of 1789 however, Schikaneder's new troupe proved its musical competence in Wranitzky's *Oberon*, an extremely demanding opera score. The director had taken on only a few of Friedel's ensemble members, but among them was the highly respected soprano Josefa Hofer, née Weber, Mozart's sister-in-law. He also employed Karl Ludwig Giesecke, an unimportant actor of minor roles but a versatile and useful property manager and theater poet, as well as the singer-actor Johann Joseph Nouseul, and his own brother Urban who was engaged as basso buffo and actor. He had brought the tenor Benedikt Schack and the bass Franz Xaver Gerl with him from Regensburg, and engaged, among others, the tenor Joseph Haibel (who was later to set Schikaneder's successful *Tyroler Wastel* to music), the beautiful young soprano Anna Gottlieb, and "the Kapellmeister and Composer" Johann Baptist Henneberg (1768–1822), whose name was subsequently to appear at least seven times alongside that of Schikaneder the text writer. We shall come across most of these names again in the program of the first performance of *The Magic Flute*.

All in all, it was a capable ensemble, even if the principal singers and actors were not as eminent as those of the Imperial National Theater; one could hardly afford to pay for "stars" in the suburbs. When we read that Josefa Hofer, the uncrowned coloratura prima donna of the Theater auf der Wieden, had to be content with a salary of 64 florins a month (supplemented by a yearly sum of 150 florins for her wardrobe), while Italian singers at the Burgtheater were raking in thousands of florins a year, we can imagine how wretched the existence of lesser-known actresses from the Theater auf der Wieden must have been. But then it was an unsubsidized, commercial theater with tickets priced for the general public. Its director had to reckon with every kreuzer—and this he most certainly did.

The financial burdens with which Schikaneder had to cope are not entirely clear. When he took over the theater he is said to have paid 1500 florins a year in rent plus 25 florins for every week of performances. This continued for 10 years; but the arrangement was altered in 1790, the year Schikaneder took over Friedel's earlier contract. Eleonore was Friedel's sole heiress, and in the meantime the Schikaneders had come together again as a couple. In any case, thrift was called for. Upon opening Schikaneder had enlarged the chorus and the orchestra, though contemporary assessments of the quality of the orchestra and its numerical strength are in conflict. In his *Materialien zur Geschichte der Oper und des Balletts in Wien* (Information Relating to the History of Opera and Ballet in Vienna), Leopold von Sonnleithner refers to an orchestra of 35 during the *Magic Flute* period, with five first and four second violins. In 1796 two members were added, but the *Jahrbuch der Tonkunst von Wien und Prag* (Yearbook of Musical Art in Vienna and Prague), printed during the same year, only credited the Freihaus Theater orchestra with 23 members, about the same strength as the Leopoldstadt Theater orchestra (25 members), in contrast to the 35 at the Kärntnertor Theater and 36 at

The proscenium arch of the Freihaus Theater auf der Wieden.

the Burgtheater. One wonders if the orchestra for Schikeneder's ambitious music theater could really have been smaller than that of the Leopoldstadt Theater. When necessary, he enlisted extra players, for example for his matinee concerts of Haydn symphonies (as early as April 1791; these were a signficant innovation) and of course for *The Magic Flute*.

Schikaneder demanded strict discipline in his company right from the start. This was all the more necessary, as most of the actors lived in crowded quarters in the rambling Freihaus. Schikaneder and his wife, for example, were in the 5th courtyard, up the 23rd staircase, on the 2nd floor. Without doubt, life in the pleasant leafy courtyard and in the inn was boisterous, inspired by the director's own joie de vivre. Although he had now become a respectable citizen, the amorous adventures of this passionate philanderer can scarcely have been curtailed by his revived marriage of convenience. Some light is thrown on this subject by his later sacking of Fräulein Hoffmann—at least temporarily—his proven remedy for avoiding petty jealousies. She played the Second Lady in *The Magic Flute*, but from time to time first lady in his heart.

In order to maintain strict order when working he established printed "House Rules" which every member of the ensemble had to swear to obey. The basic rules were "morality, good discipline and politeness of the informal kind," plus punctual attendance at rehearsals. A fine of 30 kreuzer for each quarter of an hour's tardiness was imposed. And a late appearance three successive times before a performance was grounds for immediate dismissal. No member could refuse a part, "insert additions or alterations," behave in a quarrelsome way or speak badly about the theater. The deportment of the musicians was also regulated; they had to appear punctually in the orchestra pit and forego "unseemly laughter and unnecessary chatter." And finally, "Herr Emanuel Schikaneder who made these rules, director of this theater, does not exclude himself from any one of them." Possibly by way of compensation the strict "house father" afforded his employees greater job security by extending the usual six weeks' notice of dismissal to six months.

The death of Emperor Joseph II on February 20, 1790, robbed Schikaneder of his powerful patron. During the last phase of Joseph's illness the theater was closed and remained so into April. This unavoidable box office loss had to be made good quickly—most securely, by Schikaneder's calculation, with continued performances of proven works, and especially light opera which promised the best success. The Leopoldstadt had scored a triumph with Martin y Soler's *Una cosa rara*—why not come up with a sequel? Without delay Schikaneder wrote a libretto entitled *Der Fall ist noch weit seltener* (The Case is Even Stranger), which Schack set to music. However, shortly after the premiere in June 1790, it became clear that Nestroy's later observation was proved: "however well a sequel goes, the interest is not there," a maxim which Schikaneder was to violate repeatedly. Mozart, a frequent visitor to the theater, wrote in May to Constanze who was taking the cure in Baden: "Yesterday, I went to the second part of *Cosa rara*—it didn't please me as well as the Antons." Mozart was a *Cosa rara* connoisseur; he actually quoted a few bars from it in the finale of *Don Giovanni*.

Schikaneder simply had to keep pace with the Leopoldstadt! But in the meantime, the Leopoldstadt had gone in for opera in exotic costume, scoring a hit with Hensler-Müller's *Sonnenfest der Brahminen*. It was certainly no accident that Schikaneder's heroic—comic opera *Der Stein der Weisen* (The Wise Men's Stone) appeared at the Theater auf der Wieden almost at the same time in September 1790. He had got wind of the sensation to come, and wanted to do them one better. This accounts for the haste of the production: Schack, Gerl and other contributors not even named on the program hurriedly divided the composing among themselves, as is evident from the many "Quodlibets" which were highly popular at the time. Such evening-length entertainments flourished until the late 19th century, especially when composers like Auber, Boieldieu, Cherubini and Hérold combined forces. They knew how to concoct a pastiche and bake a frothy pastry-opera to suit the public's taste.

Der Stein der Weisen oder Die Zauberinsel (The Wise Men's Stone or The Magic Isle), one of the greatest successes of Schikaneder's first season, vanished quickly, but it is important as a forerunner of *The Magic Flute*. Composed a year earlier, this magic opera probably also drew upon Wieland's collection of fairy tales, *Dschinnistan*. In both, the theme is the testing of a noble pair; there is even a trial by fire and water, and the hero is accompanied by a droll servant, a nature boy called Lubano who in the end wins his Lubanara. They too have a duet "Wo Lubanara nur miauen kann" (Lubanara can only miaow). Who isn't reminded of the "Pa-Pa-Papageno-Papagena" duet?

A farce, *Der Teufel in Wien* (The Devil in Vienna), is preserved in the Wiener Stadt-und Landesbibliothek in an edition dated 1791. Until recently it was considered to be by Schikaneder. The fact that the copy does not list the author tells us nothing definite about its authenticity, for at the time there were many pirated editions. But it has now been established that it is not an authentic Schikaneder work.[3] It well might have been: it contained a true Schikaneder role, full of trivial capering about a superstitious, rich man who is made a fool of by a prank involving the devil. The chief joker is an easygoing bachelor called Brenner who brags about his conquests in love. He is exactly as one would imagine an urban Papageno in a Viennese farce. It seems that an insignificant author made use of the popularity of such Schikaneder characters. Or did Schikaneder himself profit from these ever-popular character types, cashing in on the craze for them until the figure became entirely associated with him—Papageno in ever new costumes and situations?

This Schikaneder-like *Teufel in Wien* is worth noting, even if it was not written by him, because eight years later he was to write a completely different, socially critical comedy with the same title, and also because that rogue Brenner, in a suggestive couplet, gives a candid and entertaining account of Viennese prostitution, alluding to the contemporary connection between society morals, prostitution and the theater:

In der langen Kärntnerstasse
Giebt es Mädchen überall—
In der schmalen Naglergasse
Findet man sie nach der Wahl.

In the long Kärntnerstrasse
Girls are everywhere—
In the narrow Naglergasse
You can choose them as you care.
But if in dozens you desire them
Go every evening to the Graben.

Schellenbastey, Tuchlauben, Wildpretmarkt and Kazensteig [tr. note: all red light districts in Vienna] are duly noted:

Wer sie aber Dutzendweis will haben
Der geh'alle Abend auf den Graben.

"Grabennymphen" or "Grabenschnepfen" (nymphets or silly wenches from the street in Vienna known as the Graben) had been familiar figures in Vienna for decades. Even the straight-laced Empress Maria Theresia could not prevent the "Whores' Mass"— which was celebrated in the highly respected Kapuzinerkirche, a Franciscan Church—from becoming a rendezvous for prostitutes. The Josephine liberalization aided and abetted the growth of prostitution, as did the many public baths in the suburbs that functioned as hole-and-corner brothels. Finally in 1787 Joseph II was forced to tighten regulations: "Everyone, be he male or female, who sells his body and earns his living by fornication is a political criminal." But in view of the spreading proletarianism these regulations achieved as little as the later stepped-up snooping of the "Naderer", Emperor Franz's hated secret police. In the Josephine era the number of Viennese prostitutes was estimated at 3,000, "which would mean that every sixty-fourth person was a woman of easy virtue."[4] The enlightened Berliner Friedrich Nicolai, on a visit to Vienna, wrote of 10,000 Viennese prostitutes—but he was very critical of Vienna, and had little evidence to support his estimate.

At any rate, visitors to the theater knew what was meant when the bachelor Brenner (his colleague in the piece is called Schnaps) mentioned the Viennese red-light districts by name. That a character was allowed to do so on the stage is astonishing; but it seems that imperial censorship was more strictly enforced with obviously political matters, with the "Jacobins," than sexual morality. After all, washerwomen and chambermaids who could be bought were an established fact in the traditional pastimes of the cavalier—it had always been and would always remain so—and the petty bourgeois audiences in the suburban theater simply smiled indulgently.

Along with the spoken plays he was obliged to produce, Schikaneder was at the time trying his luck as author of several new or revived magic comedies with music which are now lost. In so doing, he was swimming with a thoroughly topical theatrical tide.

The late Baroque "Bernadoniade" with elaborate stage effects had served its purpose years ago. During the enlightened decade of Josephinism, freed from censorship, the theater had been flooded with a spate of critical and realistic dramas which flourished with the new, polemical, anti-clerical journalism. Towards the end of Joseph II's reign, however, the pendulum swung back again. A conservative reaction against his high-flown plans for reform emerged, supported by countervailing intellectual undercurrents.

The Age of Enlightenment drew to its twilight with the death of Voltaire, its uncrowned king. In the end, the dethroned goddess of Reason had made no decisive intrusion into the lives of her princely admirers, and none at all into the lives of commoners—she had neither improved their lot nor prevented wars. Seen from the theater's point of view, the public had gradually tired of Reason on the stage; it missed enchantment, it missed being transported out of a frugal daily existence. The bourgeois scene no longer satisfied. Why should fantasy, which had taken refuge in the picturesque garb of a knight of the Middle Ages, not also fly to strange and colorful distant lands and engage in unbelievable, unreal, magical adventures?

The literary ground was well prepared. In countries speaking Romance languages, fairy stories which had been in circulation for a good hundred years were collected into 41 volumes, Le Cabinet des Fées (1785). More important for Germany and Vienna was the simultaneous publication of a collection of exotic fairy tales entitled Dschinnistan, by the popular Wieland. The model philosopher of the Enlightenment had become the herald of what was later to be termed Romanticism. However, "die Blaue Blume," The Blue Flower of Romanticism, found and immortalized by Novalis, was now to blossom in Viennese theater soil. Hensler, the current idol of the Leopoldstadt Theater, deftly produced dozens of plays about knights and ghosts, and although these took advantage of the current longing for the supernatural, their effect was more sober and rational: small wonder that the traditional Viennese Kasperl, Laroche, the financial draw of the house, did rather badly in this new magic genre. As the companion-servant of noble knights he only played a secondary role. The Magical—in costumes, sets and most important of all, in view of the modest theatrical props of the time, in the imagination of the public—was absolutely essential for the new plays. Music, the chief store of magic, was included: nothing worked without it then or later in Raimund's poetically ironic play *Die Gefesselte Phantasie* (Of Fantasy in Bondage), nor in Nestroy, whose satirical plays proved to be the fulfillment of the old Viennese popular theater.

These early magic plays were a long way from his *Lumpazivagabundus* and also from the brilliantly hidden symbolism of later works like *Talisman* and *Häuptling Abendwind* (Chief Evening Wind). But the soil had been prepared and was to be fruitful for generations. It was cultivated by Hensler, a practical man of the theater. Schikaneder, with whom Hensler competed, was no less practical, but his talent, at times, went far beyond practicality. Despite Schikaneder's sense of music he could have had no idea of the timeless partnership he would enter into when he offered the impoverished and no longer fashionable Wolfgang Amadeus Mozart a contract to compose a new magic opera, in competition with the Leopoldstadt Theater. We are not even sure when he did so.

Looking back, it would seem that the Theater im Freihaus auf der Wieden, which has disappeared without trace, is only worthy of historic notice as the site of the first performance of *The Magic Flute*. On the other hand, every new work was of vital importance for Schikaneder's livelihood. Each performance cost about 150 florins in out-of-pocket expenses. The director worked independently without the aid of subsidies, so when he entered into a contract with a friend who had not composed a German opera for years, he was taking a genuine risk. Mozart was a genius, but that was no guarantee of a box office triumph. That *The Magic Flute* was to become a technical success was not a kind fate but the fruit of a process of maturing which had passed through many tentative stages, some partly successful, some failures, from the moment of conception to the moment of completion. Schikaneder, the inferior partner, by undertaking the responsibility for this venture created for himself a permanent and estimable niche in the history of music.

5 *The Magic Flute*

The evening of September 30, 1791, was to become one of the most important in the history of opera, for on that date *The Magic Flute* first saw the light of day in the Theater auf der Wieden, under imperial and royal privilege. The house, splendidly lit by wax candles, was sold out, and even if during the intermission the audience behaved in a somewhat circumspect way, at the end it applauded with enthusiasm. A theatrical success from the start (in October there were as many 20 performances and many more before the end of 1791), it was also highly acclaimed by the cognoscenti, then and now. Beethoven valued *The Magic Flute* the most highly of all Mozart's operas; Goethe was so fascinated that he immediately started to write an operatic sequel; Wagner paid it the almost superlative homage: "What versatility, what diversity . . . indeed, this genius has taken almost too gigantic a step, for in creating German opera he at the same time fashioned a perfect, masterly example of the genre, impossible to improve on, so that this genre can no longer be extended or continued."

Wagner's statement about the creation of "German opera" needs to be looked at more soberly—after all, Mozart's *Entführung aus dem Serail* had preceded *The Magic Flute*. But the intensifying of the German Singspiel form, from the episodic love story of the *Entführung* to the allegorical world theater of *The Magic Flute*, justifies Wagner's judgment. Its style and profundity indeed represented the

The playbill for the first performance of *The Magic Flute* in the
Theater auf der Wieden.

first true realization of German "Grand Opera" as promised in the playbill of the premiere: the announcement is in part typological, in part ostentatious, but it was quickly substantiated by the opera's true greatness. Few works for the theater have achieved such rapid and lasting recognition.

The list of noteworthy *Magic Flute* admirers runs into the hundreds and extends to the present day—including modern critical philosophers like Theodor W. Adorno and Ernest Bloch. In his Mozart biography, Wolfgang Hildesheimer favors a more cautious assessment, but he is the exception. The opinion of the man in the street tallies with that of the expert—it has remained a standby of the repertory for almost 200 years.

The Magic Flute is the most frequently performed of all operas, at least in German-speaking countries, where more opera performances are given than in the rest of the opera world put together. This was also true in the 19th century, when Verdi, Bizet and Puccini became strong competitors. Between 1947 and 1975 *The Magic Flute* was staged 8,142 times in the Federal Republic of Germany and West Berlin. Records of performances in the German Democratic Republic, Austria and Switzerland more or less parallel those of West Germany. *Figaro* and *Carmen*[5] are still only runners-up. Internationally *The Magic Flute* does not enjoy a similar popularity, particularly in Italy where the Singspiel with its spoken dialogue has never been popular. But *La Flûte enchantée*, *The Magic Flute*, *Il flauto magico*, the Czech *Kouzelna flétna* and various other translations of *Die Zauberflöte* continue to be among the public's favorites.

No one would dispute that Mozart's music is responsible for the stature of the opera and that his librettist's contribution is of lesser importance. What, then, did Schikaneder actually add to the opera's value and success? This is a double question, the second part of which can be answered far more easily than the first, at least from an historical and theatrical point of view. Apart from writing the text, the director of the Freihaus theater was involved as the singer and actor of Papageno, the major role. He was also the stage director, although this function was not mentioned in the original program because the director's role was not the autocratic one we know, but simply arranging entrances and exits. But Schikaneder was author, producer and director, controlling casting and the magnificence or sparseness of the scenery, all of which means that his contribution to the success of the evening can hardly be overestimated. Seen from this angle, the wording of the printed program, "Eine grosse Oper in 2 Akten, von Emanuel Schikaneder" (A Grand Opera in 2 Acts by Emanuel Schikaneder) with Mozart's name only appearing in small print following the cast list, loses some of its absurdity, especially as programs of this sort were then the general rule. Certainly Schikaneder was not intentionally slighting Mozart.

In fact, the original *Magic Flute* success was a Schikaneder success. Under the circumstances, he provided the best cast possible. Papageno could not have been more effectively portrayed than by himself.[6] The tenor Benedikt Schack sang Tamino, the bass Gerl (either Thaddeus or his brother Franz Xaver) Sarastro, the Queen of the Night was sung by Mozart's sister-in-law, the respected Josefa Hofer. She must have been a virtuoso, otherwise he would not have written such coloratura arias for her. He must also have expected a first-class performance of vocal technique and expression from the seventeen-year-old Anna Gottlieb, for the Pamina aria in G minor still has the characteristic of a solo "pièce de résistance" for prima-donnas of the 20th century, who now profit from 200 years of Mozart tradition. The theater's Kapellmeister, Johann Baptist Henneberg, conducted after the second performance. The orchestra was small, but it must have been good enough to virtually sight-read the tricky overture and to play it well; after the overture the visiting composer Johann Schenk, who had been forced to find a last-minute seat in the orchestra pit, pushed his way forward to Mozart, who was conducting from the keyboard, and kissed his hand enthusiastically.

"Herr Gayl, scenic painter and Herr Neszthaler, set designer flatter themselves that they have worked with the greatest artistic ardor, to realize the plans laid down for the work." This rather pompous announcement on the program probably did not overstate things, although we have neither the original stage designs nor exact descriptions of them. But we have Schikaneder's vivid descriptions in the stage directions of the libretto. For the trials by fire and water he demands: "The scene changes to two large mountains: from one mountain we can hear the rushing and roaring of a waterfall; the other spits out fire; both mountains have a grill through which one can see both fire and water; where the fire burns, the horizon should be light red, while a dark fog lies over the water." These instructions reveal an almost cinematic imagination. Schikaneder's verses may often be coarse and clumsy, but the poetry of his stage directions is always daring: It is poetry in images. Of course a theater then could not provide complete realism, but the 12-meter depth of the stage offered some possibilities for scenic effects which would certainly astonish the public. Twelve new set pieces served the ten scene changes. During the trial by fire and water two three-dimensional mountains with paths appeared, bathed in magical light, and the "flying machine" with its gondola decorated with flowers in which the three boys come floating aroused the greatest rapture. Schikaneder, a true theater director in the sense of Goethe's *Faust*, had surely not skimped on "back-drops and machines" and had provided "all of creation on the narrow boards."

The old, wise, but chancy theater maxim, that one has to throw one's money out of the window so that it can come in at the door again, was certainly proved once again in this presentation. According to a contemporary account, one had to stand in line as early as five o'clock in order to get a ticket for weeks after the opening night. A year later, Schikaneder announced the 100th performance—this was cheating a little: in fact it was the 83rd. Before it was transferred to the Theater an der Wien *The Magic Flute* had 223 performances, a record for the times, followed by a similar success in the new theater. Out-of-town performances started as early as 1792 in Prague, the final breakthrough coming with the Berlin performance in 1794. No fewer than 27 German theaters played the opera during that year, and performances elsewhere were soon to follow.

Schikaneder, without doubt the efficient director and chief actor of *The Magic Flute*, was also its co-author: what can be said of the importance of his contribution? His contemporaries already recognized that an immeasurable gulf yawned between the artistic qualities of the musical setting and the text; in fact it was the difference between Mozart's genius and Schikaneder's theatrical talent. This difference is not the matter for discussion, the real question being: is *The Magic Flute* an incomparable masterpiece *in spite* of Schikaneder or *thanks to* Schikaneder, however humble these thanks? "In an opera, poetry must be the obedient daughter of the music," was Mozart's esthetic credo. There is certainly no need to doubt the absolute obedience of Schikaneder's "poetry," if, without being ironic, one wants to call it that. Since Mozart and Schikaneder were in constant, in fact daily, personal contact during the entire joint production, there unfortunately are no letters or any other documents left to us of the conception, growth, alterations, and polishings, nor about possible discussions and heated arguments. Verdi's exchange of letters with his librettists, Strauss's with von Hofmannsthal give us such valuable insights into creative workshops—they would be even more helpful for the esthetically problematic *Magic Flute*, but they are totally lacking. One has to rely only on the final result.

Mozart and Schikaneder worked closely together. The composer altered no less than 50 places in the text; he made cuts and additions. No one knows whether it was Schikaneder who during the creative process emphasized the Masonic components in the libretto and the dominance of Sarastro's world over the Volkstheater-Papageno. It is certain that it was a joint labor. In 1795, when derided as an unequal partner and forced into a defensive position by Vulpius in Weimar, Schikaneder could rightfully say, "I worked diligently on this opera with the late Mozart."

In his extensive correspondence Mozart always speaks his mind freely; scarcely one of his contemporaries escapes his scornful wordplay. Yet there is not a single derogatory sentence about his librettist Schikaneder, but rather indications of a firm partisanship. In his letter of October 8, 1791 to Constanze, Mozart describes how angry he became with a stupid member of the audience who laughed senselessly at everything, even at the ceremonial Sarastro scenes, forcing Mozart to change his seat. He then joined a married couple of his acquaintance and enjoyed the performance "with pleasure until the end." He writes in the same letter that he had "the little [text] book" of *The Magic Flute* delivered to his mother-in-law to prepare her for her first visit to the opera. This may be of trifling importance, but it does confirm Mozart's maxim of the inseparability of "a good composer who understands the theater" and "a knowledgeable poet as a true phoenix." They certainly achieved this in *The Magic Flute* in which, with Schikaneder as the phoenix, one may be permitted to transfer the emphasis from the noun "poet" to the adjective "knowledgeable."

He definitely was an efficient man of the theater. If this seems too facile a judgment one can counter it by quoting W. S. Auden, an unquestionably great poet of the 20th century, highly esteemed for his craftsmanship as both Stravinsky's and Henze's librettist. Auden writes: "A text should not be judged by any intrinsic poetic worth, but according to its success or lack of success in stimulating the musical imagination of the composer.[7] Viewed from the esthetic perspective of almost 200 years later, who can deny that Schikaneder was a powerful stimulus to Mozart's musical imagination?

Many years ago some of the most illustrious minds, as well as some second-rate ones, separated the wheat from chaff in the *Magic Flute* libretto by uncovering the deeper meaning beneath the seemingly silly surface. Thus Hegel: "how often does one not hear it said that the text of *The Magic Flute* is really deplorable, and yet, it is one of the most praiseworthy opera books." His archenemy Schopenhauer at least shared Hegel's esteem for Schikaneder. In his *Aphorismen zur Lebensweisheit* (Aphorisms for a Philosophy of Life) Schopenhauer describes those experiences in life in which "though we searched for pleasure, happiness and joy, we found, instead of instruction, insight and knowledge: permanent and true wealth in place of what is transitory and illusory. So it is in *The Magic Flute*, that grotesque but significant hieroglyph." David Friedrich Strauss, who was highly regarded by his contemporaries for his research into Christ's life, wrote a sonnet in praise of the librettist. It starts with "Was schikanieret ihr den Schikaneder?" (Why do you harass your Schikaneder so?), and the last two stanzas, after a mythological comparison, praise his *Magic Flute* text which "is transfigured ever anew in Mozart's music."

Whether expressed in prose or poetry, such contemporary or near-contemporary opinions in defense of Schikaneder contradict generally held views, and even have a touch of paradox about them. According to Goethe, it required "more education to be able to recognize the worth of this opera text than to deny it." Whether these often-quoted words are authentic or not, they certainly hit the mark. Goethe is readily quoted in defense of Schikaneder, despite some inconsistencies in his views. Thus when he became director of the Hoftheater in Weimar in 1793 he had *The Magic Flute* performed as early as January of the following year, but using the not altogether advantageous arrangement by his brother-in-law, Christian August

Vulpius, the successful author of the robber romance *Rinaldo Rinaldini*. "It was virtually impossible for us to perform *The Magic Flute* in the original version," the introduction to the libretto states. Is Vulpius here using the editorial "we," or is he also including Goethe? Whether he is or not, Goethe was the theater director and he allowed the arrangement to be staged without a mention of Schikaneder's name. But it was not only the sensational success, with 82 performances of *The Magic Flute* during Goethe's management, which made it his favorite opera. It must also have enchanted him as a work of art, as a total entity which included Schikaneder's text.

Goethe, the author of six Singspiel librettos—Schubert was to set the joyful *Claudine von Villa Bella*—had long ago recognized that it was not the poetic quality of the verses that assured the success of an opera. If he had not clearly seen other merits in Schikaneder's text, from the vivid scenic effects to the moral idea, how would he have been able to start work on *The Magic Flute*, Part II, only a year after the first performance in Weimar, following faithfully in Schikaneder's footsteps? The same characters appear in the work: the wise Sarastro, who here starts on a journey to test himself; the Queen of the Night who gives voice to a fiery aria full of revenge; the cheerful Papageno who again treats us to a Pa-Pa-Prattle duet with his Papagena. In no way does the poet spurn Schikaneder's old stage jokes:

> ER: *Warum sind wir denn nicht vergnügt?*
> SIE: *Weil wir nicht lustig sind!*
>
> HE: Why aren't we happy then?
> SHE: Because we aren't merry!

Goethe added the figure of Tamino's and Pamina's son, who is now at the center of the trials and adventures, including another trial by fire and water. In the end the courage of the parents is rewarded by the rescue of the son and by a spirit, who, rising out of the coffin, greets life with an inspiring aria and then flies away:

> *Hier bin ich, ihr Lieben!*
> *Und bin ich nicht schön?*
> *Wer wird sich betrüben*
> *Sein Söhnchen zu sehn.*

In Nächten geboren
Im herrlichen Haus,
Und wieder verloren
In Nächten und Graus.
Es drohen die Speere,
Die grimmigen Rachen,
Und drohten mir Heere
Und drohten mir Drachen;
Sie haben doch alle
Dem Knaben nichts an.

Here am I, you dear ones,
And am I not fair?
Whoever would grieve
To see his young son?
Born in dark nights
In magnificent house.
Again lost to sight
In horror and night.
The threatening spears,
The grim open jaws,
They threatened with dragons
They threatened with hordes;
But none have desire
To do the youth harm.

The fragment ends with these verses; only a few notes suggesting the plot's continuation remain. But isn't the spirit who flies away a forerunner of the youth Euphorion in *Faust*, Part II? Goethe has given both of them the same dactylic speech rhythm. Verse of such quality was certainly beyond Schikaneder—and yet it was *his* theatrical fantasy that led Goethe through the labyrinthine ways of *The Magic Flute*, Part II. The poem remained a fragment because the librettist was unable to find a composer. Neither the well-established Viennese opera composer Paul Wranitzky nor later Goethe's friend Friedrich Zelter of Berlin wanted to risk comparison to Mozart.

It seems that Goethe's judgment of Schikaneder became even milder with advancing age. The Genevan Sorel, summoned to Weimar to tutor the princes, tells us of a conversation with the almost

74-year-old privy councillor: "He finds the first part full of improbabilities and childishness but rich in contrast, and credits the author with great skill in the art of conveying theatrical effects."[8] Finding improbabilities and childish pranks in the *Magic Flute* libretto neither devalues it nor prevents us from acknowledging the richness of contrast and the art of theatrical effect. A few years later, when Goethe was telling Eckermann about his recently completed "Helena" act from *Faust*, Part II, he said: "It is enough that the majority of the public should enjoy the spectacle; at the same time its higher significance will not escape the initiated, as is also true of *The Magic Flute* and other works." Such a comparison of *Faust* and *The Magic Flute*, turning on higher meanings and the initiated, comes from the lips of the *Faust* author himself! But one must not overestimate these words of Goethe, even if reflected in much more explicit praise for Schikaneder by music and theater figures of our time— Bruno Walter, Bernhard Paumgartner and Walter Felsenstein ("it is quite an outstanding work . . . including Schikaneder's part"). Nor should we overestimate how much the 20th century has done to restore honor to Mozart's friend and collaborator. Combine these accolades with the scorn heaped on Schikaneder by contemporary newspaper critics and one would be able to fill whole volumes.

In some larger measure, one of the oldest surviving accounts of the premiere of *The Magic Flute* can be blamed for the decades-long devaluation of Schikaneder. On October 9, 1791, the Berlin *Musikalisches Wochenblatt* carried an anonymous article remarking that the new opera had "not received the expected applause because the contents and the text of the work were very inferior." This observation is clearly untrue; we have no reason to doubt Mozart's private and unsolicited account in his letter to Constanze, October 7, 1791, in which he states, "on the evening when my opera was performed for the first time and received so much applause, *Tito* was played for the last time in Prague and was also unusually well received."

Applause, then, right from the start. However, the criticism of content and text deserves comment, as it is typical of the contemporary divergence between public success and critical judgment, between the music and the libretto, between the "higher significance" (Goethe) and the lower literary form.

Once more we ask ourselves: is *The Magic Flute* a masterpiece in

Schikaneder as Papageno.
From the first libretto of *The Magic Flute, 1791.*

spite of Schikaneder, or thanks to Schikaneder? The question is an oversimplification, for the subject is much more complex. It has been argued for nearly 200 years and has produced a wealth of responses, and these debates will assuredly continue in the future. Only those blind to both shortcomings and merits of the *Magic Flute* libretto will come up with simple, black-and-white answers. The author of this book is not one of them. I have been involved in this debate for decades, often as a kind of inner dialogue. An insight into this dialogue might be obtained by imagining a pair of fictitious opponents, one of them a critic, the other a defender of Schikaneder. Such an exchange might follow along these lines:

CRITIC: So, thanks to Schikaneder, you consider *The Magic Flute* a masterpiece?

DEFENDER: I was a little more modest, I said, "partly thanks to Schikaneder."

C: Does this include the wording, which isn't even correct, let alone good German? "Sie drang *in* Tempel heimlich ein" (She entered in temple secretly). And this "in temple" actually appears again!

D: Just change it to "im Tempel" (in the temple) as it cannot be heard clearly anyway!

C: Yes, praise God, one doesn't hear a lot of Schikaneder's unspeakable poetry when it's sung. He can't even form a correct imperative! "Lieber guter Mond vergebe, Eine Weisse nahm mich ein" (Dear good moon forgive me, I've been taken in by a white woman) is what he has Monostatos say.

D: Don't be such a pedant. That is simply common south German usage: after all we are dealing with popular theater. [Ed. note: "vergib" would be the correct form.]

C: And how do all those stilted, pretentious, bombastic phrases fit into the popular theater? In the Queen of the Night's: first aria "Du wirst sie zu befreien gehen" (You will go and set her free). Gehen—what a feeble word, obviously to make it rhyme, but in such a highly emotional situation! Or Sarastro's tirades and bookish subordinate clauses: ". . . wenn nicht ein böses Weib, das zwar eine sehr gute Tochter hat, den Dolch dazu geschmiedet hätte" (. . . if it were not an evil female, who actually has a very good daughter, who had forged the dagger for it). He instructs Pamina like a high school teacher rather than a high priest.

D: Yes, I have to admit that the Sarastro dialogues are not Schikaneder's strongest writing.

C: You can say that again! The more unctuous he is the more unbearable he becomes, particularly in the speech before the priests in the second act. That he calls his teaching of the highest wisdom an "object" may well be a convention of the time, when youths in love didn't thirst for their beloved but for "the beloved object." But what drivel to have Sarastro thank his assenting subjects in "the name of humanity," and earlier to call "today's meeting one of the most important of our time," raising it to the level of world history!

D: I don't find that entirely inappropriate. If you really take *The Magic Flute* seriously; that is, as Schikaneder's and Mozart's mutual aspiration towards an allegorical World Theater, then we are in fact dealing with an extraordinarily important meeting in this first scene of Act II. The prince they are discussing develops far beyond an opera tenor and lover. He is introduced by Sarastro as a candidate for his throne, he will inherit the sevenfold circle of the sun, he will become the ruler of the world in the kingdom of the good, in Utopia. If that isn't an hour of world history!

C: All right, all right, we all know the higher meaning, the good intention, but are they enough? With such miserable verses?

D: What do you think of the following verses? "Hör ich so seine höchste Art bewähren /Entbrennt mein Aug in heilgen Wonnezähren." (When I so hear his highest nature proved /My eye's inflamed with tears of bliss). That's from *Lohengrin*, and the writer derided nearly all opera texts preceding his own. Which only proves that one can write effective opera librettos with miserable verses.

C: But even in his peculiar "Ring" alliterative verse, Wagner never managed such odd exchanges as did Schikaneder: "Wo ist sie denn?" (Where is she then?), one of the three boys asks about Pamina. "Sie ist von Sinnen (She's out of her mind), replies his colleague, and we are quite dumbfounded. This is almost the modern theater of the absurd! And even you, who swear by the Volkstheater qualities, by Schikaneder's Papageno comedy, don't you find the text of Papageno's first aria, third verse, more childish than childlike? "Wenn alle Mädchen wären mein /So tauschte ich brav Zucker ein" (If all the girls were mine alone I'd swap some for a sugar cone). And so on!

D: Of course that's not poetry, but one must think of everything within the scene and within the comedy and how they relate. By the way: it can't be proved that this third verse was written by Schikaneder, because it is neither in the original score nor in the first libretto. On the other hand there are many parts that can be quoted as examples of Schikaneder's theatrical wit. Even in the much-maligned spoken dialogue. "Ich bleibe ledig" (I'll stay single), says Papageno laconically when he has learned from the priest that he must be prepared to die after he sees his longed-for Papagena. It couldn't be formulated more briefly, more to the point—and it always brings the house down. Papageno's creator even puts a breath of self-irony into his mouth, which was something rather rare in the coarse popular theater of the time. After he has lied to the Prince and told him that he strangled the serpent, he says dryly "to himself," "Bin in meinem Leben nie so stark gewesen als heute" (I've never been so strong in my life as today). That is good theater; Verdi would have called it "Parola scenica." Schikaneder has even shifted some of Mozart's Masonic humanity from Sarastro's heights to Papageno's artlessness. "Bin ich nicht ein Narr, dass ich mich schrecken liess?" (Aren't I a fool to let myself be so frightened?) With these words this child of nature brings himself back to his senses after the shock of meeting the moor Monostatos. "Es gibt ja schwarze Vögel in der Welt, warum denn nicht auch schwarze Menschen?" (There are black birds in the world—then why not black men too?) In a moral sense this was good Volkstheater, as indeed it may be for us.

C: But theater people don't find Schikaneder's dialogue at all good, but rather in great need of improvement. In performance it's always ruthlessly cut.

D: I should refrain from making the tasteless observation that neither *Hamlet* nor *Faust* have ever been played in their entirety. [Tr. note: *Hamlet* has!]

C: For my part, I should refrain from quoting the obvious "Quod licet jovi, non licet bovi" (What is permitted to Jove is not permitted to cattle). But I would like to remind you that for the last 190 years, on stages everywhere, Schikaneder has constantly

been "improved on" with ad libs. It seems to have been necessary. "Bei mir kann doch von Geist keine Rede sein" (There's no
point in talking about spirit to me). Or: "Herr, mischen Sie sich
nicht in meine Familienangelegenheiten!" (You, sir, stop inter-
fering in my family affairs!). These are two irrepressible Papageno
jokes which aren't in Schikaneder's text but go back to insertions
made in early performances.

D: What does that prove? At best that the *Magic Flute* text achieved
the highest degree of popular appeal, that of the folk song: it
becomes anonymous, everybody's property, it is sung to death!

C: Unfortunately not where it is often most necessary. In the arias the
text is so inwardly attuned to Mozart's music that the impressive
brilliance of his genius almost obscures our critical view of the
foolish text. "Ein Mädchen oder Weibchen/ Wünscht Papageno
sich" (Papageno wants a girl or a little wife for himself)—why this
curious distinction? Is Schikaneder simply thinking of the rhymes?

D: It may seem to be thoughtless "Schikanederei," but in fact it isn't
at all. Long before this, in the first act, Papageno complains to
Pamina that he has "noch nicht einmal ein Mädchen, viel weniger
ein Weib!" (Not even a girl, let alone a wife). The small difference has its point, even if his joke—sex with or without a
wedding ring—doesn't make us raise our eyebrows quite as much
as it would have raised those of the petty bourgeoisie in 1791. And
so it is, oddly enough, with many parts of the *Magic Flute* text.
What seems at first glance to be childish or badly done proves at
the second or sometimes only the third glance to be astonishingly
apt and well thought-through. Take Number 7 as an example, the
Pamina/Papageno duet "Ihr hoher Zweck zeigt deutlich an/
Nichts Edlers sei als Weib und Mann" (Its high purpose makes it
clear / that nothing is nobler than man and wife), where both of
them sing of the universal power of love.

C: It could scarcely be praised more clumsily! I know very well that
Schikaneder wants to extol the "oneness" of man and wife, their
harmonious togetherness—that's what he wants to do, but he
can't, not even in the repeated final verses which increase in inten-
sity: "Mann und Weib und Weib und Mann /Reichen an die
Gottheit an" (Man and woman and woman and man /attain the
level of divinity). "An die Gottheit *heran*" (attain to the level)

might have been acceptable; but then the rhymester would have had one syllable left over.

D: Right. And yet, being an obedient servant of his friend and artistic master, he succeeded in conveying one of the most moving messages of all music theater, formulating in two simple verses the core of this human allegory called *The Magic Flute*. I admit, though, they're technically and poetically open to criticism.

C: The dramaturgical function of this popular duet is open to criticism, not to mention how illogical it is. Both Pamina and Papageno are escaping, they haven't got a moment to lose and yet they waste time singing a totally unnecessary duet.

D: Unnecessary? This Mozart melody, which is both close to folk song and sublime?

C: Of course, Mozart is always used as an excuse to defend Schikaneder!

D: But after all, they were partners, Mozart is always the musical co-dramatist!

C: All right. Opera has its own laws of logic, there must be time and space for bel canto. But should it be at the expense of characterization? How does it happen that Papageno, the son and heir of *Hanswurst* and Kasperl who responds only to the most fundamental sensuality, how does it happen that he ends up going into raptures about "the higher purpose" of love with a princess?

D: I could answer that with Kierkegaard's philosophical interpretation of Papageno. It places the joker, the simple child of nature, among the exemplary Mozart Eros personifications, between Cherubino who is "dreaming desire" and Don Giovanni, whose advances and conquests are one and the same thing. Papageno is the second stage, "anxiously searching"; his music is always characterized by a "zest for life, bubbling with love." For these reasons, why shouldn't our Eros personification, raised to such mythical heights, allow the finest sentiments of his nature—which is also continually bubbling over with love—to resonate in harmony with this higher purpose? But I certainly don't want to read into this something that would be totally foreign to Schikaneder and Mozart. Even without calling on philosophy, this duet has a place in the overall dramatic plan of *The Magic Flute*. Early in the opera, even before the first finale, this glorification of masculine-feminine affinity tends to offset the anti-feminine Masonic passages found later in the libretto. Contrasting spheres, the natural and the sublime world, sensuous and spiritual love meld together, symbolically, in this simple melody.

C: An overall plan for *The Magic Flute*? In many ways, it's rather a work that has been patched together. You really can't ignore the contradictions, the many things that just don't fit. Is the Queen of the Night really meant to be an avenging fury, Sarastro a magnanimous wise man? Sarastro's first appearance in a triumphal chariot drawn by six lions is that of the compleat autocrat, which is confirmed by his quite unjust order to administer 77 lashes on the soles of the feet of his servant Monostatos, who has only done his duty by arresting the intruder Tamino and bringing him forward. That's the behavior of a despot, not a priest; spreading terror through unpredictable moods has always been a mark of the absolute ruler. The Queen of the Night, on the other hand, who later calls for murder and finally, armed, leads in a troup of terrorists, appears at first as an injured mother with whom we all feel sympathy. Her daughter has been abducted, her suffering is genuine. Mozart himself is our principal witness. The G minor of the aria "Zum Leiden bin ich auserkoren" (I am condemned to grief) can never be interpreted ironically, nor can Pamina's sorrowful aria in the same key which was often used by the composer to express deep emotion. No, the Queen of the Night is introduced as a good fairy; she arranges for her protégés Tamino and Papageno to be given the helpful and "good" magic instruments on their way, and Sarastro appears in the first act as an autocratic tyrant and master of slaves. The fact that they change roles after the intermission and that black is turned into white simply reveals the confusion and lack of consistency of the libretto. It is probably true, as was soon claimed, that it was radically altered and turned upside down while they were working on it.

D: Yes, this was indeed claimed but never proved. Can you really believe that Mozart would have permitted such a thing? Do you really think that he who had paid such minute attention to all the details of the *Entführung* libretto 10 years previously would, as a mature man with the experience of his masterpieces *Figaro*, *Don*

"Entrance to the Temple of Trial."
Copper engraving on the title page of the 1793 edition
of *The Magic Flute* libretto.

Giovanni and *Così* behind him, have let himself be talked into a muddled libretto for his principal venture into the field of German opera, and set it to music without taking any dramatic interest or share in it? Such a view would imply that one of the greatest of all dramatic composers was willing to be degraded into a mere supplier of "pretty tunes." What a simplification! No, the process of creating something as complicated as an opera is not that primitive and lacking in psychology, certainly not as far as Mozart is concerned, because on closer examination the seemingly straight-forward becomes more and more complicated, and nothing, absolutely nothing, is simple. If the two main protagonists, the Queen of the Night and Sarastro, don't remain as they appear to be at first, if seen from the audience's perspective they change and reveal new characteristics—which is the case with other characters as well—isn't this a sign of dramatic quality? Nothing was more foreign to the mature Mozart than to draw his characters in obvious black and white. The Countess in *The Marriage of Figaro* is by no means the angel which a bowdlerized German translation makes her out to be, Masetto is not a jealous village idiot, and though even the animated marionettes of the *Così* joke are on the brink of the absurd, Mozart has us guessing about what is true feeling and what is irony. And as with Da Ponte, we must give Schikaneder his due as the partner of a dramatic composer who knew exactly what he wanted. It may be that the basic plan was altered more than once and modified during the many months of cooperation, for Mozart a relatively long period. But this long gestation wasn't just a matter of chance, but a period of enriching and deepening meaning.

C: Then how can you explain the unmotivated sudden change of character in the serious main parts, in contrast to Papageno, the comic figure, who always remains the same?

D: He is certainly not always the same. A couple of times he even reveals almost Figaro-like, rebellious characteristics; for instance when after their arrival in Sarastro's territory he describes his well born master Tamino as a coward and generally seems very cheeky. He hasn't seen anything of the allegedly helpful "noble boys" who will point the way. Here we already have a hint that the initially sympathetic Queen of the Night has lost authority. Then there is the sudden reversal of roles we have already spoken about, which actually by Schikaneder's standards—and these were indeed also Mozart's carefully considered standards—is an astonishingly subtle dramatic effect. Is Sarastro really transformed from a militant tyrant into a humane high priest? One should not forget that before he appears in his warlike chariot in the Finale of Act I, his true character has already been announced in the previous scene in the grove with the three temples. There Tamino, who is looking for a "cowardly villain," is gently told that he will not find such a one here, but a ruler in the temple of wisdom who is ready to proffer him the hand of friendship.

C: Of course that could be a later insertion.

D: Possible. But what would that prove? Nothing more than that colorful raw material, drawn from many sources and worked through to its final form, has been given shape. And only this final form should be judged, not the stages of its coming into being.

C: And the three boys in the final form, have they really been shaped logically? At first, for no apparent reason, they change sides, leaving the Queen of the Night and entering Sarastro's service. Right at the end they seem to act rebelliously even against their new master. They even lead Pamina in to go through the trials at Tamino's side, which had never been mentioned before—and then they allow this woman to pass the test together with the aspirant to the temple of wisdom. This could never have been laid down in the original design of such an all-male organization and its high priests.

D: Originally perhaps not. But couldn't Sarastro himself have undergone an inner transformation, a process of learning, as one would call it today? In any case he has learned to do without; one hears it in his words, and in a good production and presentation one senses it in the first finale. He gives up the vague hopes of an aging man. The situation is almost like that of King Mark: Sarastro is able to turn from the tragic to wise resignation when he says to Pamina, "Du liebest einen andern sehr. Zur Liebe will ich dich nicht zwingen . . ." (You love another very deeply. I will not force you to love me. . . .) In the end he even learns how to do without the power of ruling. In some modern psychological versions one sees Sarastro handing over the insignia of the sevenfold circle of the sun to Tamino and withdrawing quietly into the background. This seems to be entirely legitimate and follows Schikaneder's clues (even if not his text) and the intentions of Goethe, who in the second part of *The Magic Flute* sends Sarastro off on a journey to self-realization.

And as far as the three boys are concerned: They are probably fulfilling Sarastro's wishes when they lead Pamina to her lover prematurely, giving a woman the opportunity of "initiation". The high priest (the Freemason master—the voice of Mozart and Schikaneder) is a reformer of the Masonic male organization, that is, symbolically of patriarchical society—what a perspective for Schikaneder's popular suburban theater!

And to return to the three boys changing sides—they aren't just cheap little messenger boys or simply the decorative occupants of an impressive flying machine. Their real function is explained in the first printed libretto, where they are called "the three genii." Genii are not at the beck and call of anyone. If you interpret them as the personification of the voice within us, the "good genius" in man, then they act logically throughout all their rather confused journeys, steadfastly obedient to the fixed star of enlightened reason. They are willing to enter the service of the Queen of the Night because they know "Zum Ziele führet diese Bahn" (This road leads to the goal). On the way there, of course, they must lead their charges along a tortuous path, imparting a few words of wisdom to them every now and again, always producing the magic instruments at the right moment, and preventing two suicide attempts. . . .

C: A record that is true to form for Schikaneder!

D: He had to offer his public something, above all a good, exciting story. If you don't believe that the three boys are simply meant to be errand boys, if you are prepared to recognize them as important symbolic figures, then you really must listen to Mozart's music. Each bar the three boys sing has its own completely unmistakable aura of sound. This is true even when they are only the subject of conversation: The Queen of the Night's three ladies, who have always sung in a very human, rather feminine and coquettish tone, resort to one that is quite different, transfigured, when they announce that the boys will be their companions along

The Magic Flute, Act I. Tamino enchants "animals of all kinds" with his flute, here only apes. Copper engraving from a series of stage sets by the brothers Joseph and Peter Schaffer, c. 1793. The series presumably goes back to a production in Brünn (Brno); at any rate to a very early style of performance.

the journey. And the boys sing like this throughout the entire opera: like higher beings who have had the great good fortune to be given such unearthly melodies by Mozart. Their music would sound unconvincing if sung by Pamina. After all, she's a human being and the boys belong to another sphere, that of the genie.

C: Again Mozart has to stand in for poor old Schikaneder, and the irrational charm of the music is used as an argument to compensate for the lack of dramatic logic! Should this be allowed to go on and on? Does the divine Mozart really transfigure all of Schikaneder's sins? How for example, can you explain the fact that the seemingly wise Sarastro, who is presented as superhuman, even if he is perhaps corrected as an afterthought, behaves so unwisely, even foolishly, when he orders a lecherous Moor, of all people, who can't find a sexual partner for himself amongst all these "noble" whites, to guard the desirable young Pamina? The great slave owner—a nice job on the side for an enlightened priest, by the way—surely had unlimited choice among his servants. But no, it had to be the lustful Moor.

D: To be honest, Monostatos is indeed a problem. One could enlist well-trained Freudian and Jungian psychologists of today as expert witnesses for and against Schikaneder in this nearly 200-year-old case. They believe that they can prove scientifically what he at best could only have guessed at—but that at least would speak for his so often denied poetic talent, in which poets are seen as seers. It is the opinion of a leading Jung disciple[9] that the Moor Monostatos obviously represents the "dark side" of Sarastro's court and is associated with the positive priestly figure "as his shadow"; in this respect the figure of Monostatos represents the ambiguity which lies within every position in the "diversity of life with all its opposites" which Mozart supposedly found in Schikaneder's text with its "many layers." And as far as the shadowy Monostatos is concerned; "while the abduction of Pamina was 'consciously' carried out for the sake of the gods, Sarastro's original selfish intention has become unconscious and projected onto Monostatos whose presence in Sarastro's realm can only make sense when so explained."

C: My God, how clever the inventor of the notorious "Schikanederei" (chicanery) was! He even provides Jung's disciples with material!

D: Your sarcasm is understandable but superficial. Behind it lies the realization that what is of prime importance in dealing with these old, naive texts is whether, and how far, decades, indeed centuries after their more or less accidental date of birth conditioned by the times, they are still open to understanding, being thought about and thought through anew. Are they good enough and open enough for posthumous interpretation? Schikaneder achieved this with his *Magic Flute* libretto. Not one of his contemporaries nor his later competitors, for a time much more successful than he, managed it. There lies the difference, and it's a fundamental difference, historically seen, a truly essential difference that separates the wheat from the chaff.

C: Then it probably doesn't disturb you when characters repeatedly sing texts which don't belong to them—texts that probably are leftovers from an original version, later recast.

Bekämen doch die Lügner alle
Ein solches Schloss vor ihren Mund;
Statt Hass, Verleumdung, schwarzer Galle
Bestünden Lieb und Bruderbund.

If every liar one and all
Had such a padlock on his mouth;
Instead of hate, of libel and black gall
There would be love and brotherhood.

The three ladies sing this verse, and Papageno, whose punishment is a padlock on his mouth, senselessly agrees. All right, he does it for the sake of a beautiful quintet. But how come "Love and Brotherhood?" They are ideals from Sarastro's masculine world; how do they get into the mouths of the Amazons, the adversaries from the militant matriarchy? And how is Papageno allowed to sing the following verses in the second quintet, Act II Scene 5:

Von festem Geiste ist ein Mann
Er denket, was er sprechen kann.

A man is of the firmest mind
Whose thought and speech are of one kind.

Papageno, who never thinks before he starts chatting!
D: Here he is merely singing along with the other four voices. I shall content myself with an historical operatic explanation. In an 18th-century Singspiel there were no textually independent, individual voices in an ensemble such as you find in the *Rosenkavalier* trio. But if you listen more carefully, you will hear that a reason for music dominating the text has in fact been established here. Papageno has just sung "dass ich nicht kann das Plaudern lassen / Ist wahrlich eine Schand' für mich" (That I cannot give up chattering / Is really a disgrace). So he has come to realize exactly what he then sings in the quintet.
C: Should we really be so adventurous as to take Schikaneder at his word? We would stumble on a wealth of sensless rhymes!
D: Certainly, as far as the formulation is concerned, for he was no poet. But he was an imaginative playwright and a much better

dramatist than many people think. If you are going to take him at his word in this capacity you must accept his words where they are most effective—and that is on the stage. But what happens in usual practice? The parts of the text that were set by Mozart are left untouched. But the dialogues, for which Schikaneder was first and foremost responsible, are weeded out at the director's whim, if only to suit the many foreign singers who speak broken German. Then, as you know, even the greatest and most exemplary opera houses cut half a scene, a practice which simply precludes a deep musical and dramatic understanding of Mozart. The dialogue between the Queen of the Night and Pamina, before she forces the murderous dagger on her daughter and sings her brilliant revenge aria, is so often reduced to a few miserable remains! But the complete dialogue, which by the way isn't at all long, solves many of the seeming contradictions in the plot and characters of *The Magic Flute*, for in it the Queen recounts the earlier events which explain her motivation; and so enlightens the audience as well as her daughter.

C: But why only then, shortly before the end of the opera? Probably one of the careless ways in which Schikaneder turned the original plan upside down. If the Queen had told Tamino the whole story after her first entrance some things would have been a little clearer.

D: Certainly. But Schikaneder and Mozart did *not* do this although it wouldn't have cost them any additional work, and that decision gives us something to think about. Everything need not be clear at once. Isn't the work more exciting when the public is astonished and puzzled to start with? It's only the story told later by the Queen of the Night, so often deleted, that illuminates the action. She clarifies, motivates, and reveals the real nature of the main characters. Is Sarastro really the "barbarian" as represented by his enemy? No; because as she has to admit, his abduction of Pamina simply fulfilled the will of her dying husband who, as mythical ruler of the circle of the sun, handed over to the "initiated"—to Sarastro the priest of whom he thought highly—the symbol of rule, as well as his daughter whom Sarastro was to educate. The ambitious widow opposed his wishes: Her effort to overturn his last will and testament, which one has to view as fundamental law in the symbolism of the allegory, this power-lusting rebellion, was the cause of the girl's abduction. Her disobedience lets Sarastro off and puts the Queen in the wrong. The replacement of matriarchy by patriarchy, implied and hinted at, adds profundity to the magic opera, played on a suburban stage for a petty bourgeois audience. Seen in this perspective even the anti-feminine parts of *The Magic Flute* appear in a new light. At first sight, from the present-day view, these parts seem disconcerting; at second sight, if we view the Masonic components historically, they seem dispensable, and perhaps could be cut. At third sight, when aside from the music one is trying to grasp what is behind the popular, simple words, they achieve a symbolic multiplicity of meanings. But in order to grasp all this one must hear the text, from the stage, and not cut scenes of crucial dramatic importance.

C: That implies taking the old barnstormer and versifier seriously, as if we were dealing with *Faust*, Part III!

D: Well, the author of *Faust* went on to write *The Magic Flute*, Part II. Who knows if it would have enjoyed Schikaneder's success had it been completed and not remained a fragment!

C: And who knows how much of the text really is Schikaneder's!

With that we shall end this imaginary dialogue. It could go on endlessly as have the *Magic Flute* debates in the past, for the opera provides a seemingly inexhaustible supply of food for thought. The artistic difference between composer and librettist; questions about how the opera was written—questions which cannot be clarified because they were not documented; the multiplicy of forms—magic farce, opera seria and buffa, German Singspiel, fairy tale and mystery—all these questions have a place and are woven into a great work of art. Then there is the unique and harmonious mixture of the "popular" (Mozart's father had once anxiously advised his son to write that way) and the esoteric. All these problems are inherent in the sources of the material used which are as diverse as the artistic end product and much more complex than Schikaneder's detractors of any period care to admit.

The extensive, jumbled literature about *The Magic Flute* still cites the fairy tale "Lulu oder die Zauberflöte" as the main source—and as in most things, the simpler the statement the less true it becomes.

Christoph Martin Wieland, an enlightened Freemason, is usually cited as author, which is also inaccurate. In reality the story is by J. A. Liebeskind and was simply included in Wieland's collection of fairy tales *Dschinnistan oder auserlesene Feen-und Geister Maerchen* (Dschinnistan or Selected Fairy and Ghost Stories). Such an oversimplification of the opera's origin, augmented in some accounts by a mention of Terrasson's Egyptian novel *Sethos*, goes hand in hand with the generally accepted view that the libretto had been suddenly "turned upside down," and black transformed into white.

It is true that the early scenes of *The Magic Flute* follow the "Lulu" fairy tale from which it also borrows the magic title instrument. Lulu is a noble prince from the kingdom of Korassan whom Perifirime, a "radiant fairy", persuades to recapture the gilded thunderbolt, the emblem of authority, from her enemy, the wicked magician Dilsenghuin, who stole it, and return it to her. She offers two magic instruments, a flute and a ring, to aid Lulu in this venture. Lulu sets off, and in the end, disguised as an old minstrel, he not only returns the thunderbolt but also frees the imprisoned virgin Sidi.

This is an oriental fairy tale—the exotic was very fashionable at the time—and undeniably a source for *The Magic Flute*, but at the most only to Scene 15, and in no way, as is often thoughtlessly maintained, to the finale of Act I. But the influence of other sources is also evident. To start with, there is again Wieland's *Dschinnistan*. This collection of fairy tales was, after its publication in 1787, widely read and was well known throughout Germany and notably to Schikaneder, who was not ill read and who had already based his heroic-comic opera *Der Stein der Weisen* (The Wise Men's Stone) on a *Dschinnistan* story of the same name. The test motif from *The Magic Flute* was also taken from this story: a raging torrent and a sea of fire which have to be crossed. The three boys derive from the *Dschinnistan* story *Die klugen Knaben* (The Wise Boys). Soffra, a tyrannical magician who remarkably enough reigns in exotic Asia as both "King and High Priest," holds the shepherd's daughter Alinde prisoner in a dungeon, from which she is freed by the courageous goatherd Salamor. Wieland's sentence, "Three beautiful boys who eat beneath three silver palm trees with golden leaves," contained in this story is almost literally repeated in Schikaneder's scenic directions for the first scene of Act II—they give Salamor astonishingly enlightened Masonic advice: "Sey standhaft, erdulde gelassen, alles was dir dabey begegnen wird, und hüte dich einen Laut von dir hören zu lassen!" (Be steadfast, endure patiently everything that you will encounter and let no syllable cross your lips). Schikaneder took both the "flaming starry" Queen and the portrait of a girl capable of arousing sudden love from other *Dschinnistan* tales. "The hideous black slave" comes from "Adis und Daly" and is as lecherous and vengeful as Monostatos.

The obvious visual and oral appeal of some contemporary theater images must have been more important to Schikaneder, the man of the theater, than printed literature. The opera *Das Sonnenfest der Brahminen* (The Sun Festival of the Brahmins) by Hensler-Müller, produced with immense success in the Leopoldstadt Theater in 1790, had as its central theme a love story with appropriate decor and costumes which followed in the well-established footsteps of *Die Entführung aus dem Serail*. A brave Englishman frees his beloved, who has been selected as a sacrificial victim in India. Substantial scenes with priests frame this plot. It seems to anticipate Louis Spohr's opera *Jessonda* of half a century later, but elements of it suggest *The Magic Flute*. There is the noble Brahmin high priest; a sun temple which symbolizes the final victory of the good; and Barzalo and Mika, the inevitable, cheerful Volkstheater pair, who provide Papageno— Papagena joy: "ich werde dein Weibchen / Du wirst mein Männchen" (I'll become your little wife / you my little husband).

The premiere of a work less frequently performed than *The Sun Festival*, the German opera *Oberon* by the court opera composer Paul Wranitzky, was directed by Schikaneder at almost the same time (1789). Its music was artistically far above the norm of contemporary Singspiel, and has led to some notable revivals, right into the 20th century. But more importantly it shares important textual associations with *The Magic Flute*, not only because the librettist was Ludwig Giesecke but also because Wieland provided the subject matter, so the plot has many closely related motifs. In this re-shaping of Wieland's famous verse epic, Giesecke had adapted a libretto by Friederike Sophie Seyler, a theater veteran and successful actress. We can sense in it, toned down by the conventions of a magic opera, a premonition of the Romantic, curbed though it is by the spirit of the Enlightenment. Although there can be no real comparison with

Mozart's and Schikaneder's symbolic World Theater, without this *Oberon* which was staged a full generation before Weber's last work, many *Magic Flute* motifs would be inconceivable. The role of the cheerful servant Scherasmin who accompanies the hero may simply be typical of the Volkstheater, but when he sings his E major aria,

> *Heisa! lustig ohne Sorgen*
> *leb ich jetzt als Salomo!*
> *und war noch vergangnen Morgen*
> *povero Diabolo.*
> *Heisa! hier ist gut zu leben!*
> *Wird mir dann Freund Oberon*
> *noch ein hübsches Mädchen geben,*
> *geh ich ihm nie davon.*

> Heisa! happy without care
> Now I live like Solomon!
> Yet I was this early morn
> povero Diabolo.
> Heisa! life is really good here!
> If my good friend Oberon
> Lets me have a pretty maiden,
> then I'll leave him nevermore.

And here is Scherasmin's duet with Fatime: Can't one almost hear Papageno?

> *Komm herein mein liebes Weibchen,*
> *hier hast du meine Hand schlag ein!*
> *Wir wollen wie die Tutteltäubchen*
> *uns schnäbeln und des Lebens freun.*

> Come in, my dearest little wife,
> Come take it, here's my hand!
> And like the little turtle doves
> We'll bill and coo, enjoy our life.

In passing, observe how pale this Scherasmin is, when seen in Wranitzky's work on the stage, and how anemic even Weber's musically much richer Scherasmin seems! How infinitely inferior they both are compared to Papageno!

Even though the following motifs occur in similar fashion in other contemporary operas, they remain important models for *The Magic Flute*: firstly, the lovers are willing to make sacrifices, to find each other through trials involving life and death. Secondly, a magic horn brings help in moments of dire distress. And lastly, the higher conflict of a pair of opposites—here a couple of royal elves quarrelling, but without any ideological implications.

Nor, in tracing origins, may previous works of Schikaneder and Mozart be overlooked. Komorzynski has tried to prove that Schikaneder's Augsburg operetta *Der Luftballon* (1786) was a forerunner of the *Magic Flute*.[10] But this topical work, written for the occasion of the ill-fated balloon extravaganza, is worlds apart from the *Magic Flute* allegory.

Thamos, König in Ägypten, an earlier drama which both Mozart and Schikaneder considered, is much closer. Its author was a prominent advocate of enlightened Josephinism, a Freemason, and Vice Chancellor of the Bohemian court chancery, Tobias Philipp, Baron von Gebler. The similarities between this work and *The Magic Flute* are too striking to be ignored, as I have already mentioned in connection with Schikaneder's Salzburg period. An Egyptian temple to the sun, in which the wise priest Sethos rules, has a central place in both works.

In order to win Sethos's daughter Sais and the royal throne, Prince Thamos must prove his strength and loyalty against intriguers, who are lead by a passionate and ambitious woman called Mirza. The author placed the action in scenes of "enlightened" pathos with elaborate sets and decor (which must certainly have caught Schikaneder's interest), for which Mozart composed dignified choral music which anticipates the priests' music in *The Magic Flute*. Sethos's relationship to Sarastro and to Shakespeare's wise magician Prospero is clear. Mira's relationship to the Queen of the Night is worth mentioning in that in both cases a domineering woman embodies the evil principle, some proof to contravene the reversal theory seen by some in *The Magic Flute*. Komorzynski believes that he was the first to discover that Prince Tamino inherited his name from Prince Thamos. Recent Egyptology research has revealed that the final names Tamino and Pamina are of Egyptian origin, but have mistakenly changed their sex: Pa-min was the male servant of the god Min, Ta-min his female servant.

But Schikaneder could not have known anything about this, as ancient Egypt was a romantic mythical fairyland at that time. It was not until 1824 that the young French orientalist Jean-François Champollion deciphered the Egyptian hieroglyphics. However, much that seemed Egyptian at the time, and therefore much Masonic material, found its way into *The Magic Flute*. From the start Masonic rites and ethics were based on romantic notions of ancient Egypt and its wisdom. Two prose works, certainly known both to Schikaneder and Mozart, had a decisive influence on their opera, probably greater than all other sources. First, the novel *Sethos, histoire ou vie tirée des monuments anecdotes de l'ancienne Égypte, traduite d'un manuscrit grec* (Sethos, a History or Life Drawn From Anecdotes of Ancient Egypt Translated from a Greek Manuscript) by Abbé Jean Terrasson; and secondly, the essay *Über die Mysterien der Ägyptier* (On the Mysteries of the Egyptians) by Ignaz von Born which appeared in the first issue of the new *Journal für Freymäurer* (Journal for Freemasons) in 1784.

Terrasson's expansive novel was published in Paris no later than 1731, but first became known in Germany through the 1777/78 translation by Matthias Claudius, and even later in Vienna, where it was of great topical interest. It was an early "novel of development" with an attractive and exotic setting. Prince Sethos, who seems to have lived a century before the Trojan Wars, is initiated into the priestly mysteries of Egypt by the "Interlocuteur" Amedes—here we are reminded of the speaker in *The Magic Flute*. The following two volumes of the novel are devoted to these initiation rites. Sethos is found to prevail against numerous intrigues perpetrated, characteristically enough, by a woman, Queen Dalucca, who is Sethos's chief antagonist and the embodiment of the principle of evil. He survives three tests, passes through labyrinths and a fiery "vaulted chamber" and swims naked across a branch of the Nile, thanks to strength of character imparted by his devotion to the god Isis and the goddess Osiris. Schikaneder quotes almost word for word from Terrasson in Sarastro's aria. Here is Terasson's version:

O Isis, grosse Göttin der Egypter.
gib deinen Geist dem neuen Diener.

O Isis, great goddess of the Egyptians,
Give your spirit to the new servant.

The two armored men's chorale text, "Der, welcher wandelt diese Strasse voll Beschwerden / Wird rein durch Feuer, Wasser, Luft und Erden" (He who walks this toilsome road of care / Is cleansed by fire, water, earth and air), appears in the Sethos novel as an inscription carved into the rocks at the entrance to the labyrinth: "Wer diesen Weg alleine geht, und ohne hinter sich zu sehen, der wird gereinigt werden durch das Feuer, durch das Wasser und durch die Luft" (He who goes this way alone without looking behind him will be purified by fire, water and by air).

Schikaneder and Mozart probably owe even more to the essay by Born, first of all due to his eminent position. Ignaz Edler von Born (1742–1791), Master of the Lodge "Zur wahren Eintracht" (Of Perfect Harmony), was generally considered to be the leader of the Viennese Freemasons, and was also a highly esteemed scientist. Maria Theresia had appointed him as the founding director of the "Naturalienkabinett" (Natural History Collection), and during the reign of Joseph II he was responsible for many improvements in mining and was a member of numerous European academies. His sudden resignation from the Lodge in 1786 was puzzling; it was possibly to protest the Imperial Freemason Decree which reduced the power of the Lodges by putting them under state supervision. It could also have been due to his delicate health—he was only 48 when he died—or discouragement arising from his failure to stem growing obscurantism. (The Bavarian Elector forbade the formation of the so-called *Illuminaten* Lodges for which the enlightened, controversial and anti-clerical Born had struggled.) His example, however, continued to be of great influence, so it is easy to believe that Born reappeared, commanding and transfigured, as Sarastro. Schikaneder and Mozart, both involved in Freemasonry, knew and respected him, and "the initiated" could recognize him clearly in the figure of the wise and powerful man whose sun's rays "destroyed" the darkness. Born had just died in July 1791, and the followers of the Queen of the Night again came to the fore. "Porcheria Tedesca" (German piggishness) hissed the new Empress, criticizing Mozart's mildly enlightened *La clemenza di Tito* in Prague.

Born's essay in *The Journal for Freemasons* seeks old venerable sources in support of Masonic teachings and customs. He sees both rooted in the Egyptian priesthood. The article was not intended to be an apologia for the Lodges which were under the constant, suspicious scrutiny of both the church and the monarchy and not infrequently forbidden, but rather to provide a rational foundation on historic principles for Masonic beliefs insofar as this was possible without an understanding of hieroglyphics and only resting on Hellenic literary sources (Apuleius, Heliodorus, Diodorus and Plutarch among others).

Born makes the case that the admittance rites of the Freemasons corresponded to those of the ancient Egyptian priesthood which was a secret male society, open only to the initiated: "the female sex was forever excluded from service of the gods." The god Osiris, symbolized by the sun, and the nature goddess Isis were particularly venerated. The beautiful temples in Memphis and Heliopolis and those "immense colossi," the pyramids, were praised as sublime witnesses to ancient Egyptian wisdom, even more so the virtues of the priests: discretion, truth and wisdom. Born then draws practical applications to which Freemasons were to adhere: "Submission to the king and the laws, reverence for religion, and decorum were the essential virtues of the Egyptian priest and are also those of the Masons." And: "Is it not our destiny to oppose vice, ignorance and stupidity and to spread enlightenment? To encourage the daily practice of virtuous deeds, to practice all that is good and to oppose all that is evil?"

Born's ethical program, located in an exotic Egyptian setting, clearly stimulated the imagination of his readers—and until recent times no *Magic Flute* production could manage without pyramids. Everything was dressed in Masonic symbolism, to which the intellectual establishment of that time was sympathetic—and does this not conform to the ideological outline of *The Magic Flute*? Whether Born was the model for Sarastro or not, his essay which reassessed the Enlightenment in terms of ancient mysteries certainly added the Masonic element to the diverse sources of the motifs in *The Magic Flute*. Mozart had been a member of the Lodge "Zur Wohltätigkeit" (To Charity) since 1784, and took an active and lively part in Masonic life. Schikaneder had been a Mason in Regensburg, and though it is not certain whether he belonged to a Lodge in Vienna, we must assume that he was in close contact with the Freemasons of Vienna if only for business reasons. After all, virtually all of the culturally influential Viennese were involved in Freemasonry: aristocrats like Prince Esterházy and Count Thun; high court officials Gebler, Born, and Baron Joseph von Sonnenfels, who was an economic and political adviser to Joseph II; publishers like Toricella and Artaria who disseminated the works of Haydn and Mozart; rich citizens like the businessman Michael Puchberg; prominent persons like Johann Reinhold Forster who had sailed round the world; composers and writers of all kinds, from Mozart, Haydn and Wranitzky to Schikaneder's factotum Gieseke. As a private theatrical entrepreneur, Schikaneder, dependent at all times on the financial resources of his colleagues and on rich and influential contacts, would not have been able to distance himself from the influential lodges. His own ideas and beliefs also led him to swim with the same "enlightened" tide, as both his earlier and later works prove.

Is *The Magic Flute* therefore a Masonic opera? This is another point upon which the opinions of interpreters differ. Earlier writers, including Bernhard Paumgartner and Alfred Einstein, answered the question largely in the affirmative. But recently the cultural influence of the Freemasons has declined and this aspect has been downplayed, for example in Felsenstein's famous 1954 production at the Komische Oper in Berlin. An interpreter should never over-emphasize aspects of the work "like the Masonic or the Egyptian," otherwise the immediate and sensory world of popular theater is lost, wrote Götz Friedrich, the intellect behind this production.[11] Even the frequent symbolic use of the number three in *The Magic Flute* is generally common in fairy tales. True enough—but such tokens are integrated into an extended network of other Masonic symbols: the "northern portal" where Tamino seeks an entrance; the covering of the two initiates' heads; the minimum age of 20 for admission; the inquiry into initiates' intentions; the testing for silence, steadfastness, and courage; the three highest virtues, praised in the choral finale:

> *Es sieget die Stärke*
> *Und krönet zum Lohn*
> *Die Schönheit und Weisheit*
> *Mit ewiger Kron!*

Strength is the victor
And crowns as reward
Beauty and Wisdom
With its eternal diadem!

All these symbols accord with the traditional Masonic teachings and practices as set down in the literature of Freemasonry, for example in the *Alte Pflichten* (The Ancient Duties) from the second half of the 18th century. Strength, beauty, and wisdom also symbolize the three "great pillars" of the Lodges. The condescension towards, if not contempt for women, which is frequently expressed in the libretto, as when Sarastro instructs Pamina in the first finale:

Ein Mann muss Eure Herzen leiten,
Denn ohne ihn pflegt jedes Weib
Aus seinem Wirkungskreis zu schreiten.

A man must guide your heart
Without that every woman tends
To overstep her natural sphere.

is also characteristic of Masonic thought. However foreign such views, coming from a purportedly wise man, might seem to modern minds, one must make allowances; one knows the previous history, that "that proud female," the Queen of the Night, has in fact overstepped her natural sphere. The general tone of the opera, however, is as anti-feminine as that of the Speaker who represents Sarastro two scenes before: "Ein Weib tut wenig, plaudert viel./ Du, Jüngling, glaubst dem Zungenspiel?" (A woman does little, chats a lot./ Young man, do you believe in wagging tongues?). Or again in the second quintet in which Tamino berates the Queen of the Night who is after all his mother-in-law to be: "Sie ist ein Weib, hat Weibersinn" (She is a woman with woman's sense). This tone is indeed consistent with Masonic thought; we have already met it in the ancient Egyptian references, and in their male-only Lodges which parallel the patriarchical structure of 18th-century European society. It must be said though, that the principle of male-only organizations was not rigorously pursued. The so-called "Adoptionslogen" allowed women to take part in Masonic life, and according to Marie Antoinette's account, "tout le monde," meaning aristocratic society, joined these Lodges in the Paris of 1781. We cannot be so certain about Vienna.

Certainly Schikaneder and Mozart would have readily accepted responsibility for the Masonic features in *The Magic Flute*. Although the composer was the more active member, it seems that he was willing to make a little fun of his all too anti-feminine Lodge brothers. The priests' duet of warning (Act II, Sc.4) "Bewahret euch vor Weibertücken" (Guard yourselves from women's wiles), using the example of a wise man who has been deceived, is certainly not composed as if Mozart were seriously nodding his head in agreement with the final verses. The moral "Tod und Verzweiflung war sein Lohn" (Death and despair were his reward) hops about in a cheerful C major, staccato, musical irony which would produce an even more ironic effect if modern interpreters (when indeed they let us hear the duet and don't cut it) did not follow their careless predecessors, changing Mozart's original Allegretto into a pseudo-ceremonious Andante.

Wise teachings in verse never appealed to Mozart the music dramatist, and in fact in some other places he crossed them out. Apart from that, his composition was faithful to Schikaneder's Masonic allusions. One of the copper engravings for the original libretto, with its pyramids, five-pointed star, quadrant and trowel, clearly illustrates these allusions. (See illustration on page 108). Schikaneder's text may be chiefly responsible for the frequent symbolic use of the number three, from the three ladies and the three boys to the three appearances of several of the main characters. Here the magical three relates specifically to the symbolism of Freemasonry and not general mystical beliefs: three "large portals," three movable treasures (quadrant, spirit-level and plummet) and three immovable ones (a drawing board, rough stone, carved stone), three large and three small lights, and so on. Mozart highlights this symbolism in his music, starting with the Overture which begins with three chords in E-flat major, and after the exposition brings them to our attention again in another rhythm. We hear them in the three-fold trombone chord before Sarastro's speech at the beginning of the second act as well as in many other more or less esoteric musical allusions which would have been understood by the "initiated" in the audience.

Did they really understand? We do not know. Mozart's often-

Scenic designs for *The Magic Flute* for the Berlin Royal Opera House,
1816, by Karl Friedrich Schinkel.

quoted statement (in a letter to Constanze October 7 and 8, 1791) "what pleases me most of all is the silent applause," could mean that he welcomed understanding by a peer group. Schikaneder hit the audience with a sledgehammer. Just what his inner convictions as a Freemason were, we may never know, but the practical man of the theater kept them firmly in view, even if at the weekly Masonic gatherings in which he took part the joys of the dining table refreshed him at least as much as the joys of "games and music" which were simultaneously offered according to Kapellmeister Ignaz von Seyfried. But the Freemasons as a target group hardly existed any more then.

The first Masonic Lodge was founded in England in 1717. It looked to the ethical code of the medieval knightly orders for its ideological foundations as well as a new enlightened humanism of individual responsibility for the education of man, an end to which most Freemasons also subscribed. The builders' associations connected with the construction of the Gothic cathedrals, entirely independent of town guilds, provided the organizational model. The "secrets" of the cathedral builders, working masons employing the quadrant and trowel, formed the basis for the sacred ceremonies and rituals of the Freemasons. After its founding in England the movement spread rapidly to the continent. By the middle of the 18th century the cultural elite of Germany gave its support to the new organization. This elite included monarchs like Frederick II of Prussia and Francis I of Habsburg-Lothringen (to the chagrin of his wife, Empress Maria Theresia), and intellectuals from Klopstock, Lessing, Herder, Wieland, and Goethe to Matthias Claudius and Chamisso. In the Anglo-Saxon world it extended from Swift and Pope to Benjamin Franklin; in France from the encyclopedists to Stendhal. It was considered proper and progressive to be a Freemason. Opposition understandably arose among the Catholic clergy who were accused of being "obscurantist," the enemies of enlightened progress.

The clerically-minded and pious Empress Maria Theresia ordered the first Viennese Lodge closed in 1742, but when her son Joseph became co-regent he was able to institute some degree of tolerance. As Emperor, he published the Freemason Edict of 1785, subjecting the movement to the control of the imperial government and reducing the number of Lodges in Vienna from eight to three. He remained well-disposed towards Freemasonry, however. This is not surprising, as its enlightened liberalism paralleled his own views, and the highest court officials—even the imperial censors Joseph von Sonnenfels and Gottfried van Swieten, the son of Maria Theresia's personal physician and the librettist of Haydn's great oratorios— were members of Viennese Lodges. Emperor Joseph II, having the Lodges well under control, saw them as his allies against determined clerical opposition to his reforms. This official support continued, even though in the meantime all kinds of colorful sects had formed: from the Bavarian Rosicrucians who endeavored to make kindred spirits of magic, alchemy, mysticism, and the Enlightenment; to the avowedly anti-clerical Illuminati, the "Illuminated Ones," who had also found numerous adherents in Bavaria. Ignaz von Born, revered by Mozart and Schikaneder as the prototype of Sarastro, sympathized with the Illuminati. But the movement was soon dissolved in Bavaria.

After the death of Joseph II and the short reign of Leopold II, who kept the Freemasons under his wing, the lot of the movement became very difficult. Under the arch-conservative Franz II, the Jesuits at court took the upper hand, leading to the linking of the Enlighten-ment to Jacobinism, so in 1794 the Lodges were again suppressed. In such a climate stage productions such as the comedy *The Freemasons,* by the famous actor and director of the Burgtheater Friedrich Ludwig Schröder, or the historical drama *Die Tempelherren* by Johann, Knight of Kalchberg—which appeared half a year before *The Magic Flute,* singing the praises, in Schikaneder's words, of a temple "built with wisdom, beauty, and strength"—could no longer be mounted.

Franz II and his supporters did not consider *The Magic Flute* to be a harmless fairy-tale opera as is documented by the official regional police reports from Prague on the occasion of the first Czech produc-tion of the opera in 1793. The amateur company performing it was listed as a dangerous, secret society and a "veritable order," and so was placed under police supervision.[12] Two years later the *Geheime Geschichte des Verschwörungs-Systems der Jakobiner in den österreichischen Staaten* (The Secret History of the Conspiratorial System of the Jacobins in the Austrian States) appeared in London, probably launched by Viennese court officials. In it the opera was interpreted as a revolutionary allegory, Sarastro incorporating the wisdom of enlightened legislation, Tamino the people, Pamina freedom, and so on.[13]

Such a political objective was certainly not Mozart's and Schikaneder's intention. But no doubt their ethical concept had political implications. Tamino's journey, his purification through experiencing life and the tests, is typical of the education of princes, a favorite pedagogical and political theme of German Enlightenment. Its model was Wieland's novel *Der goldene Spiegel oder die Könige von Scheschian* (The Golden Mirror or The Kings of Scheschian), then a later literary masterpiece, Goethe's *Wilhelm Meister*. In the latter the education of a ruler is broadened to include a humanistic education. The political component of this classical "Bildungsroman" (novel of education) is evident in spite of its symbolism, and multiple links bind it to *The Magic Flute*. Wilhelm Meister's long "Wanderjahre" (journeyman's years) are reflected by Papageno, who is incapable of growth or education, when he complains (Act II, Sc.7.), "so eine ewige Wanderschaft" (Oh this eternal wandering!). In the year that *The Magic Flute* was first performed it seems that political innuendos in the theater may have been less dangerous than they were to become later. Still, it must have seemed daring enough to the political snoopers when they heard the following lines, which showed little respect for the established society of the realm and must have sounded altogether too Jacobin for their ears:

> *Sprecher . . . Er ist Prinz.*
> *Sarastro: Noch mehr—er ist Mensch!*

> Speaker . . . He is a Prince.
> Sastro: More! He is a human being!

We have already mentioned the many unmistakable and conspicuous Masonic symbols. Is *The Magic Flute*, then, a Masonic opera? It is, but at the same time it is much more. Certainly the Masonic symbols were consciously included; they comprise the esoteric side of the work, sufficient for the cognoscenti, unnecessary for general audiences of popular theater. By the same token we can penetrate Bach's works more deeply after we understand the composer's number symbolism that Friedrich Smend was able to trace, but this does not mean that Bach is inaccessible *without* such knowledge. Also much that is unappealing and dogmatic in Freemasonry, especially the male society's contempt for women, is offset by the positive representation of Pamina. In contrast to the custom of the Lodges, we find in Schikaneder's text a courageous young woman who in fact is worthy to assume the lead during the trials of life and death, and is initiated: "Ich selbsten führe dich, / Die Liebe leitet mich!" (I myself will guide you,/ For it is love that guides me). A modern production can dispense with Masonic symbols and with pyramids in the scenic design: if it can project the humanistic idea, the human allegory within a fairy tale, then it will have conveyed what is most essential in the opera.

Thus we have exotic fairy tales that are characteristic of the time; scholarly novels about Egypt; and Masonic treatises as sources; moral allegory with an intentional political bias; the petty bourgeoisie of a suburban theater as the principal audience, the balance those of "higher level," the initiated who would support a new German opera as the ideal public; a secular composer of genius and a deft practical man of the theater as an unequal team. When one considers these glaring differences, one can only be astonished at the well-rounded quality and harmony of the finished work, rather than at its inner contradictions. In his Mozart monograph Alfred Einstein coined the beautiful sentence: "*The Magic Flute* is one of those works that is capable of enchanting a child; at the same time it can move the most experienced of men to tears and uplift the wisest." Adorno, who is certainly no apologist, recognizes in the opera another vortex of diverging opposites: the spheres of "higher" and "lower" music. "The last time they were reconciled, as if on the narrowest border line of extreme stylization, was in Mozart's *Magic Flute*; works like *Ariadne* by Strauss and von Hofmannsthal reveal a longing regret for the passing of this moment."[14] If this is true, this "last time" was a great moment in theatrical history, and both Mozart and Schikaneder are responsible for it, even when considering the music. We know that the melody of Papageno's popular song "Ein Mädchen oder Weibchen" was not Mozart's invention, but is a typical "roving song," existing in many versions, so that however much we mistrust legends about *The Magic Flute* which are difficult to check, it is quite possible that Schikaneder brought this tune to his friend, whistling or singing it for him. The tune was known in both Viennese, "Der Kaiser ist ein lieber Herr" (The Kaiser is a dear Lord) and in Prussian "Üb' immer Treu und Redlichkeit" (Always be faithful and honest).

Many years earlier when he was guest artist in Memmingen, Schikaneder would have heard it in Swabian and remembered it.

Pamina and the Three Genii.
From the cycle of *Magic Flute* frescoes
painted in 1866 by Moritz von Schwind
for the Wiener Hofoper—today the Staatsoper.

6   Theories and Legends

"... nicht nur ... meine Musick, sondern das Buch und alles zusammen" (not only my music, but the text, and the whole work), to Mozart's great joy, pleased his rival Salieri (letter to Konstanze, October 14, 1791). This complete and complex *Magic Flute* includes much that is inconsistent and inadequately edited, much that is fantastic and illogical. I have already discussed many of these characteristics. At first, contemporary criticism held Schikaneder to be a hack writer of limited intellectual aspirations, a scapegoat. Since 1841 there has been a theory that both plot and characters were reversed halfway through the creative process, when it was discovered that the rival Leopoldstadt Theater planned to put on a piece by Joachim Perinet also based on Wieland's (that is, Liebeskind's) *Lulu oder die Zauberflöte*. It was called *Die Zauberzither oder Kaspar der Fagottist* (The Magic Zither, or Kaspar the Bassoonist), with music by Wenzel Müller. When it was feared that this would be performed earlier, Schikaneder quickly turned the good fairy into the evil Queen of the Night and the tyrant Sarastro into a wise high priest of wisdom, thus supposedly standing the plot on its head. "As a result, some inconsistencies have arisen between the beginning and the end, for example the ambiguous behavior of the genii."

This quotation is taken from the novella *Zauberflöte, Dorfbarbier, Fidelio* (Magic Flute, Village Barber, Fidelio) by the drama critic Georg Friedrich Treitschke who was active in Vienna. We would hardly know anything about him were it not for the fact that his name has gone down in music history as one of the librettists of *Fidelio*. Although the novella is a product of pure literary fantasy and can claim no documentary worth, it was bolstered by the authority of Otto Jahn's great Mozart biography (1859); the legend of the plot's reversal has haunted the growing *Magic Flute* literature, particularly the more popular writing, ever since. This legend has had its supporters up to the present, from the English musicologist Edward J. Dent, who in his book on Mozart's operas (1913) held that Monostatos and not Sarastro was the original opposite of the good fairy; to Kurt Pahlen's *Zauberflöte* monograph of 1978, which without furnishing any evidence, offers indications of the sudden break in the plot attributed to the *Zauberzither* competition. ("Schikaneder must have had one shock after another during its performance".)

Other anecdotes or amusing details originating with Treitschke's story also hang on tenaciously. There is the one about Schikaneder, seemingly on the point of bankruptcy, appearing "in the spring of 1791 at the bedside of Mozart, the late riser" and crying out in despair, "Help me, friend and brother, or I am lost! I need money, money!" He purportedly brought the first sketch based on the Lulu fairy tale with him, although the ending was still obscure and he had left much of "the metrical design" to the prompter Haselböck. Or again, as has often been repeated, Schikaneder had reserved the role of Papageno for himself, or that Mozart composed "mostly in the summer house in Schikaneder's garden, a stone's throw from the theater" (the famous *Magic Flute* summer house)[15], out of which grew the legend that Mozart was locked up to keep him at work, but that he used the house instead for drinking and sexual orgies. That Schikaneder's despairing cry for help was simply a pseudo-dramatic insertion into a late romantic novella, that the director was actually in good financial shape, and that his reasons for a partnership with Mozart were purely artistic—these are facts that have been verified by the thorough Mozart research of Komorzynski and Rommel, so we can ignore these other anecdotal embellishments.

Where then did Treitschke, who otherwise had no particular connection with the origin of *The Magic Flute*, get his details, remembered exactly half a century after the premiere of the opera? They were based on information from Kapellmeister Baron Ignaz von

Seyfried (1775–1841) who was a very close witness. We would certainly class him as only a minor composer, but as a conductor at Schikaneder's theater and previously a Mozart pupil, he was without doubt close to the scene. We have to thank Rommel's almost detectivelike acuteness as a researcher for a fragment from an undated and unaddressed letter of about 1840 which has been identified as the source of the story that has caused so much confusion.[16] Written by Seyfried and meant for Treitschke it is today preserved in the archives of the International Mozarteum Foundation. The letter contains most of Treitschke's fantastically spun stories, especially the "about-face" of the whole plan. Incidentally, according to Seyfried "this happily saved the whole work; otherwise Mozart, in his dramatic swansong, would hardly have been able to leave such a magnificent poetic and romantic masterpiece, as a model for posterity." This is Seyfried's tribute to Schikaneder. There is no mention, incidentally, of that which will occupy us later—of any part of the text having been written by Giesecke. Seyfried simply mentions that Giesecke "informed" his director about Wieland's *Dschinnistan*—from which Schikaneder had already taken the material for the libretto of *Der Stein der Weisen*!

What are we to make of Seyfried's testimony relative to the theory of reversing the plot? Not much, when we consider the circumstances, and make allowances for some obviously false details attributable to the failing memory of a 65-year-old who died a year later, and who was reporting complicated matters from half a century previously. He took lessons from Mozart as a talented youngster of 15—could he at this age have succeeded in obtaining intimate insight into the extremely involved creative process of a work like *The Magic Flute*?

Later on, Seyfried may have had some difficulties with Schikaneder, of the kind that can seldom be avoided between Kapellmeister and director in a theater. But whether he was really unfavorably disposed towards him or not seems to be a matter of secondary importance when compared to the obviously petty mentality of a man who could reduce the subtleties involved in the reshaping of musical and dramatic material, enriched by enlightened symbolism, to a mere matter of competition between two theaters.

We have little firsthand historical information, but what we do have contradicts the theory of the break-in-the-plot and the alteration of it. In a long letter dated June 12, 1791, Mozart told his wife in Baden of his visit to the *Zauberzither*, that is, the work which had its premiere four days earlier and is supposed to have sent Schikaneder into such a panic. There is no such panic to be felt in Mozart's letter. "In order to cheer myself up I went to see Kasperl in the new opera about the bassoonist, which has created such a stir—there is nothing to it." There speaks the expert. He could not have been more relaxed about it. In fact, the work was well received by the public, and Wenzel Müller was an able and extremely prolific composer of popular Singspiele. But scarcely any reasonable man would have seen any competition for *The Magic Flute* in *The Magic Zither*, let alone such experienced men of the theater as Mozart and Schikaneder. We are here dealing with one of the usual, straightforward, amusing pieces in the old tradition of the magic fairy tale with its magic instruments, which had been doing their duty by their titles for decades: *Die bewundernswürdige Bassgeige*) (The Admirable Double Bass) or *Die magische Violine* (The Magic Violin), for example. Perinet added to them considerably, for in addition to Prince Armidoro's magic ring and magic zither as well as Kasperl (his cheerful companion's magic bassoon), he invented magic hair and a magic ball.

The outline story of the good fairy Perifirime, who moves the prince to retrieve the treasure stolen from her by the wicked magician, here named Bosphoro, is based on the Lulu fairy tale. It includes all the magic adventures and the marriages of two couples: Armidoro and Sidi, the abducted fairy's daughter, and Kaspar and Palmire, Sidi's confidante.

Both couples, one sentimental, the other comic, were already typical of the "Oberon" opera. The many scene changes with spectacular tableaux at the ends of acts, like sea storms with grandiose collapsing of bridges, were typical of the magic comedies or comedies with machines of the post-Baroque era. As they are both based on the same fairy tale sources, there are of course parallels between *The Magic Zither* and *The Magic Flute*. In the fat and lecherous Zumio, who is employed by the magician as watchman over the women, one recognizes a model (obviously slimmed down and demonized) for Monostatos. That his master, with tyrannical arbitrariness, wants to punish him "with 100 strokes across the belly" obviously left an impression on Schikaneder. Pizichi, who is a helpful "little genie" and on the side of the good forces, will later divide into three to become the famous boys or genii. And Kaspar Bita and Papageno are obviously related.

Perinet's Kaspar the bassoonist is of course far more in the Kasperl tradition of the Leopoldstadt Theater, and in this work he is completely in the limelight. It must have been his "lazzis" and little jokes which firmly ensured the success of *The Magic Zither*; the dialogue Perinet put into his mouth was effectively taken straight from the mouth of the Viennese man in the street. When the fairy provides a balloon as a travelling conveyance, Kaspar says, in the tones of a Viennese cab driver, "Fahren wir Euer Gnaden? Aber das sag' ich gleich, mit dem Rucken gegen die Pferd kann ich nicht sitzen, sonst—" (Are we off, your Grace? But I must say it straight—I ain't sitting wi' me back against them 'orses, otherwise—). The bassoon, whose tone even then was used for all sorts of comically indecent effects must here have been an excuse for very vulgar stage gags. At one point Kaspar squeezes the instrument, and "red wine squirts out of it"—one can just imagine the guffawing in the balcony. Then he teaches the clumsy harem guard Zumio how to play the bassoon:

KASPAR: *Blase! Blase!*
ZUMIO: *Durch die Nase?*
KASPAR: *Nein durchs Maul, du dickes Schwein.*

KASPAR: Blow! blow!
ZUMIO: Through my nose?
KASPAR: No, through your mug, you fat pig.

Certainly there was much to laugh about, but in all three acts there isn't the slightest hint of an original idea. Thus the happy couples sing in the final chorus:

KASPAR: *O du herrlicher Fagott*
halfst uns allen aus der Noth.

O bassoon, my lovely
You've saved us all from misery.

. . . .

ALLE: Lacht und scherzet, tanzt und singet,
Wenn ihr Dankesopfer bringet,
Nennt das erste Pizichi,
Vivat, vivat pizichi!
(Sie machen eine Gruppe und heben Pizichi empor)
Ende des Stücks.

ALL: Laugh and joke and dance and sing,
If you an offering of thanks will bring,
Call the first one Pizichi,
Vivat, vivat Pizichi!
(They form a group and lift Pizichi on high)
The End.

And was this the competition that induced Mozart and Schikaneder to a sudden change of plans? But perhaps the *Magic Flute* authors, simply in order to distance themselves more clearly from the "Kasperliade," embellished the plot with the enlightened ethics of Sarastro's world. This would clearly have had to be done with breathtaking speed, because Mozart was already working on the instrumentation of the second act by the beginning of July, that is, on the final form, which is confirmed by his letter of July 3, 1791, to Constanze. And as early as June 11, 'before he had even been introduced to *The Magic Zither*, he closed a letter to Constanze, after informing her that he "had composed an aria for the opera," with the sardonic words "ich küsse Dich 1000mal und sage in Gedanken mit Dir: Tod und Verzweiflung war sein Lohn!" ' ((I kiss you a thousand times and say: my thoughts with you: Death and despair were his reward!), which is the text of the Masonic priests' duet from the second act. Thus he must have already had the libretto before him in the form that places Sarastro's world on the "daylight" side of the allegory. Many people date the start of Schikaneder's and Mozart's collaboration on *The Magic Flute* as spring 1791, but it could possibly go back even further. A letter from Schikaneder to Mozart dated September 5, 1790, now in the municipal library in Vienna, reads as follows:

Dear Wolfgang,
I'm returning your Pa Pa Pa; it is quite all right by me, it will

do nicely. Until we see each other this evening,
Your E. Schikaneder.

If the letter is genuine—Kormorzynski questions it because of Schikaneder's graphologically dubious signature, but Rommel and other Mozart experts accept it—then it is a rarity, that is, the only written document from the creative workshop of *The Magic Flute*. As it can only refer to the Papageno-Papagena duet, the letter would then verify that both composer and librettist had been working together for some time, and that the Treitschke-Seyfried story of Schikaneder's cry for help in the spring of 1791, and the large number of coincidences and improbabilities that led to the changing of the plot, contain more fantasy (by reason of an old man's faulty memory) than reality. Even if we accept that Seyfried could really have gotten his information from Mozart, his teacher at the time, and had remembered it correctly, is it thinkable that the composer would have told him such a tall story and would have had a reason for doing so? The enlightened and ethical message of the opera was certainly close to Mozart's heart; such an important and deeply felt work as the *Masonic Funeral Music*, K.477 implies powerful inner involvement, and Schikaneder was responsible for the text for Mozart's *Little Masonic Cantata* K.623.[17] So that this message, which could very well have been a basic intention right from the beginning, should not be endangered in a time of growing reactionary pressure, Mozart may have consciously led people up the wrong track. "And the pretence that concern for another contemporary opera had led the authors' pens to transform their own material was a most effective means of protection." This is the opinion of Friedrich Dieckmann, who advocates this theory.[18] Such camouflage would have strengthened both the political intention and the effectiveness of *The Magic Flute*: would have—let us leave it in the conditional. That Mozart would have used an unknown pupil who was still only a child as a decoy is scarcely credible.

Two years later yet another legend was added to that of the plot inversion, namely that Karl Ludwig Giesecke, an actor at the time and later a mineralogy professor, and not Schikaneder had written the *Magic Flute* text. This Gieseke (spelled without ck) appeared as "First Slave," a very minor role, on the playbill for the first night of

The Magic Flute. There was no more talk of his having any further connections with Mozart's last opera for over half a century. In fact he was long dead when Julius Cornet, who had been the director of Vienna's Hofoper at the time, claimed in a brochure dated 1849 (its actual concern was the present situation of the German theater)[19], that Giesecke, a Professor at Dublin university, had disclosed to him on a visit to Vienna during the summer of 1818 that he was "the real" author of *The Magic Flute*. "G. only credited the figure of Papageno and his wife to Schikaneder." The musicologist Otto Jahn supported this view in his Mozart Monograph which appeared in 1859, and so, together with the spreading regard for this work, Giesecke's fame as the "real" *Magic Flute* librettist also spread.

Two generations of *Magic Flute* commentators were to follow Jahn, although the first Schikaneder biography by Egon Komorzynski (1901) adduced many convincing counter-arguments and took up the cudgels on behalf of Schikaneder. But at the time the author was an unknown young man of 23. His courage and perception were first rewarded in the new edition of Jahn's standard work: in 1919 Jahn's editor Hermann Abert dropped the Giesecke theory, even if he was of the opinion that some participation could not be ruled out. But in spite of this, the earlier claim by the authoritative Jahn was perpetuated by writer after writer. Editions of the libretto appeared with the wording "By Schikaneder after Giesecke"; even the Staatsoper in Vienna listed on the program "An opera by Giesecke and Schikaneder," 70 years after Jahn. Komorzynski's enlarged Schikaneder monograph of 1951 and Otto Rommel's standard work on the old Viennese *Volkskomödie*, which followed a year later, thoroughly demolished the Giesecke legend. Rommel's work is not well known and is difficult to find. Wolfgang Hildesheimer, the youngest and (thanks to his brilliance as a writer) quite justifiably the most noted Mozart biographer, ignores both these Schikaneder researchers, referring to secondary English sources instead. And so in 1977 he once again revived the old stories. As far as he is concerned, "although Giesecke was a relatively unimportant member" of those having a part in the *Magic Flute* text, he does not doubt that "he was the creator of Sarastro and the realm of *The Magic Flute* that is his domain."[20]

What is this Giesecke legend supposed to mean? We must begin with the originator of all this confusion. In his 1849 discourse on the theater, Julius Cornet (already mentioned) tells us, more or less in passing, how in the summer of 1818 "a fine old gentleman in a blue frock-coat, with a white cravat and adorned with an order" sat down at his table at an inn in Vienna. This old gentleman was Giesecke, the "former choir member" and now professor of mineralogy, who then confessed himself to be the real author of *The Magic Flute*. Cornet names five other members of this company at the inn, among them Kapellmeister Ignaz von Seyfried, already known to us through the reversal-of-plot theory. Jahn, who also supported this theory, appropriated from Cornet's report the name of the author of the allegedly added scenes with Sarastro and the priests. Jahn came from Kiel in northern Germany, and knew little about the Viennese Volkstheater of Mozart's time, for little research had been done on that subject. Only in this way can we explain how such a respected musicologist as Jahn would draw upon the Cornet source so uncritically—a source that later proved to be rather murky.

There are many things in Cornet's report that do not make sense. He writes that Seyfried "had a feeling" that Giesecke was "the real author of *The Magic Flute*." Why then did Seyfried remain silent about this until his death in 1841? In view of the extraordinary and growing popularity of the opera he, as a crown witness, would scarcely have kept his knowledge secret. But he said nothing about Giesecke, even in his informative letter to Treitschke to which we have already referred, and in which Schikaneder is clearly cited as sole author. Nor did Ignaz Castelli or the authors of the "Eipeldauer" letters, well informed about the Viennese theater scene, mention anything about Giesecke's authorship. On the contrary: Seyfried had known Giesecke for years, both having worked together in the same Schikaneder theater, but he was only able to report that Giesecke, a factotum as actor, stage-manager and hack writer, had drawn his director's attention to Wieland's *Dschinnistan*.

Why did Giesecke himself remain silent for most of his life about his "real" part in the writing of this famous opera? After that meeting in the inn in 1818 (more likely to have been 1819, as 30 years later one cannot trust Cornet's memory to have been entirely accurate), Giesecke lived for another 15 years, yet he never wasted his breath on the subject again.

The English musicologist Edward J. Dent approached the Giesecke legend in two books written shortly before World War I.[21] He believed he knew the answer: the scholar of "European standing" had no reason to pass himself off as co-author of an "opera text known for its foolishness." The Danish mineralogist K. J. V. Steenstrup, however, in a biographical sketch of his colleague, wrote that Giesecke, after emigrating to Ireland, remained a passionate friend of opera and in fact lost his fortune backing a theatrical enterprise.[22] Why then did he not confess to his collaboration with Mozart? Dent does not go so far as to applaud Giesecke as the "only" librettist of *The Magic Flute*, saying that one cannot "clearly define" his part, but he does consider him to be "the creator of Sarastro."

Who then was this Giesecke? He was certainly a remarkable man, and his career was hardly less adventurous than Schikaneder's. Like Schikaneder he lived under an assumed name. Karl Ludwig Giesecke (or Gieseke) was born in Augsburg in 1761 as Johann Georg Metzler, son of a tailor. He attended the Latin gymnasium there and studied law for three years in Göttingen, but at the age of 23 the theater lured him away. Six years later the usual ports of call for itinerant players led him to Friedel at the Freihaustheater, and he stayed on working under Schikaneder. His theatrical talent was only sufficient for small parts. "Mr. Giesecke has no distinct specialty and plays whatever roles come his way," remembered Castelli. Aside from that he edited and wrote plays, and as stage manager he saw to it that the performances ran smoothly. He must have known as early as 1794 that his future in the theater would earn him no laurels, because he turned to the study of mineralogy, later to trading in minerals, and here lay his true professional future, which was to prove very successful. It is not clear how he acquired the title "Royal Prussian Mining Advisor," but equipped with it he went to Copenhagen in 1805 and spent seven and a half years working for a trade commission, living like an Eskimo and doing soil research on the island of Greenland, which then belonged to Denmark. He published a scientific diary on the subject which was highly esteemed—a mineral discovered by him bears his name, Gieseckit—and finally went to Dublin as professor at the university there. The Danish king raised him to knighthood, as did the British monarch. He presented specimens from his magnificent collection of minerals not only to the Emperor in Vienna, but also to his natural-scientist-colleague Goethe in Weimar, with whom he was in correspondence. While in Vienna he joined the Masonic Lodge "Zur gekrönten Hoffnung" (To Crowned Hope). He remained a bachelor all his life. On his death in Dublin in 1833 his obituaries honored him as a scientist but not in the least as a writer, although he had actually written 33 plays and librettos during his years in the theater. All had been long forgotten by the time of his death. Most of them were simply adaptations which were put aside after a few performances; only a few, parodies of the kind universally popular at the time, can be termed moderately successful.

This honorable man, who has certainly taken his place as a mineralogist in the early history of that science, gained posthumous fame as one of Mozart's partners solely on the strength of Cornet's report, which was ignored for 10 years but then made public in Jahn's famous Mozart monograph. In addition his name is found in an interleaved libretto of *The Magic Flute*. This is certainly some evidence. But why shouldn't a stage manager, an assistant producer, have owned just such a libretto to control the entrances and exits? A critical examination of the question as to whether Giesecke was in any way capable of a partnership with Mozart deserves scrutiny. The composer never once mentioned him, and entered *The Magic Flute* in his list of works quite objectively as: "A German opera in two acts. By Emanuel Schickaneder." We could argue: what did Mozart care about the provenance of the libretto?—but that would underestimate Mozart as music dramatist. Assuming that he knew Giesecke not only as the minor actor in the role of "first slave" but also as author of Sarastro's lines—but had ignored this addition to the libretto as unessential—would do nothing to support the Giesecke story. Komorzynski's strong denunciation of Giesecke really isn't necessary ("a plagiarist without character, without scruples".... "simply a vulgar swindler" ... "a runaway tailor's son from Augsburg who wasted his youth as a good-for-nothing") in order to discredit Giesecke's role as writer of *The Magic Flute*.

Two thorough experts on the Vienna Volkstheater of Mozart's time, Otto Rommel and Otto Erich Deutsch, reach the same conclusions quite independently of each other. Deutsch summarizes: "Giesecke, a modest poet, was an honorable man. He never claimed to have written the text of *The Magic Flute*. Cornet has made a mountain out of a molehill."[23] Rommel, who is the only historian to have examined 12 of the extant Giesecke manuscripts critically, judged Giesecke's "original dramas" to be "without exception awkward, often conspicuously clumsy variations of a theatrical genre in vogue in Vienna at the time," and concludes: "briefly, seen from Giesecke's point of view, *The Magic Flute* would have been an unlikely event, because it had neither a forerunner nor a successor among his dramatic works, while from Schikaneder's point of view it was fulfillment and promise."[24]

Supporters of Giesecke's authorship credited him with the final concept of the work, and particularly with the Sarastro and priests scenes, as already mentioned, while doubting that Schikaneder could have written them. Such high-flown speeches call for an educated author, and Giesecke, after all, had achieved a professorship. But the dialogues and verses connected with Sarastro, apart perhaps from the Tamino-Speaker scene (I/15), are the weakest in the whole *Magic Flute* text. Schikaneder's reputation as an author would only be slightly impaired if here and there he had really had some help in formulating the text, perhaps as time was pressing. On the other hand, many similar texts can be found in his other opera librettos that effuse pathos, noble courage and false spirituality. He always gave his best when he used the language of his own common folk. But when necessary he could wield an educated pen, as we shall see in his later quarrel with Vulpius who, unasked, adapted his texts.

So, if nothing can be made of Giesecke, Cornet's statement which has caused such confusion for decades must rest on a faulty memory. Cornet is clearly incorrect when he writes that Giesecke had come to Vienna "directly from Iceland and Lapland," for he is confusing these countries with Greenland, and there can be no question of "a direct" journey. Why should his memory of the main point not also be wrong? It could have been that Giesecke might, half ironically, have passed himself off as the "true" author because he was the first to draw Schikaneder's attention to the *Dschinnistan* fairy tale, and perhaps because as an employee, he had helped his director out a little. This may have been the case, but not as Cornet wrote it and as Jahn took it over. "Giesecke could not have made the remark put into his mouth by Cornet," concluded Rommel, who however is very critical of Komorzynski, the Schikaneder apologist. Rommel summarizes his argument so convincingly that even the obvious question, "Why did Cornet keep silent for so long?" resolves itself in very human forgetfulness.

Quite apart from Giesecke, other cooks may also have been at work in the *Magic Flute* kitchen. It was soon doubted that Schikaneder could have written every single word of his almost 100 plays with his own pen, and such doubts were only logical. In his most fertile and creative 10-year period until about 1800 he would have had to write five works a year, in addition to his activities as theater director and producer which required much time and were much more essential to his existence. Even then such productivity would have been unusual, although the public constantly expected something fresh, and directors endeavored to satisfy this demand with ever new variations on old and well-tried models. Anonymous writers willing to help the authors whose names appeared on the programs were a dime a dozen. They were probably as miserably paid as the nameless gag men of Hollywood's most prosperous years, who guaranteed Chaplin's and Harold Lloyd's successes. Very early on, behind-the-scenes gossip in Vienna, that flourishing theater metropolis, circulated the names of all sorts of people as ghost writers for successful authors. A certain Pater Wüst (or Wiest), another Pater Cantes, or a so-called prompter called Haselböck or Helmböck were mentioned as Schikaneder's "versifiers," and arbitrary observations of this kind were not all that far-fetched. Today when most theaters, although highly subsidized, "live" by offering different productions of old plays, it is almost impossible for us to imagine that a private theater at the end of the 18th century had to constantly stake its existence on new works, one premiere after another. A suburban theater public's demand for new plays was insatiable and could not be satisfied by the "classical" dramas of Shakespeare, Lessing, Goethe or Schiller (at the time they had not even been acknowledged as such): the works produced had to be new. Inevitably esthetic value ranked far lower than sensational topical attraction.

We must try to imagine Schikaneder's Theater auf der Wieden in light of the studios of the most famous early Baroque painters whose work was in constant demand, and where the masters, whether a Rubens or a Rembrandt, could only meet this demand by providing the idea and the basic concept of a painting, leaving most of the actual execution to pupils. The idea was the decisive factor in the painting's value, the unmistakable trademark of the master.

It could well be that even prompters contributed this or that verse to Schikaneder's effervescent productiveness, but Giesecke's name does not appear once over a period of almost 60 years. Nor would Schikaneder have had any reason to feel at all disturbed by such contributions. But as far as the definitive authorship of *The Magic Flute* is concerned, it was left to Joachim Perinet, a former rival as a writer, to strike a blow for Schikaneder. This he did as early as 1801 in a poetically conceived fictional "theater conversation"; and two years later in the *Wiener Theater-Almanach auf das Jahr* 1803 (The Viennese Theater Almanac for the Year 1803): "It has been proved that the plan and the dialogue are his own. Herr Winter, who is also stage manager of this theater, can attest to this, for he and he alone can read Schikaneder's hieroglyphics, and he is always the first one to have to read them. But Schikaneder himself would be the first to deny that he has written all the verses for his operas."

The more soberly one investigates the Giesecke legend, the less meaningful it becomes, as can also be said of another witness whom Jahn introduces. The composer Sigismund von Neukomm is said to have confirmed Giesecke's authorship. Neukomm made Giesecke's acquaintance later, but when *The Magic Flute* was written he was a boy of 13. He was born in Salzburg and went to Vienna for the first time as a student in 1798. Similar gossipy accounts of Schikaneder's authorship flourished in Vienna at the time. It was said that Schikaneder had spoken disrespectfully of the dead Mozart, who owed his best melodies to him, and that he had exploited the needy composer shamelessly. In 1828 Georg Nikolaus Nissen, author of the first comprehensive Mozart biography, spread it abroad that Schikaneder had run about screaming, "His ghost pursues me everywhere!" Such exclamations were effective—after all, a new generation wanted to compensate for their fathers' neglect of Mozart.

But Nissen, as Constanze Mozart's second husband, was biased. She was the source of all his information, and Constanze was ill disposed towards Schikaneder because she believed he had cheated her out of her financial share of the *Magic Flute* success. This was unjust. At the time royalties for further runs in the theater were not paid: composers simply received one lump sum for a new opera.

Mozart was never very highly paid during the last year of his life: he was given a mere 200 ducats for his previous opera *La Clemenza di Tito* even though the work had been commissioned by none other than the Emperor of the Holy Roman Empire of the German Nation. His fee for *The Magic Flute* is unknown, like so many other elements surrounding this miraculous work. If we can really believe Ignaz von Seyfried, Mozart received 100 ducats paid in coin from his employer Schikaneder, a high fee for a private theater. Schikaneder also passed on the net profits from the score to the widow.[25] Schikaneder, then, had been generous to his esteemed friend. Perhaps as he was himself very liberal in running up debts, he later forgot the debt of the score? No one knows exactly. But we are certain the widow Constanze was no friend of his. However, even in Nissen's biography, which was inspired by her, there is no mention of a *Magic Flute* librettist called Giesecke.

7 In the Freihaus Theater Auf Der Wieden II

The Magic Flute proved to be Schikaneder's most lasting and success-ful draw for his theater. He presented 223 repeat performances of the opera and it remained the mainstay of his repertoire. But if we relate this number to the yearly average, around 20 performances during a season, they are too few to attribute the financial success of the Wiedner theater entirely to Mozart's work. This period of more than 12 years under Schikaneder's direction represents the fullest blos-soming of this entrepreneurial Volkstheater and of the productivity and highly versatile talent of its director.

It was not only due to *The Magic Flute* that these were the best years of his life. Only the Theater an der Wien, founded later and Schikaneder's second historical achievement, was able to outdo them in external brilliance. But never before or after did his many-sided talent flourish so opulently, the talent of a man of the theater, of an organizer and director of theatrical performances. During a dozen years he was to launch at least 404 operas, ballets, tragedies and comedies in "new productions" (the term was not yet used then). Until the final years at the Freihaus theater, when he had to look for a partner with stable capital, they were also financially successful. At the same time his own creativity as a dramatist was to bear much fruit. He wrote 57 operas and plays for his Theater auf der Wieden, which comprised more than half of his total oeuvre.

The number implies hasty writing, and this it doubtless was, as year after year he turned out four plays. There must have been a lot of routine work among them; in fact most have disappeared without trace. However, as we have already mentioned, this prolific grinding out of plays was not unusual then. Joachim Perinet, Schikaneder's *Magic Flute* rival and later the resident playwright in his theater, produced 110, considerably more than his director. Even in the middle of the 19th century when the public had Raimund's and Nestroy's excellent works at its disposal, it was still so insatiably keen on premieres that the crafty director of the rebuilt Carl Theater committed Karl Haffner, one of his dramatists, "to furnish at least eight new works, written by himself, for Director Carl, in each year of contract."

Schikaneder's prolific output was considered perfectly normal by his contemporaries so that they scarcely pilloried him for it: more so for the outcome—carelessness, a lack of logic and detailed working out, making up for literary weakness by more and more pompous theatrical spectacles. His undeniable success as a man of the theater did not concur with contemporary asessments of him as a writer. Indeed the opposite is true, and it was ironically his most important work, *The Magic Flute*, which contributed most greatly to his devaluation by established literary criticism. The ever-growing success of the opera led to a closer examination of Mozart's partner. He had previously been thought of as a south German provincial talent, but now he was measured against Mozart and the budding High German literature of the Enlightenment. Esthetically this certainly was a mistake.

Spellbound by Lessing's and Schiller's power with words, the critics had lost their feeling for the more naive but no less vital imaginative force of the south German Volkstheater. In 1792 they were presented with the first two issues of Schikaneder's *Sämtliche theatralische Werke* (Complete Works for the Theater), containing six plays written after 1788 but excluding *The Magic Flute*. Even if these had been better, blistering condemnations such as the one in the *Allgemeine Literaturzeitung* in Jena, which concluded that Schikaneder was a "vollkommen elender dramatischer Sudler" (an utterly miserable dramatic scribbler), would have been more than understandable. A mere reading of the plays was of little avail, for they were anything but reading matter, but even the weakest of them was effective on the stage. Of course, Schikaneder himself bears some responsibility for the denigrating slogan "Schikanederei" coined by critics and which remained fashionable for two generations, until the reassessments of Jean Paul and Börne, but not as early as *The Magic Flute* in which spiritual idealism compensated for the rather modest stage sets and inferior rhyming.

It was not until the middle of the 1790s that Schikaneder began himself to "schikanedern" and increasingly to take exhibitionistic refuge from the text in scenery, from an "enlightened" logical plot to post-Baroque delight in visual display. By so doing he was the author of his poor reputation. It was in part an externally downhill path that he had begun to tread, in part a following of his own inner compulsions.

The limit, as far as it can be ascertained at all, is reached in the comic opera *Die Waldmänner* (The Woodmen) of 1793. "Man hat auch nicht einmal Zeit zum Nachdenken, ob's Stuck gut oder schlecht ist, weil man vor lauter Schaun keine Zeit zum denken hat ("You don't even have time to consider whether it's a good or a bad piece, because with so much gawking to do there's no time to think), reported the journalist Josef Richter after attending a performance at the Theater auf der Wieden. Richter is disguising himself here, as he was able to do for 28 years with enormous popular success, as a naive man from the country, from the Eipeldau (today Floridsdorf) who wrote to his cousin in Kakran (today Kagran) about the goings on in Vienna. His observations, clever and entertaining in a stylized Viennese dialect, provide comment on contemporary social and cultural affairs.

Richter or "Eipeldauer", as he was called (1749–1813), for his part was not only a highly productive journalist but writer as well. His 36 works for the theater and 15 novels have almost vanished behind his peasant character, as Jaroslav Hasek was later to do behind his *Good Soldier Schweik*. In his youth he had been a progressive Josephine liberal; he finished life as an arch-conservative police informer. If one wanted to survive as a writer during the reign of Emperor Franz, whose name was embellished by court propaganda with the title "the good", one had to make accommodations. It was not only their being contemporaries that drew the two popular artists Schikaneder and Eipeldauer together. Eipeldauer talked of "our dear Schikaneder," and when the latter's star began to pale, he remained well disposed towards him throughout his decline. After all, Schikaneder spoke in the voice of the same people who bought Eipeldauer's weekly newspaper. Schikaneder, on the other hand, reduced liberal-Josephinistic leanings in his works from year to year—even when they were in code. He also had to survive in an authoritarian state which was becoming increasingly autocratic.

When in 1792 the reactionary Emperor's birthday was celebrated in the Burgtheater with Haydn's song "Gott! erhalte Franz den Kaiser" (God preserve Franz the Emperor), Schikaneder obediently repeated the song in his Theater auf der Wieden, as indeed all directors did, for deference was officially demanded. Further, he could count on full public support in so doing. The French, with whom Austria had been at war for years, were naturally unpopular at the time, so "the good" Kaiser Franz (in reality a pedantic, cold man of limited vision) was considered the hope of all patriotic Austrian forces, from the liberals to the reactionaries. And now the good patriot Haydn had even dedicated a song to him! The text was written by Leopold Haschka, a creature of the court. His obsequious verses soon disappeared while Haydn himself turned the inspired melody into an immortal set of variations for string quartet. However, the Austrian monarchy raised it to a hymn of the people which in turn led the Social Democrat Friedrich Ebert to encourage the singing of it to words by August Heinrich von Fallersleben, "Deutschland, Deutschland über alles," making it the official national anthem of Germany. Hitler was later to couple it with the trivial Horst Wessel Song, while Theodor Heuss tried to reduce the text to the harmless liberal third verse. What a destiny for a beautiful melody, what a strange and twisted path it was to follow, a path that also crossed Schikaneder's theater in the suburbs!

But let us return to the theater's history after the Mozart period. The success of The Magic Flute grew from evening to evening, but the composer was able to delight in his last opera for only a few weeks. His funeral procession from St. Stephen's Cathedral to a pauper's grave was a lonely journey, although recent research[26] has divested it of its sentimentality and reduced it to sober historical fact. At the time, mourners did not bid the deceased a last farewell at the burial, but at the blessing in the chapel for the dead on the north side of St. Stephen's Cathedral, in accordance with the austere Josephine burial rites still in force. Neither Schikaneder nor Constanze Mozart were among the small band of mourners, however. We do not know why he stayed away while Josefa Hofer, Gerl and Schack, all members of his company, paid Mozart his last honors. Was he ill? Or did he, like Constanze, make deep shock his excuse? We do not know. But Schikaneder's absence cannot be related to the rumors which coupled growing criticism of his theater to a vain and presumptuous devaluation of Mozart. He exhibited all kinds of signs of vanity, but none whatsoever of foolish arrogance towards his dead friend. Schikaneder was neither so stupid nor so base. The facts largely point to genuine admiration for Mozart, and this during a time when the composer had not yet been put on the pedestal of sacrosanct genius.

Only a few months after Mozart's death, in March 1792, Schikaneder arranged for a performance of a Mozart symphony (we are not sure which one) to be given in his theater, as part of a musical academy. He was to develop such academies, which did his orchestra credit, into events that were presented several times a year. They were a clear sign of his cultural ambitions. Haydn's symphonies were played, Beethoven appeared as pianist, and works such as Mozart's opera *La clemenza di Tito*, which was less attractive to the general public, could at least receive a concert performance. During the course of his years at the Wiedner theater, Schikaneder staged all the Mozart operas, except the early Italian ones, in accordance with the standards of the time and the amenities of the house. All of them were played, from *Die Entführung aus dem Serail* on, even *Der Schauspieldirektor*, and of course all were done in German. This practice was natural, for Schikaneder could not afford to stage works in a little understood foreign tongue, in the way snobbish, sub-sidized producers could. So instead of *Don Giovanni* he produced *Don Juan*, though "arranged by Christian Heinrich Spiess." *Cosi fan tutte*, at the time an opera of no great appeal, became *Die Schule der Liebe* (School of Love) in an arrangement by Giesecke. Six Mozart operas: in all probability more Mozart than any other German opera house at the end of the 18th century could boast. If we consider the limited resources of the Wiedner Theater and the chancy finances of its director, and compare them to the far less ambitious programs attempted by rival theaters—especially by the Leopoldstadt, which was based on Kasperl-Laroche rather than on Mozart—it becomes clear just how capable Schikaneder's private-enterprise theater was of transcending its inherent limitations. During his final eight years in the Freihaus theater, until he moved to the new theater on the other side of the river, Schikaneder produced 75 operas and Singspiele, including works by masters who had already made their names—Haydn, Gluck, Paisiello, Méhul and Salieri—while the Leopoldstadt Theater scarcely offered half this number in the same genre—only 40 new productions.[27]

The operas and Singspiele for which Schikaneder himself had written the texts were by far the most lucrative box office draws, though none came close to *The Magic Flute*. The *Tyroler Wastel* was repeated 118 times in the Wiedner theater, the *Spiegel von Arkadien* (The Mirror of Arcady) 98 times, the *Waldmänner* 96 times, and *Babylons Pyramiden* 64 times. Although all were played throughout Germany and some elsewhere, they were artistically immeasurably inferior to *The Magic Flute*, due not only to the mediocre craftmanship of the musical settings, but also to Schikaneder's texts. Those of his works not titled "Comic Operas" but "Grand Heroic-Comic Operas" were all based on the *Magic Flute* pattern, variations on the underlying theme of the trial and purification of a noble pair. As poetry, if such a designation is even applicable, not a single one of them approaches the standard of *The Magic Flute*—which clearly proves just how important Mozart was as a partner and co-dramatist. The unruly fantasy of Schikaneder's metaphors needed the discipline of a superior and reflective partner. Without him too much was immature, sloppily formulated, dashed off in the frenzy of meeting public demand.

After Mozart's death Schikaneder first tried his luck as a writer of plays rather than operas. Two of these were clear successes: the one-act play *Das abgebrannte Haus* (The Burnt-Down House), first performed at the end of August 1792—the theater was open even during the high summer, as the only time it was closed was at Easter—and in the following November the comedy *Die Fiaker in Wien* (The Coachmen in Vienna). In the first the drunken shoemaker Brandl whiles away his life with schnapps and idleness, in the ruins of his burnt-down house with a vain and hideous battle-axe of a wife, one of Schikaneder's most brilliant parts: the whole is an early little masterpiece of transparent character comedy, a model for the future. Without the drunken shoemaker Brandl, Nestroy's shoemaker

Knieriem could scarcely have been conceived, although Knieriem's grotesque philosophy is obviously more profound. The honest Hansjörgle Dreyfuss, "a shoemaker's apprentice from Swabia," also enriches the Viennese Volkstheater's tradition of featuring popular, good-natured fellows from Swabia, which have Raimund's magician Ajaxerle (little Ajax) as its crowning glory.

The plot of *The Burnt-Down House* is more typical than original. The shoemaker who has come down in the world is tormented by the wicked squire of Silberberg, but in the end is rescued, *deus ex machina style*, from his misery by the noble king. Today the following scene seems like a parody, but was not so intended at the time. It was rather a brave but disguised posthumous homage from faithful subjects to the unforgotten Emperor Joseph II who had been fond of going among the people incognito and doing charitable deeds but had become somewhat suspect in more autocratic times.

> KING (alone): Men like myself live here, but they are unhappy, and yet joy prevails when they see their prince . . . Truly, to know that we are so loved by our subjects is worth more than a hundred bloody victories.
> KING (opens his cloak).
> BRANDL (falls to his knees with all the others): O dear! O dear! I am dead as a mouse!

We recognize here the sure-fire effect of the king opening his cloak, revealing himself as His Majesty—an effect used earlier by Schikaneder which obviously served its purpose here, too. The scenes in which Schikaneder sharply and unerringly reproduced the common speech of the people are yet more important. For example, when the stupid and vain shoemaker's wife saucily imitates an upper-class lady: "In der Stadt heissens auch nicht Schusterweiber, sondern Fussakkomodirersgattinnen" (In town they're not called shoemakers' wives but foot accommodators' spouses). And if any one of Schikaneder's many hundreds of scenes comes close to Nestroy it is this:

> SYBILLE *(vor dem Spiegel): Bin ich etwa nicht die Schönste im ganzen Dorf?*
> BRANDL: *Ja, wenn man von hinten anfangt.*
> S: *Wer hat so schwarze Augen?*

B: Was Augen—hol du mir einen Brandwein!
S: So rothe Backen—
B: Ein Brandwein!
S: So eine schöne Nasen!
B: Ein Brandwein!
S: So einen schönen Mund—
B: Was Mund? Schustern haben nur ein Maul.
S: So schöne weisse Zähne—
B: Ein Brandwein sag ich.
S: So einen hübschen kleinen Fuss—
B: Ein Brandwein!

SYBILLE (in front of the mirror): Aren't I the prettiest in the whole village?
BRANDL: Yes, when you start at the end.
S: Who's got such black eyes?
B: Eyes indeed—get me a brandy!
S: Such red cheeks—
B: A brandy!
S: Such a lovely nose!
B: A brandy!
S: Such a beautiful mouth!
B: What mouth? Cobblers just have a mug.
S: Such lovely white teeth—
B: I say a brandy!
S: Such a pretty little foot!
B: A brandy!

In about double as many lines of dialogue the drunken basso ostinato calls six times for his brandy which is "parola scenica," dramatic theater. It is much more inspired than the countless pseudo-poetic rhymes with which Schikaneder endeavored to meet the poetic conventions of the times. Literary critics took no notice at all of this vulgar but masterly one-act play, but the actors and their public recognized its qualities by putting it on decade after decade.

The theater of the late 20th century is notable for both its lack of new productions and its turning back to older plays. Were it prepared to undertake a Schikaneder renaissance, it should not overlook *The Burnt-Down House*, although since the work was never printed a revival would depend on its greatly varying manuscripts.

After two years Schikaneder naturally followed up this box office success with a sequel called *Der Hausfrieden* (Peace in the House) which has vanished without trace. The contrary is true of his "coachman" plays, which were even greater box office draws. The original *The Coachmen in Vienna* has disappeared, but the sequel which was first performed a year later, *The Coachmen in Baden*, has been preserved. Perinet praised the original as Schikaneder's "most triumphant and important local work," which the 115 presentations before 1825 substantiate. Eipeldauer lauded the plays in his down-to-earth reports. "Da habn s' d'Fiaker aufgführt, und die gfalln den Wienern noch besser als der dumme Anton. Ich hab glaubt, die zerplatzen vor Lachen" (They 'ad put on the Coachmen, and the Viennese, they likes 'em better than the silly Anton. I thought they would burst theirsels laughing). If originals are always better than "follow ups," as Nestroy's theatrical words of wisdom contend, *The Coachmen in Vienna* must have been among Schikaneder's best. *The Coachmen in Baden* is certainly an above-average product of his pen.

Of course, the Dramatis Personae in each "coachmen" play remain basically the same. The upright coachman is called Rosschweif (Horsetail)—the fact that he every now and again beat his wife did nothing to tarnish his honest image among the public. His wife, blinded by vanity and striving for a place in "high society" is almost taken in by a false lord. In a high-class watering place she gives herself out as Baroness von Rosschweif, and tries to pair her daughter off with a nobleman, Lord Holzwurm (Woodworm) who turns out to be a common bootblack and a Frenchman at that (public displays of dislike for the French among theater people went hand in hand with the state police's search for Jacobins). The plot is a stereotype: Philip Hafner had used the same scheme repeatedly. But of prime importance to a Volkstheater audience was Schikaneder in the main role of Rosschweif the coachman, for he gave his best in a role personifying petty bourgeois folk-wisdom. This role sometimes recalls the higher wisdom of *The Magic Flute* but more closely gives voice to the sentiments of middle-class society, as for example when the upright Rossschweif says:

Gentlemen, as long as I have my wits about me, neither my

wife nor my daughter may overstep the bounds—as soon as people seek more than their position allows [NB. His wife wanted to play at being genteel by wearing a pompadour] there's always misery at home afterwards. Let the genteel and rich go as they please. . . . a pompadour like that isn't even good for starting a fire because it's been completely ruined by too much hair powder and pomade . . .

The play opens with an extremely realistic scene involving servants: the petty bourgeois comedy of marriage is anticipated at the lowest proletarian level. The chambermaid wants to better herself ("I don't want to mix with the common people any more"), but is forced to submit to a lecture delivered by the honest bourgeois coachman: "Now I've had enough, young lady. Don't you grumble about common people; you belong to them just as much as we." The applause in the balcony must have been thunderous, as it certainly was after the repentant final words of the wife Lenorl: "I beg you for just one thing, don't put any more money in my hands, give me another chance . . . you can beat me every day"—which is exactly what the valiant coachman-husband had done only twice up to then—practically not at all.

This small-town satire had been preceded in 1792 by a so-called "country family portrait" entitled *Der redliche Landmann* (The Honest Husbandman). It dealt with a soldier's life in five acts; had a typical ranting colonel; an equally typical honest peasant; and a handsome lover, a cornet who is unjustly accused of having stolen the regiment's funds. In the end it is discovered that the culprit was a raven. The motif is the same as Rossini's *La gazza ladra* (The Thieving Magpie).

In his opera *The Woodmen* which followed a year later, with music by the theater Kapellmeister Johann Baptist Henneberg, Schikaneder was again to engage in an idyllic country romp, this time as librettist. The noble property owner Heinrich wishes to test his bride; he has it given out that he is dead and goes to live with his servant in a house in the forest. The new property owner and rival for the girl's affections is a naval officer, a braggart, but a good man notwithstanding, abounding in the same uprightness as the country folk. The bride too proves to be virtuous and faithful, so that nothing can prevent a happy ending once the true circumstances have been revealed by the hero. The success of the opera, which was of course nothing more than a naive Singspiel, can only be explained by Schikaneder's flair for staging—I have already quoted Eipeldauer's impression.

The idea of the test, if one may speak about an idea here at all, vaguely reminds us of *The Magic Flute*, but the pseudo-realism indicates rather the area of the *Volksstück*.

Schikaneder's desire to go further along the *Magic Flute* path, even without Mozart, is shown much more clearly in the most important operas after 1793. *Die Eisen-Königin* (The Iron Queen), a so-called "magic play" with music again by Henneberg, has been lost, so one can only gather from press notices that it was another test or trial story. The first performance of a "comic and magic play" called *Der wohltätige Derwisch, oder Zaubertrommel und Schellenkappe* (The Charitable Dervish, or The Magic Drum and Fool's Cap) took place three quarters of a year later, in September 1793. Komorzynski was able to locate the production book from which the plot can be reconstructed. What kind of music the team of composers Schack, Gerl and Henneberg produced, obviously in extreme haste, remains unknown.

Again two fairy tales from Wieland's *Dschinnistan* collection provide the source. The dervish in the title is a king who has been robbed of his power by his enemy; he seems to be descended from Sarastro, just as the other characters remind us of *The Magic Flute*. The lyrically soulful prince Sofrano, the dervish's son, derives from Tamino, but his beloved Zenomide is no true and devoted Pamina, but rather a vain and ambitious young woman. Therefore at the end the audience has some insight into wisdom, but there is no love marriage. Papageno's descendant Mandolino, the usual prince's companion along dangerous paths, also has no roguish second Papagena in his Mandolina. Instead he has landed a "terrible female" who beats him thoroughly because he keeps running after other girls. Of course this was again just the role for Schikaneder, and the following quotation is worthy of Papageno.

> PRINCE SOFRANO: O I am the happiest of mortals! Does that not move you, Mandolino?
> MANDOLINO: Yes, everything is moving me, especially hunger and thirst!

Of course, there is plenty of magic. Magic key, magic drum, magic bag and magic cap make for all kinds of scenic drolleries, causing "very misshapen huge noses" and arranging for monkeys' heads to pop out of dishes. Schikaneder's scenic imagination could let off steam in producer's directions: "Scene change! the shores of the sea—Lightning, thunder, night. Two ships from the left . . . two ships from the right . . . fighting from both sides."

The scenic designers had plenty to do and the audience much to marvel at. Speculations about a new *Magic Flute* success, however, did not come to anything: the music was thrown together haphazardly and a far cry from Mozart. Komorzynski, who calls the work "one of Schikaneder's best efforts," has also tried to claim that it was the source of Raimund's first play *Der Barometermacher auf der Zauberinsel* (The Barometer Maker on the Magic Island), but he ignores a more complex situation. It is true that Schikaneder, Raimund and Karl Meisl (who was commissioned to hand in a first act for *The Barometer Maker*, which was rejected and rewritten by Raimund) all drew inspiration from the same *Dschinnistan* source. Schikaneder no doubt had hopes for many repeat performances of his routine play. By 1823, after the experience gained through a generation of theatrical development, this theme, in Raimund's hands, heralded the beginning of a new and poetic genre which was no longer merely effective theater. The traditional nobleman's companion becomes Raimund's comical Bartholomäus Quecksilber, the title role. Raimund was charged with plagiarizing older plays and did little to help himself by using Schikaneder's term "Magic Play."

It is not clear why late in 1793 Schikaneder applied (without success) for the lease of the Burgtheater. Was it a megalomaniac urge to expand? His intentions are made much clearer when, a short time later, he asked to be allowed to put on so-called "Herculean or Olympic games after the custom of the ancient Greeks" four times a week in the Prater. Spectacular open-air shows had always been one of Schikaneder's fortes, and were here inspired by the objective of luring visitors away from the neighboring Leopoldstadt Theater. But the director of the latter, Marinelli, immediately complained so forcefully that Schikaneder's offer was rejected. Schikaneder had every reason to fear the completion of the Leopoldstadt Theater, although his Wiedner Theater was flourishing. His company was about 40 strong, versatile and hard working—most of them lived in the Freihaus so that Schikaneder had them well under control. But shortly after Mozart's death Schikaneder lost Anna Gottlieb, the lovely young Pamina of *The Magic Flute*. She gave up singing, perhaps shocked by her friend's and teacher's early demise, and then went to the Leopoldstadt Theater as an actress, appearing there with great success in leading roles. Benedict Schack, the original Tamino, and Gerl, the original Sarastro, also left the ensemble about three years later.

But Schikaneder always managed to provide reinforcements. He found a new and attractive Mozart singer in the soprano Marianne Willmann. He engaged the Italian choreographer Giov.Batt.Checchi, a well-regarded pupil of Noverre, to build up the Wiedner Theater's own first-class ballet company, but it was disbanded in 1796, as Schikaneder was forbidden to put on ballet. In Vincenzo Sacchetti the younger, son of a famous Baroque court designer, he had his best stage designer for years, particularly for the new production of *The Magic Flute*. Finally he engaged Ignaz von Seyfried as Kapellmeister and was able to win over Joachim Perinet, Marinelli's successful theater dramatist, to join him.

Perinet had enticed tens of thousands of people to buy tickets at the Leopoldstadt, not only with *The Magic Zither* but also with its new version, *Pizichi*, and other works. In 1798 another even more successful dramatist, Hensler, managed 222 repeats (up to 1824) of the *Donauweibchen* (Little Woman of the Danube) at the same theater. This was indeed competition for *The Magic Flute*. The two most successful suburban theaters, Schikaneder's auf der Wieden and the other in the Leopoldstadt, remained intense rivals. Lesser competitors quickly fell by the wayside, as for example in 1793 when the solid theater in der Landstrasse, which had tried for three years to become a cultural suburban center, finally gave up and became a lowly tax collector's house. Other theaters opened and then petered out. Eipeldauer reports a true blossoming of Viennese theaters in 1794: "For the last fortnight I have been kept running from one theater to the next. Earlier, only the Leopoldstadt had its Kasperl, but now every suburb has its own. With the National Theater in the new Lerchenfeld there are seven suburban theaters in Vienna, so you can imagine what a lot of money there must be in Vienna." Most of the newly founded theaters were unable to remain solvent, but even so the buildings were solid, no longer the provisional huts and stalls of the first boom in theaters in the 1770s, and certainly not "Kreuzer-theater." This was the name given to the "Schmieren" (this word first appeared in the 19th century), where members of the audience had to pay a kreuzer for every act, before the next one was played to satisfy their curiosity.

The suburban theaters in Hietzing, at the Neubau, in the Lerchen-feld and the Landstrasse came and went, but the rivalry between the Wieden and the Leopoldstadt endured and became theater history, even surviving the pulling down of both houses and the deaths of their directors Schikaneder and Marinelli. The new Theater an der Wien was to become the first Nestroy stage with the glorious *Lumpazivagabundus*; the Carl-Theater which replaced the dilapidated Leopoldstadt in 1847 was the home of Nestroy's late works, and when the Viennese operetta took over Singspiel and musical farce, the rivalry continued. When the Theater an der Wien produced Offen-bach's *Bluebeard* and *Die Grossherzogin von Gerolstein* (The Grand Duchess of Gerolstein), the Carl-Theater in the Leopoldstadt proved its mettle by producing a new Suppé within a month. With the advent of Johann Strauss the Theater an der Wien won control of the drawing cards. *Die Fledermaus* opened there in 1874, quickly outdis-tancing Lecocq's *Giroflé-Girofla* at the Carl-Theater; Leha's epoch-making opener of the Silver Age of Viennese operetta, *Die Lustige Witwe* (The Merry Widow, 1905) was also staged at the Theater an der Wien, although the Carl-Theater countered with Oscar Straus' *Walzertraum* (Waltz Dream). But it was the Kálmán premieres, with *Gräfin Mariza* (Countess Maritza) as the central attraction in the 1920s which finally gave the decisive lead to the Theater an der Wien. It is standing and playing today, while the Carl-Theater was pulled down long ago. Schikaneder as Papageno, carved in stone, still looks down from the frieze of the theater, the ultimate victor in the one-and-a-half centuries of rivalry with the Leopoldstadt.

During his time Schikaneder had to fend off not only Marinelli's popular Kasperliaden, but also the growing contempt of critics. He did not live long enough to enjoy Goethe's effort to save his honor. What he did know was that this prince among poets who was pro-ducer at the Court Theater in Weimar allowed *The Magic Flute* to be played in a version by his brother-in-law Christian August Vulpius, which did not even mention Schikaneder's name on the program. Vulpius was an extremely successful hack writer and Goethe's dramatic factotum at the Weimar Court Theater. His arrangements fed the Weimar repertoire, and his novel of an aristocratic robber, *Rinaldo Rinaldini,* became so popular that Hensler was able to distill no less than six Rinaldini plays from it for the Leopoldstadt. In his preface to his *Magic Flute* arrangement Vulpius promised to "impose a plan" and to clean up "at least the nonsense" of the verses. When one compares the original and Vulpius's version, that dramatic intention seems a clear-cut case of braggadocio: the alterations in the text are irrelevant and merely cosmetic. Yet Vulpius was doubtless clever and musically sensitive. What strikes today's listener is that Mozart sometimes accentuates incorrectly, which also occurred to Vulpius, and no reverence for an untouchable Olympian (although at the time Mozart did not yet count as one) kept him from making corrections.

> *Dies Bild o! wie bezaubernd schön*
> *welch Glück, die Schöne selbst zu sehn!*

> This portrait O! how bewitchingly fair;
> What joy to see the beauty herself!

So begins Vulpius's Tamino portrait aria, and it does indeed bring the accents of verse and magic into clearer harmony than the original. Komorzynski is of the opinion that Vulpius "never improved" anything, but this view is not supportable—however, it scarcely alters the fact that his version is sterile and pedantic. Schikaneder was quite right when he protested in the preface to his opera *Der Spiegel von Arkadien* (The Mirror of Arcady) against such presumptuous nitpicking and lack of regard for the original version. With Vulpius's reply, Schikaneder restated his points in a "Pro memoria" which he published as a preface to his new opera *Der Königssohn aus Ithaka* (The King's Son from Ithaca). This preface reveals Schikaneder's talent for polemics. "There are no more plagiarists today, only revisers (or rewriters) who get hold of other people's work and diminish it by their strident claims, like circus barkers praising their wares which have been gathered together by begging." Schikaneder then takes aim at Vulpius: "As far as you're concerned, rewriting means taking a word out and stitching in another which sounds the same!". This observation hit the mark indeed, for everyone could see Vulpius's makeshift botching for himself. It was evident not only in *The Mirror of Arcady* which Vulpius arranged, again without mentioning Schikaneder's name, but also in *The Magic Flute*. For example, he turned Sarastro's "Hallen" aria ("in diesen heil'gen Hallen") into a "Mauern" aria:

In diesen heilgen Mauern
Kennt man die Rache nicht.
Nicht strafen, nur bedauern
Ist der Geweihten Pflicht.

In these sacred walls
Revenge is not known.
Not to punish, only to regret
Is our sacred duty.

Nevertheless, for many decades *The Magic Flute* was almost always played in Germany in Vulpius's version. Modern opera goers may be surprised that Goethe, as a theater director, acquiesced, but Vulpius's dull pseudo-logic and aversion to anything fantastic reflected the Zeitgeist, insofar as it was anti-romantic—a path Goethe pursued at that time. But in Schikaneder the irrational, rampant imagery of the Baroque theater constantly breaks through the shell of "enlighten-ment," and to such a writer the balance, the reason, and the "classically" committed esthetics must have remained unintelligible, even contemptible. But Schikaneder could hold his own in polemics; he knew all the right jargon. In the "Pro memoria" mentioned above he actually uses several Greek words, written in the Greek alphabet in order to put down Vulpius the know-it-all as the one who was lacking in classical knowledge.

The Mirror of Arcady, with music by Franz Xaver Süssmayr, was put on in November 1794 and had a lasting success. It was an easy target for the critics who applied the term "Schikanederei" to it, but the public admired the gods in the clouds of Mount Olympus, a romantic magic castle, thunder, lightning and sea battles on the stage. The plot is a crude variation on *The Magic Flute*. The wicked magician Tarkaleon entices people onto his island with a concave mirror in order to enslave them. (Shades of Klingsor!) He has already entrapped Metalio and Giganie, two children of nature, and he intends to snare the sentimental pair of lovers, Ballamo and Philanie. But the gods, with Jupiter at their head, amicably intervene using magic, and are responsible for the happy end. Schikaneder's most original idea was that the father of the gods is able to sow human beings on the Arcadian isle like plants, a race of peasants emerging from the furrows. The librettist wrote a new Papageno role to suit himself: the bird catcher becomes a viper catcher, Metalio is required to deliver the brood of snakes to his magician master who then concocts poisonous potions—not an attractive transformation. Still, the Papageno clone seems to have been the best thing about the piece. In aria No. 4, a kind of "register" aria (as in *Don Giovanni*: "he likes them thin, he likes them round, this one likes them with black hair, that one, blond . . ." the refrain recalls Papageno's song: ". . . doch ich wär nur dann zufrieden / wenn sie alle wären mein" (. . . yet I would only be happy / if they all were mine), and even more so in no. 13:

> *Seit ich so viele Weiber sah,*
> *so schlägt mein Herz so warm,*
> *es summt und brummet hie und da*
> *als wie ein Bienenschwarm.*
> *Und ist ihr Feuer meinem gleich*
> *ihr Auge schön und klar,*
> *so schläget wie ein Hammerstreich,*
> *mein Herzchen immerdar*
> *Bum bum, bum bum . . .*

> Since I so many females saw,
> my heart beats e'er so warm,
> it hums and bumbles here and there
> just like bees in a swarm.
> And if her fire mine is like,
> her eye so bright and clear,
> so beats my heart with hammerstrokes
> forever, evermore
> Bum bum, bum bum . . .

The refrain is repeated at the end 42 times in fast sixteenth-notes. Süssmayr's music surely contributed to the success of the day, for the yellowed pages of the vocal score show that Mozart's pupil could effectively imitate his master's handiwork, at least to the extent that common musical phrases could be copied. Süssmayr had already shown this kind of talent in the secco recitatives for the opera *Tito* in Prague and in his completion of the Requiem. At any rate, among the 17 "Arcadian" numbers, he offers us a well-composed quartet and a full-fledged soprano aria with accompagnato recitative—real opera music. No one can lay at his door the burden of his inability to replicate his master's genius! Rather, it is to be regretted that there is only this one Schikaneder and Süssmayr collabortion, seemingly because the composer could earn more at the two court theaters. The writer-director's other partners were certainly not better.

This is evident in the "grand heroic-comic opera" which followed, *The King's Son from Ithaca*, with music by Franz Anton Hoffmeister. The composer came from Swabia and combined the profession of extremely facile composer with that of a music publisher in Vienna, rather as Diabelli had done for Schubert and Beethoven. Beethoven called Hoffmeister his "most beloved brother" which was honor indeed for an unoriginal hack. But his "Paperl" song from *The King's Son from Ithaca* was to become a popular hit—most certainly thanks to Schikaneder, who once again played the part of a prince's cheerful companion, the greedy, cowardly, love-thirsty Colifonio:

> *Bey grossen und mächtigen Herren*
> *möcht ich wohl ein Papagey sein.*
> . . . .
> *Ich schickte mich herrlich darein*
> *ein Paperl, ein Paperl zu seyn.*

> With great and powerful masters
> I'd like to be a parrot.
> . . . .
> It'd suit me so wonderfully well
> A Polly, a Polly to be.

In the end Colifonio predictably gets his nymph Pratschina, after many changes of scene with thunder and lightning, disasters at sea, nymphs' dances and gods on thrones of cloud, while Telemachus gets his aristocratic nymph Tillina. The main tragic figure is the mythical lady Calypso, who here falls in love with the son of her erstwhile lover Odysseus. Bowed down with suffering, she hands him over to a younger woman in the end.

Kurz-Bernardon had already staged a "Telemachus magic play" in Vienna, based on the French novel by Fénelon. Later Grillparzer was to elevate Calypso's fate into the highly poetic blank verse of his *Sappho* tragedy.

But Schikaneder was only able to set his *King's Son of Ithaca* at the basic level of the naive "machine play." His scenic directions are more imaginative than his conventional opera verses: "The stage represents a broad alley of great trees; the branches of the trees bend towards each other in the wind. A broad view of the sea. A marble staircase leads right to the shore. As the curtain goes up, Calypso appears to tell of a very disturbing dream . . ." Or: "The rocks cave in, Minerva with her retinue appears in a sun chariot. The scenery is transparent, the trees a brilliant green, the sea like silver. Neptune appears with his sea horses, accompanied by Telemachus and Tillina, after them water gods and nymphs in silver shells."

However, Schikaneder looks more than a century ahead in his little operetta jokes. The nymph Pratschina, a "soubrette," is quite roguish about men:

Euch, ihr Herrn mit stolzen Blicken,
lacht ein schönes Mädchen aus . . .

You men with proud looks,
a pretty girl laughs at you . . .

And the refrain is:

Denn wir machen es nur so
so-so-so
und das Herz brennt lichterloh.

For we only do it so,
so-so-so-,
and your hearts are all aflame.

The women in Lehar's *Merry Widow* of 1905 were to find their lesson rather hard, but were also doing it "so-so-so"! Only the texts of the songs of the opera *Der Höllenberg oder Prüfung und Lohn* (The Infernal Mountain or Trial and Reward) of 1795 have been preserved. The music is by Joseph Wölfl from Salzburg, a pupil of Leopold Mozart and Michael Haydn. The texts are as hollow as most of Schikaneder's opera texts after *The Magic Flute*. The humanistic quality of Mozart's opera lingers on in the figure of the good magician Harmoneus who sings of the happiness of unity attained by love of humanity. We are also reminded of Shakespeare's *The Tempest*. Prospero's magic isle here becomes a magic mountain where the noble Batto, banished from the royal court by intrigues, must overcome all kinds of adventures until he can free the daughter of the helpful magician Harmoneus. Of course, one of Papageno's descendants is at his side, a wandering musician called Klingklang, and his female partner, the quick-tongued Nierra.

The opera was much acclaimed, but *Der Tyroler Wastel*, with music by Jakob Haibel (Mozart's brother-in-law and tenor at the Wieden), which followed in May 1796, was an even greater success. Here Schikaneder departed from the *Magic Flute* track, and turned to popular local subject matter.

Again it was an old theme harking back to Philipp Hafner: the honest head of the house, Herr von Tiefsinn (Mr. Deepthoughts), is tormented by his wife who is dazzled by high society and is making every effort to gain admittance to such circles. To accomplish this she wants to pair off her daughter with the vain old dandy, Herr von Tulippan. But the daughter, needless to say, loves another: the baker's good son, Joseph. So that the right pairs get each other in the end, someone has to straighten things out, and this is the role of the Tyroler Wastel of the title. He is an earthy fellow from the country who visits his titled brother, Herr von Tiefsinn; finds the madness of the Viennese city quite foreign to him; gets caught up in its turbulence especially during a visit to the Prater; but in the end manages to set everything right by virtue of his healthy common sense and delving deep into his well-filled purse to help his brother out of a tight spot.

Wastel was to be Schikaneder's most successful role after Papageno, and this Singspiel with its biting social criticism was almost as important in the development of the Viennese local comedy as *The Magic Flute* had been for romantic German opera. As a matter of fact, new wine had been poured into old bottles: the naive cliche enriched by many sharp observations and striking theatrical turns of phrase; the topical text, the contrasts between town and country, moral decay and earthiness which are incorporated in *The Tyroler Wastel* were routine dramatic features by the middle of the 1790s. The long war fought by Austria and revolutionary and Napoleonic France had resulted in widespread land speculation, impoverishment of the poor and the birth of a new, narrow class of exploitive purveyors to the court and the newly rich who had been given titles. The world was no longer an ideal world—the proletarian chambermaids, washer-women and waitresses provided a reservoir of poor to support the growing prostitution which Kaiser Franz's "vice squad" could not possibly stem. Anyone who denounced this new world and its increasing corruption, who endeavored to put forward the virtues of an older and more wholesome world could count on applause from the theater balcony where the petty bourgeois sat. Even if a play was in no sense revolutionary—the strict censorship would not have allowed such a presentation—but simply recalled the merits of the good old days (the expression existed even then!) and their deeply rooted honesty, it could count on large, appreciative audiences.

The Tyroler Wastel fulfilled these demands in full measure. Schikaneder added a cheerful couple as servants to the young lovers, who come from a bourgeois background. Marianne the cook confines herself to what is purely human and animal in her aria:

> *Ein schöner Mann ist delikat*
> *Wie ein Kapaunel mit Salat*
> *Und weiss ein Mann dies nur einmal*
> *So ist er gleich damit brutal.*

> A handsome man is as tempting
> As capon with salad
> And once he knows this well
> He is at once quite brutal.

In the meantime the honest baker sings of his pride in his higher social standing:

> *Drum fühl ich stolz die Würde*
> *Ein Bürgersmann zu seyn.*

I'm proud of the dignity
Of being a citizen.

Wastel, who addresses everyone with "du" (the familiar form),
seems to come from the backwoods, but he turns out to possess true
peasant cunning and is rich in the bargain. He sings an aria which
practically became a folk song:

> Die Tyroler sand often so lustig, so froh,
> sie trinken ihr Weinel und tanzen a so.
> Früh legt man sich nieder, früh steht man dann auf,
> Klopft's Madel aufs Mieder und arbeit' brav drauf.
> Da kriegen's dann Kinder, wie die Kugeln so rund,
> Die zappeln und springen, wie die Hechten so g'sund.

The Tyroleans are merry and cheerful just so,
They drink up their wine and dance yes, just so.
Early to bed and early to rise,
Give a pat to their girls, and to work they then go.
And then they have children as round as a ball,
Who wriggle and jiggle like pike in a pond.

The continuation of the human race is best done by honest
Tyrolean women for which Wastel praises them in another aria:

> Die Weiber sind a nit so g'naschi,
> Sie bleiben getreu ihren Mann,
> Sie machen kan Wischi kan Waschi
> Und schau'n kan andern nit an.

Women don't go around sampling,
They always stay true to their man,
They don't do no wishy nor washy
Nor look at another one once.

When he does not have to rhyme but can let his view of human
behavior flow in colorful prose, Schikaneder is, as always, at his best.
Nestroy himself would not have been ashamed of the dialogue the
Prater innkeeper carries on with his servants.

INNKEEPER: Hey you, Seppel, is there any champagne?
SEPPEL: Haven't ever seen any, as long as I've been here.

Zum Fensterln hast
ka Schneit.

Schikaneder as the "Tyroler Wastel".
Engraving by K. Hanauer in a calendar of 1797.

INNKEEPER: True! I guzzled it up myself last year then! But that doesn't matter, bring me some Tyrolean wine and a lump of sugar—later when they have had a skinful and are really sozzled they'll think they're drinking the best champagne.

Even running out of venison does not embarrass the hardworking Prater innkeeper. He first orders "a couple of large rabbits" from a neighboring farm and then 12 kreuzers' worth of smoked sausages . . . "so that we can offer stuffed meats," from which the kitchen boy produces the dish of the evening:

INNKEEPER: Hey you, tell me, what happened to the two ravens that Mick the hunter gave me as a present yesterday?
SERVANT: I've plucked and gutted them!
INNKEEPER: Good! Now light the fire quickly, and put on some water and sauerkraut . . . later I'll put the ravens into the sauerkraut so that people will think they are eating partridge and pheasant.

This is almost black humor, but the public so enjoyed it that *The Tyroler Wastel* was played 118 times. Eipeldauer reports in 1796: "You really can laugh yourself to death at this play, you would swear that a real Tyrolean peasant with goitre is standing on the stage, so completely was the actor able to create the whole personality and the swollen throat."

Schikaneder was quick to supply a follow-up called "Österreichs treue Brüder oder die Scharfschützen in Tyrol (Austria's true Brothers or the Sharpshooters in Tyrol), but it was a dull copy although he had tried to exploit the patriotic war mood. The original Wastel had a long career. He can be traced to the time when the Silver Age of Viennese operetta was fading. After all, isn't Leo Fall's *Fideler Bauer* (Merry Peasant) a late variation, though containing far less social criticism?

It is hard to place the comedy *Der Fleischhauer von Ödenburg* (The Butcher of Ödenburg) in time, as only a producer's copy survives.[28] It is a repeat of the old theme: the upright husband (Herr von Springerl), tormented by a megalomaniac wife; the sentimental pair of lovers who only find each other after the usual confusion and after the wife has been cured of her infantile and overbearing conceit. Here too, Schikaneder gives of his best in the minor characters and their local color. The factotum called Stössel—barber, apothecary, and advisor in matters of love—is the perfect, sly detective. "Largo al factotum della città"—although not quite: Rossini is missing.

Early in 1797 Schikaneder fell seriously ill and had to take to his bed, but a fortnight later was back on stage as Wastel. His vitality must have been boundless at the time: directing the theater, settling intrigues, writing and producing plays, not to mention the resources that his activities as "Don Juan of the Wieden" demanded—the title is Frau Schikaneder's and she must have known!

Popular plays and *Magic Flute* operas alternated henceforth in Schikaneder's repertoire. We now know more than Komorzynski did about *Die bürgerlichen Brüder oder die Frau aus Krems* (The Bourgeois Brothers or The Woman from Krems). He "knew little more than the title," but since then a copy was found. The three-act play was first performed in May 1797 and with such great success that it was repeated regularly until the March revolution of 1848. It even bore the message of social criticism: responsible behavior and social degeneration are here personified by two brothers. Through scenes complicated by love, lust for money and vanity, Lorenz Schlegel the dyer, a solid craftsman well aware of his social standing, sets the example of the moral repeated at the end by all the characters: "Es leben alle rechtschaffenen Bürger!" (Long live all upright citizens!). His brother Sebastian, on the other hand, who is a potter by trade, has given up his honorable craft, married a rich woman on the lookout for a title, and moved into a mansion in Vienna which is far beyond his means. In keeping with the tried-and-true pattern the daughter Theresa is to marry a baron:

> SEBASTIAN: Don't you know the sort of company I keep? No one crosses my threshold who isn't a least a "von" . . . everyone calls me Herr von Schlegel.
> THERESA: Father, I am honest!
> SEB: Now you just listen to me—no one will give you a kreutzer for that! You must be politically astute and detach yourself from the common rabble as best you can.

In the end, of course, this conduct trips up the degenerate snob

Sebastian as well as his wife who has long since refused to wear a modest bonnet. The ex-craftsman Sebastian, in financial straits, thinks of trying his fortune as a theater director in Warsaw—interesting from the point of view of theater history: a director's craft in Schikaneder's time was expected to rest on solid ground!

The most brilliant role is given to Poldel, the potter's apprentice. Poldel is not a bad boy but a sly one, who draws the logical conclusions from his former master's megalomania:

> POLDEL: Don't call me Poldel anymore, now my name's Leopoldinus . . . I'm no longer an apprentice but a house assistant.

When he moves into the town palace in Vienna, this intelligent member of the proletariat who has risen in the world speedily turns into an arrogant creature having no time for anyone else:

> POLDEL: Dear lady, I have important business to attend to . . . if anyone should ask for me, I am in my chamber.

Poldel becomes completely unhinged when he discovers how the art of acting can bolster his prestige, at least with the chambermaid. He presents himself as a talented but unappreciated actor ready for the Burgtheater, adding that one of his friends is a distributer of theater bills, "and believe me, girl, I learned a lot by heart . . . for example, the part in *Richard III*." As the chambermaid wants to see it, Poldel acts the scene from Shakespeare, exaggerating it grotesquely, of course. This scene was a "pièce de résistance" of the old Viennese Volkstheater, which lived on parody (from the sublime to the ridiculous).

Schikaneder was so apt at including such scenes that the generation of actors after him was able to shine in these minor roles. This was the case of the comedian Anton Hasenhut (1766–1841), a Leopoldstadt rival of the aging Schikaneder. The son of a ruined director, he had made his way forward in the late 1780s, and after 1800 shone in plays often written especially for him by Hensler. In these he created the role of a new comic figure called Thaddädl. His descent from Taddeo of the Commedia dell'arte is clear, but Hasenhut transformed the typical improvising Italian into a contemporary Viennese. In contrast to his older Leopoldstadt rival Laroche, the thick-set, phlegmatic Kasperl, Hasenhut created a new popular comic figure, the "apprentice" comic. These characters were appealing youngsters, really still children, scatterbrained, distracted, just out of puberty. Later, after Nestroy (we think of *Einen Jux will er sich machen*) they became "trouser roles" which verged on transvestism. Schikaneder also contributed some powerful theater types, if not archetypes; for Kurz-Bernardon had already used locksmiths' and barbers' apprentices in his comedies.

In "the grand heroic-comic opera" *Babylons Pyramiden* (October 1797) Schikaneder once more took refuge in the exotic and spectacular. Sacchetti designed no fewer than 21 amazing scenes: trees set afire after being struck by lightning, pyramids opening to reveal secret underground passages, etc. They were certainly a more powerful attraction than the music, which was once again the result of teamwork. Johann Gallus-Mederitsch, a native of Bohemia and later Grillparzer's piano teacher, wrote the first act; Peter von Winter the second. The play once again had to be put together very quickly, perhaps because Schikaneder wanted to outdo the rival Leopoldstadt Theater's brilliant new production of *Die Zwölf schlafenden Jungfrauen* (Twelve Sleeping Virgins) by Hensler and Wenzel Müller which had just come out, or perhaps because there was talk of an even greater hit in preparation, the *Donauweibchen* (Little Woman from the Danube). The director and playwright honestly admitted in the printed program that "because time was short, the music has been composed by two masters."

The plot harks back to the Semiramis myth which had already made its way onto the Viennese stage, Voltaire's *Semiramide* being the best known dramatization. The Queen of Babylon and the ambitious Artandos have murdered her husband; she now wants to marry the young and noble Timoneus, but he loves the beautiful Cremona. The ghost of the murdered man appears and torments the conscience of the Queen; but after a great deal of magic, the true lovers find each other. Inevitably a comic couple provides contrast and humor, but Papageno's descendant, called Forte, has to contend with the jealousy of his girlfriend Piana, and has the distinctly unpleasant job of "Head Tiger Boy." Cruelty and sadism are both offered for excitement: the gentle Cremona is thrown to the tigers, but her foster-mother, a magician, is able to frighten the beasts away with thunder and lightning.

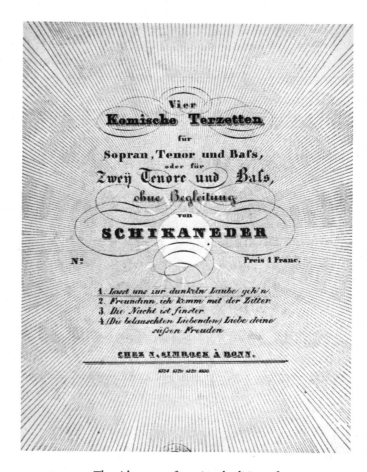

The title page of a printed edition of
"Four Comic Trios" by Schikaneder.

Effects that worked well in *The Magic Flute* are mobilized anew. The young hero plays a shawm rather than a flute, while Forte plays the barrel organ rather than a glockenspiel to attract the girls:

Ich liebte schon im zwölften Jahre
Die schönste allerliebste Ware;
Ich war von einem lockern Schlag,
Zwölf Mädchen küsst' ich alle Tag.

I was in love from my twelfth year
With things so sweet so tender,
The lightest touch just knocked me down,
Twelve girls a day I kissed in town.

Masonic symbols are once again invoked, at first in a three-fold warning to keep silent: "Strebt nach Tugend euch zu neigen / und zu schweigen, schweigen, schweigen" (Strive to attain virtue/ and to be silent, silent, silent!), yet more clearly in the vocal score arranged by Schikaneder; which along with engravings after Sacchetti's decorations also contains definite Masonic objects, from compasses to the lodge symbol. This Babylonian opera may be nothing more than a jumble of shallow phrases and sumptuous staging, but its many Masonic allusions to the better, more liberal Josephine era were significant.

Certainly Schikaneder was neither a hero nor a particularly outspoken figure; as a director he survived this authoritarian period by toeing the official line. But he was not entirely a characterless opportunist. One must recall that after the mid 1790s the Viennese theater was ruthlessly controlled by the censor. The theater censor Karl Hägelin's manual noted: "Executions of rulers of monarchical states may not be shown in the theater . . . all words which signify a spiritual office or character, such as pope, bishop, vicar etc. shall be avoided . . . cohabitation must never be portrayed." These strictures led to strange distortions of texts, as in Schiller's *Kabale und Liebe* when Ferdinand at the Burgtheater had to cry out at his disappointment in his father by substituting the word "uncle." In Schiller's *Die Räuber* Moor, the father, is likewise converted to an "uncle," and the censor struck out the line "Franz heisst die Canaille" (The scoundrel is called Franz)—for his Apostolic Majesty's name was Franz. These practices even incensed the good Emperor himself. He is reported to have said "Our censor is really stupid!"

But such remarks little affected the reality of censorship in the theater. Seven years after the death of Emperor Joseph II even the making of veiled Masonic allusions required a certain courage, especially from a director who possessed an old license for a new theater, and could therefore not afford to fall out with those in power. Nor should we overlook the social criticism which Schikaneder slyly tucked away in seemingly innocuous or patriotic passages. Johann Gottfried Seume, the famous traveller, humanist and writer of travelogues, was astonished at the daring of the Theater an der Wien, even in 1802. "I have heard things from him [Schikaneder] about the foolishness of the Viennese courtiers and the rich that one would not dare say aloud in Dresden."

Schikaneder remained true to Masonic ideas in the grand heroic-comic opera *Das Labyrinth oder Der Kampf mit den Elementen* (The Labyrinth or The Struggle with the Elements) which followed in June 1798. Such elements were implicit in the subject, for it was given out as "Part II of *The Magic Flute*." Schikaneder had long hesitated about a sequel, knowing well that any composer would be measured against Mozart and every libretto compared—for it was popular, even if many critics derided it. Peter von Winter (1754–1827) dared to venture the comparison. The composer was announced as "Kapellmeister in the service of the Bavarian-Palatine court." He had studied with Abbé Vogler in Mannheim and with Salieri in Vienna. He had travelled to Italy, and for years enjoyed a reputation sufficiently respectable for Lorenzo da Ponte to mention him (in his memoirs written in America) in the same breath with Mozart: "I, who inspired Salieri, Weigl, Martini, Winter and Mozart!" Winter tried as best he could to imitate the *Magic Flute* style, but like Süssmayr before him he had little more to offer than empty, pleasant-sounding formulas. But in 1978, as part of today's post-modern nostalgia, the opera was dug up and performed in a lavish production at the Cuvilliés Theater in Munich, being given a friendly if somewhat restrained reception.

Schikaneder did all he could to repeat the *Magic Flute* triumph, providing impressive spectacle and a cast of his best singers. The Queen of the Night was given another brilliant "revenge" aria; sung by the original queen, Josefa Hofer, who in the meantime had become Madame Mayer. Her husband Sebastian Mayer sang Sarastro and Schikaneder, of course, sang Papageno.

But even had its music been more original and exciting, *The Labyrinth* could only have emerged as a coarse rehash. Although Schikaneder had added to the *Magic Flute* cast and included some spellbinding scenes, he could offer nothing grippingly new, in contrast to Goethe's *Magic Flute* fragment which boldly introduced a new generation to the play. In Schikaneder's sequel we find new intrigues by the Queen of the Night, who now displays some sadistic qualities; Monostatos is paired with a mooress called Gura; Papageno's parents and siblings are introduced; and King Tipheus, his companion Sithos, and a high priestess to help the Queen of the Night are added. The ideals of enlightened princely education shine through in Sarastro's charge to the young couple: "Nun müsst ihr wandeln durch des Labirinthes Krümmungen wie jedes Fürstenpaar" (Now you must walk through the labyrinth's twisted ways like every princely pair). The noble wiseman reveals himself to be a loyal Hapsburg monarchist when he demands of his priests that they "fight for fatherland and throne." The music is decidedly operatic, with trios and quintets, but Papageno's antics seem duller and more shop-worn than the rest of the opera, even when Schikaneder shows off yet again as a braggart:

> *Man glaubt von den Männern izt nimmer,*
> *dass einer beständig mehr sey.*
> *Ihr Mädchen, ich bessre mich immer,*
> *nur ich bin alleine noch treu.*

> Of men you think it's never so
> That one can constant be,
> But girls, I do improve each day,
> And I alone am true.

Perhaps the dialogues were wittier, but we do not know for only the songs have been preserved, which is more than what survives from Schikaneder's other contemporary operas. Of his fantastic, legendary or gruesome plays with which he sought to swim on the tide of the *Donauweibchen* success, only the manuscript of *Konrad Langbart von Friedburg oder Der Burggeist* (Conrad Longbeard from Friedburg or The Castle Ghost) has been preserved. As in

Grillparzer's first play which came later, an ancestress haunts the castle of Friedburg, appearing in many forms until she is finally freed from the curse thanks to the steadfastness of the last member of the family. The play was a success for decades, and the public's taste for murder plays about ghosts and knights lasted even longer. We may turn up our noses at this sort of theater today, but should not forget that there were no horror films as esthetic alternatives then. The theater had to provide fare for all manner of tastes.

Little can be learned about the half-dozen or so local plays, with or without music, presented in the last years of the Wiedner Theater. We only know that the three-act comedy *Der Teufel in Wien* (The Devil in Vienna), staged in 1799, must have contained some social criticism. The devil in the title, unlike the one in the comedy already discussed of the same name and written eight years earlier, is no bogey from the standard costume wardrobe but a monster of a tenant who tries to turn out his landlord. The latter is no better than the devil because he has bought an impoverished girl from her father for 100 ducats and forced her into prostitution. The landowner's good brother, although cast as a typical bullying colonel, brings about the inevitable happy ending.

As the play was a great success, Schikaneder followed it promptly with a sequel, *Die Reise nach Steyermark* (The Journey to Styria). In this, it is "an honest Jew," (characteristic of the petty-bourgeois attitude of the time towards the Jews) who brings the lapsed landowner back to middle-class morality.

Schikaneder's spectacular operas swallowed up a great deal of money. Even so, he continued to set great store by scenic magnificence, threw money about to support his extravagant private life, and expanded his company: in 1798, Joachim Perinet was wooed away from the Leopoldstadt to be the Wiedner dramatist in residence. Admission prices were raised in the hope of supporting this munificence: the large boxes for *Babylons Pyramiden* cost 9 florins; the smaller ones 4 florins 30 kreuzer; orchestra seats were 1 florin 20 kreuzer; and the cheapest seats 17 kreuzer. The strategy resulted in the unbelievable taking of 1,045 florins the first night, but in the long run higher ticket prices could not be maintained, and in spite of his great success Schikaneder ran into financial difficulties. What neither the Shakespeare performances—according to the custom of the time always an adaptation, for example *The Taming of the Shrew* as *The Tamed Cantankerous Lady*—nor the popular local plays and courtly romances had been able to achieve, now was to be accomplished by *The Magic Flute*, which was added to the repertoire again.

On November 24, 1798, Schikaneder presented the most brilliant work in his repertoire afresh. Three years previously he had added new verses to the bird catcher's song for the ostensibly 200th performance of *The Magic Flute* (in reality the 135th). He had Vincenzo Sacchetti partly re-stage the opera; it was certainly more lavish than it had been seven years before. Stage design technique had improved, and both Sacchetti and Schikaneder were surely of the opinion that only the best was good enough.

Of course, a suburban theater could not afford the luxurious post-Baroque decor lavished on the Italian operas in the two court theaters. Palaces as architectural works of art designed by the Galli-Bibiena dynasty displayed an unbelievably ingenious perspective which was accomplished by a system of diagonal painting on cut-cloth and backcloth, but this kind of "scena per angolo", which was imitated in many theaters offering Italian opera, was beyond the means of the Freihaus theater. In the meantime, fortunately, the designer Josef Platzer had developed the backdrop of arches, which were able to support scene transformations and provide the illusion of depth with more modest financial outlays. The "flying machines" and trap doors mentioned earlier also contributed to these effects. Sacchetti was as keen on magical effects as his director, but only if he did not have to pinch pennies. So that these effects could be employed for the big productions, as they certainly were in all the Schikaneder operas, other entertainments, especially those with a bourgeois setting, were staged as cheaply as possible.

But the stage effects for the new *Magic Flute* were not stinted. Unfortunately neither the cast list nor illustrations for the scenic designs have survived. Six engravings, which have finally been identified as the work of the brothers Josef and Peter Schaffer, were issued in Brno as early as 1795. They show the three ladies in hoop skirts and Papageno in an unusual costume, which differs from the illustration in the original libretto, on a tiny stage. It is certainly not the Freihaus production, but an earlier one, in some unknown town. Nevertheless, even taking into account the customary freedom with which others may have treated Sacchetti's original drawings, a study of the 21 engravings in the vocal score of *Babylons Pyramiden*, which came out shortly before, points to an opulence of design that would surely have engaged Sacchetti's fantasy and Schikaneder's purse for the new *Magic Flute*.

A fortnight later a near catastrophe occurred in the Wiedner Theater. During the premiere of Wölfl's magic opera *Der Kopf ohne Mann* (The Head Without a Man) it was a child, and not a man, who lost his head, and yelled, "Fire!" starting a panic. Two days later Schikaneder tried to play the event down in an "announcement" to the "most worthy public," calming them and "vouching for everything." But Prince Starhemberg, the owner of the entire Freihaus complex, had become suspicious about the large debt amassed and terminated the lease for the theater. Thanks to Schikaneder's great skills of persuasion he was able to interest the rich merchant and former Masonic Lodge brother Bartholomäus Zitterbarth in becoming a partner. The new partner not only took on all the debts to date —they had risen from 63,000 to 130,000 florins—but also invested in the future plans which Schikaneder had long had in mind by purchasing the site 26 Laimgrube, only a few hundred meters away as the crow flies, on the other side of the river Wien. This was where Schikaneder had thought of establishing his new, more magnificent theater.

He still had Emperor Joseph's license in his pocket, entitling him to build a theater. Emperor Franz had confirmed it in a private audience in April 1800, while at the same time rejecting the protest of Baron Peter von Braun, leaseholder of the court theater, who sensed rivalry: ". . . I will grant Schikaneder permission to build a theater; the memorandum from Baron von Braun, however, is to be laid *ad acta* without a reply." In so doing, the Emperor had taken the recommendations of the court chancellery into account, according to which a refusal to allow construction "would cause great discontent, especially among the lower class of the public."

The remaining years of the Wiedner Theater were conducted under the mutual "directorship of Herr Zitterbarth and Schikaneder." The financially powerful merchant was now the owner, but Schikaneder remained "artistic director" and in practice general manager. Although he had no more great successes,

Schikaneder did not entirely abandon his artistic ambitions. He repeated the concert performance of Mozart's *Tito*; during other performances had Mozart sonatas played during the intermissions; continued his academy concerts of contemporary music; and brought out the Wiedner Theater's own version of *Faust*, "a romantic play with songs, scenic transformations and flying machines" by the theater dramatist Matthäus Voll with music by Johann Georg Lickl. It had as little success as several further works by Schikaneder, now lost. There is a certain irony in the fact that the author who brought the most money into the box office after 1800, otherwise quite a second-rate writer, was Karl Ludwig Giesecke with his comedy in rhyming verse *Der travestierte Aeneas* (The Travesty of Aeneas)—the same Giesecke about whom such a fuss was made after Schikaneder's death.

The magic Singspiel *Holga* shows just how anxious Schikaneder was to satisfy the box office simply by dazzling his public with spectacular effects. In the third act he "tried, with the author's permission, to create more variety with new songs, various devices, flying machines and scenes," and indeed he managed a run of over 30 performances. The author's identity was not revealed; perhaps it was Schikaneder himself who was, for once, ashamed of a trashy production. Toward the end of the theater's existence there seem to have been some decided flops: an anonymous one-act play entitled *Kopf, Magen und Herz* (Head, Stomach and Heart) was booed so violently that its first performance had to be called off before the end.

But these setbacks, combined with a dull last season at the Freihaustheater, did not dispel the euphoria which had overtaken Schikaneder's company. In spirit they were already in the newer, safer and more beautiful theater which the Emperor had granted permission to build in April of 1800. A month later the "Citizen Builder" Joseph Reymund began building, an event which the ever-resourceful Schikaneder managed to turn into a splendid, public, open-air performance. With all the members of his company, "from the director down to the program seller," he marched to the building site and, under the gaze of hundreds of curious people, helped dig the foundations.

Baron von Braun shattered this mood of high jubilation by putting on the first Kärntnertor Theater performance of *The Magic Flute*

"in German" (based on Vulpius) and making no mention of
Schikaneder's name. Since 1794 this, the second of the court theaters,
had been playing musical theater exclusively, and two years later
after the success of Johann Schenk's Singspiel *Der Dorfbarbier* (The
Village Barber), which was repeated over 100 times, it had begun to
rival the Wiedner Theater in earnest. Doubtless Baron Braun could
generally afford better singers as he was supported by a "higher
quality" public. It was his misfortune that there were some scenic
hitches during the premiere of *The Magic Flute* in February 1801. The
Queen of the Night had to crawl away into the wings because the trap
door would not function, and Papagena was only able to get out of
her old woman's garb with the helping hands of others, spoiling the
effect. Schikaneder, well trained in parody, was prompt in making
fun of his wealthy rival's scenic mishaps, and apart from the laughter
of his petty-bourgeois public, he had his one-time rival Perinet on his
team. In an anonymously published pamphlet which most certainly
was launched by Schikaneder, entitled *Mozart und Schikaneder, ein
theatralisches Gespräch über die Aufführung der Zauberflöte im Stadttheater*
(Mozart and Schikaneder: A Theatrical Discussion about the First
Performance of *The Magic Flute* in the City Theater), the current
Wiedner Theater dramatist Perinet called on the late Mozart to speak
and save Schikaneder's honor:

> *Du hast verstanden was ich kann und vermag,*
> *Und warst ein Freund vom echten Schlag.*
> *Du gabst mir Gelegenheit, mich zu zeigen,*
> *Und ich machte deinen Plan mir eigen . . .*
> *Du warst der Vater, ich der Erzieher;*
> *Hätte der Vater keine Kinder gemacht*
> *Hätt's auch mit der Erziehung gut Nacht.*

> You understood what I could do,
> And were a friend at once and true,
> You gave me chance to prove my worth,
> I took your plan and made it mine . . .
> You were the father, I the teacher:
> If father no child had brought to birth
> The teaching too were nothing worth.

Another anonymous pamphlet had Mozart himself, now in Olympus, criticize the Kärntnertor Theater's *Magic Flute*. And Schikaneder did his bit from the stage when, three weeks after the rival *Magic Flute* premiere, he treated the audience to some new bird-catcher verses:

> *Dass Mozart hier mein Bruder war,*
> *Weiss ja die ganze Priesterschar.*
> *Und ewig bleibt sein Bild in mir,*
> *Ja, dankbar bin ich ihm dafür;*
> *Denn Mozart's Geist und Feder*
> *War Freund und ist Schikaneder.*

That Mozart was my brother here,
Knows every pater, priest or friar
His image in my heart is fixed,
I thank him for it evermore:
For Mozart's pen and Mozart's mind
Were friends of Schikaneder.

Naive verses, and certainly an obvious piece of self-justification—but more important is the realization of the lively way in which actual events were presented in the theater, of how much freedom for intellectual argument existed within the institution of the theater, even under the censorship of Emperor Franz's reign.

To mark his farewell to the Freihaus Theater, his final performance on the Wieden, Schikaneder called upon all the available theatrical and polemical resources available to him. The opera *Torbern* by Antonio Bruni was already in the repertoire, and on June 11, 1801, it was followed by *Thespis*. The latter was done in Greek costume, and the hero of the title was played by Schikaneder as the mythical ancestor of all popular, from Schikaneder's point of view, all "modern" theater. Agathokles the villain probably symbolizes Baron von Braun. The allegorical play in costume, with the inevitable love story and equally inevitable music (by A. F. Fischer), glorifies the Theater Director auf der Wieden and his noble intentions. "Geist der Philosophie, Geschmack, Gefühl der Kunst, / Dies ist Dramaturgie, das andere ist Dunst" (Spirit of philosophy, good taste, a feeling for art / this is dramaturgy, the rest is but a mist); in addition to lauding his past successes it also holds out the promise of even more magnificent productions: "Wir sehen uns ja morgen / Im glücklichen Athen" (We shall see each other tomorrow /in happy Athens)—which the public understood to mean the new, larger Theater an der Wien. The play was repeated once on June 12, 1801, "Zum letztemale, beym Beschluss der Schaubühne im hochfürstl. Starhembergischen Freyhaus auf der Wieden" (For the last time, at the closing of his Highness Prince Starhemberg's Freihaus an der Wieden)—read the announcement of the farewell performance. Schikaneder tried to recruit his new public with improvised verses:

Der Weg ist nicht zu weit,
Der Fluss ist nicht zu breit,
Ein Sprung, und Ihr seid da!
Nicht wahr, Ihr saget ja!

The way is not too far,
The river not too broad,
A hop and you are there!
Isn't it so? Say yes!

We can imagine the jubilant shouts of "yes" from the orchestra and balcony. Only a few days later the pickaxes were turned to the demolition of the theater that had given birth to *The Magic Flute*. But even earlier, the evening following the farewell performance, Schikaneder opened his new theater with a new opera. It had been a move like no other in both its speed and creativity: a "Schikanederei" in the laudable sense of this notorious word.

8 Vienna's Largest and Most Beautiful Theater

Over the months as the walls rose and Vienna's newest theater began to take shape, crowds of curious people were drawn to the banks of the river Wien. The evening the theater opened, June 13, 1801, proved to be an important event in the restless life of Emanuel Schikaneder. As author he had contributed two works, *Thespis' Traum* (Thespis' Dream) as a prologue to a new opera, *Alexander,* with music by Franz Teyber. Although he played the main parts in both pieces, the real hero of the evening was Schikaneder the theater entrepreneur. What he offered the Viennese was first and foremost a new and magnificent theater, the largest, most beautiful and technically the best equipped in the entire city.

When it is recalled that Vienna was at that time the most lavishly equipped theater center in the Empire—it had five theaters including those in the suburbs—the superlatives employed in the *Allgemeine musikalische Zeitung* of Leipzig to describe Schikaneder's theater as the most comfortable and satisfactory in the whole of Germany do not seem to have been off the mark.

The Viennese were equally astonished. "If Schikaneder and Zitterbarth had had the idea . . . to charge admission simply for looking at the glories of their Theater an der Wien, Schikaneder would certainly have been able to take in vast sums of money without giving one single performance," were the admiring words of Adolf Bäuerle, a Viennese man-of-the-theater and feature article writer.[29]

The new theater was thoroughly elegant, with five tiers (boxes and balcony) "decked out in imperial blue with silver right up to the last tier." There was no comparing it with the modest and now deserted Freihaus Theater. It was also larger and the seats more comfortable than those in either of the court theaters. It could accommodate no fewer than 2,200 admissions, which is more than the Vienna Staatsoper can today. But this was made possible by the large area for standing room—1,400 behind the orchestra and balcony seats. The horseshoe-shaped auditorium could seat 700 people. The boxes at the Freihaus Theater had been plain, but these were richly decorated. Silvered caryatids supported each tier; a chandelier and many candelabra illuminated the scene with hundreds of candles. The stage curtain, designed by Sacchetti and depicting numerous allegorical figures from *The Magic Flute*, produced exclamations of pure delight.

That the new theater was designed in keeping with the wishes of Schikaneder, a practical man of the theater, was reflected in the elaborate stage equipment, superior to any other theater in Vienna. The main curtain rose and fell noiselessly on a set of pulleys, which was a great sensation on opening night, even among the aristocracy and members of the royal household in attendance. Until then "jumping curtains" were usual in the theater: a couple of stagehands would leap from the rigging-loft, and acting as counter-weights pull the curtain up with their weight. Wings had always been pushed onto the stage from left and right; now they could be let down, or elevated from below stage, which made for quicker scene changes. But the stage measurements were the most unusual feature: the overall dimensions of the theater were considerable—45 meters long × 21 meters wide, compared to 29 × 15 for the Leopoldstadt Theater—but the depth of stage was 13 meters (Leopoldstadt 10), extended 10.5 meters by a back stage, which opened up quite new sight-line possibilities. Sacchetti, who according to theater historian Heinz Kindermann was "one of the best scenic designers" of that time, and his technical assistants were better able to mesmerize the public in the Theater an der Wien with its new, superior equipment. This facility was both a blessing and a curse when considered in terms of the demands the imagination of a scenic spendthrift like Schikaneder could place on it, particularly now that he set less store on inspiration and more on stunning effects.

The Theater an der Wien.

Interior of the theater.

Yet Schikaneder's realization of his theater dream, with which he had pushed ahead so persistently during the 15 years after receiving the Kaiser's permission, proved quite practical. The site constraints of the neighborhood in some measure forced some practicality upon him and his financier Zitterbarth—both had signed the planning documents. Number 26 in the Margaretenstrasse on the Wien river (today the Linke Wienzeile) was an old four-story house, which had to be incorporated in the new structure; its many rooms served not only as theater administrative offices but also as apartments. Schikaneder and many of his company lived in the apartments, as did Beethoven when he was working on *Fidelio*. The theater itself was connected with this older building. The "Citizen Builder" Joseph Reymund did his work well, in constant compliance with Schikaneder's practical wishes. He even found space for decorations on the facade which faces the Böhmisches Gassel (today Millöcker Gasse), although this entrance for the gentry, with three large round-arched entrances under an "empire" pediment, was actually the side of the theater. The official name of the theater, "Kaiserl.königl.privil.Schauspielhaus" (Playhouse under Imperial and Royal Privilege), is impressively displayed on a marble tablet under a stone double eagle [the symbol of the Dual Monarchy— ed.]. Beneath this symbol Schikaneder had had himself immortalized as Papageno, blowing his pan flutes surrounded by little Papagenos. The "Papageno portal" remains today an important ornament of the Theater an der Wien, despite the changing fortunes of the house.

The director always considered the curiosity and the comfort of his highly-esteemed public. Very early on he employed an umbrella rental service, an amenity that season ticket holders of the late 20th century have to do without. In case of rain, those wanting to reach home dry after the performance could rent an umbrella for a small deposit and 52 kreuzer—it could be returned later to the theater or "to Herr Joseph Zitterbarth's establishment" in the Graben. How the poor Zitterbarth, who had paid off Schikaneder's debts and built a new theater, must have suffered during the first night festivities at the Theater an der Wien, for all praise was lavished on Schikaneder. Bäuerle's description of the event is amusing: when the actress Wipfel recited a poem in praise of her director "Du Mensch, als Mime wie als Dichter gross" (Oh you who are great as both actor and poet), the co-director who had been consistently ignored exploded with rage: "Bin i nit die Hauptperson? . . . hat der Schikaneder nur so viel g'habt, um eine Fuhre Ziegelstein bezahlen zu können? Nix hat er g'habt. . . ." (Am I not the most important person? . . . did Schikaneder have enough to pay for even a load of bricks? He had nothing). Some members of the company managed to calm him down, and the festivities continued.

Had Schikaneder realized his wish, Beethoven's name would have been on the program of the opening night alongside his own. The composer had already taken part in an academy concert at the Freihaus Theater, and now Schikaneder offered him his *Alexander* libretto. It is likely that the *Alexander* verses were no worse than those of the future *Fidelio* text, but only a highly exalted ethical theme might have had enough appeal to win the critical symphonist over to write an opera—and this was more than Schikaneder could offer.

Alexander the Great falls in love with the Queen of India and creeps incognito into her palace. In the end there is a wedding with massed choirs. The opening of the theater was for Schikaneder the appropriate occasion for a grandiose spectacle, or even better, an exotic opera. Once again, his poetry is more apparent in his scenic instructions than in his verses. "At the oracle's pronouncement the whole figure, including sword and torch, starts glowing. At the back of the stage is a long descending stone staircase. To the right is an archway which leads to the tomb of the kings and is embellished with urns: to the left an iron gate leading to even deeper vaults." A great tableau closes the opera: Alexander's warriors and the Indians sing of each other as brothers and embrace, and the Queen enters in a golden chariot drawn by four horses, accompanied by 40 riders on horseback. The humor of the indispensable comic figures is less impressive: one is in charge of monkeys and parrots, while the other—"Makuro, an Indian great man"—is an erotic philanderer—Schikaneder's first role in the new theater. Beethoven's substitute, Franz Teyber (1756–1810), Schikaneder's Kapellmeister during his strolling player years, turned out a poor scene, and the newly engaged singers—Antoinette Campi and Josef Simoni, the court opera tenor—proved not to be the attractions everyone expected: their German was terrible (the Alexander singer probably had a heavy, Bohemian accent; his real name was Simon).

In the prologue *Thespis's Dream*, a continuation of the farewell allegory from the Freihaus Theater reduced to three characters, Schikaneder courted, in a quite obvious way, imperial favor as a "Greek theater director" by having marble busts of the Emperor and his spouse and of Alexander brought onto the stage: "I have long carried these three monuments in my heart; they shall remain forever in my thankful soul . . . we can wish for nothing more beautiful than that a man, after a long day of toil, should come to our theater so that we can cheer his soul." He tried to repay his arch rival, the banker Baron von Braun, for the insult in connection with *The Magic Flute* at the Kärntertor Theater: when Agathokles the intriguer (von Braun) tries to thwart Thespis's (Schikaneder) conquest of Athens (the Theater an der Wien), he is forced to flee into the wings tossing off a knavish "a curse on you!" The real Baron Braun, however, did not flee into any wings at all, and remained a potent competitor.

Schikaneder travelled to Upper Austria—with his wife—for a couple of months' rest, one of the last journeys that this man from Straubing, now a resident of Vienna, was to make after the opening of the new theater. Early in 1802 he struck out again at the competition from the Kärntnertor by presenting a newly designed production of *The Magic Flute*. Sacchetti made full and generous use of the high flies in the new theater; during the trial by fire and water, for example, the audience was amazed by "a sea of fire and a column of flames, steam and smoke which rose up towards the clouds" and then quickly "transformed itself into foaming waves and a cascading torrent," as the *Allgemeine musikalische Zeitung* rapturously reported. Mme. Campi sang the Queen of the Night; Simoni, Tamino; Mme. Willmann, Pamina; and of course Schikaneder, Papageno. He announced in the program that he had "taken the liberty here and there to put new words into Papageno's mouth," and six months later, to celebrate the first anniversary of the Theater an der Wien, he sang three extra stanzas added to the birdcatcher's song:

> *Heut' zählt die Zeit ein Jahr herum,*
> *Wo mir das Herz schlug um und um;*
> *Da wagten wir zum erstenmal,*
> *Zu öffnen dieses Tempels Saal.*
> *Wir gaben Alexanders Bild*

Und eure Gunst war unser Schild.
Drum sing, ich la, la, la, la, la!
Aus teutscher Brust mein Hopsassa.

Today it is a year ago
Since my heartbeats went to and fro;
We braved it through for once and all
To open up this temple's hall.
Of Alexander was our play
And for your favor we did pray.
So now I sing la la la la!
My German breast cries out hurrah.

However, Schikaneder could no longer sing this as the owner of the theater license, for a few days earlier he had handed it over to Zitterbarth for 100,000 florins. In practice this transfer had no effect on Schikaneder's participation as Zitterbarth needed him as both actor and dramatist and engaged him for an enormous fee: 50 florins for each appearance as actor, 200 florins for each new play and 400 for each new opera. Schikaneder spent the indemnity wisely. For the modest sum of 10,000 florins he bought at first half and then the whole of a beautiful baroque house in the rural suburb of Nussdorf, rebuilding and redecorating it. Sacchetti painted the ceiling of the largest room with an allegorical scene from *The Magic Flute*, with the Queen of the Night as the central figure. The Viennese named it "Schikanederschlössl" (Schikaneder's little castle). Franz Lehár, the operetta king who had come into a great deal of money, later acquired it, and it remains a residence today. Schikaneder as the owner of a stately home—surely this was a high point in the career of the sometime minstrel and itinerant director.

But artistically, as a creative man of the theater, he had long passed his prime. He was no longer able to produce anything significant, though now and then he managed to pull off a sly coup against Baron Braun. When the most popular work of the season, Cherubini's opera *Les deux journées* (translated into German as "The Water Carrier") was advertised by Braun for the Kärntnertor Theater, Schikaneder managed to beat him to it by a day producing the opera, calling it *Graf Armand oder Die zwei unvergesslichen Tage* (Count Armand or The Two Unforgettable Days). *The Magic Flute* remained in the repertoire of the Theater an der Wien as a major attraction, but

Schikaneder's more recent works from the Wiedner Theater enjoyed only variable success. *Babylons Pyramiden* drew only small audiences, and the tearjerker *Der Grandprofoss*, though a well-tried, old favorite and now staged with dozens of horses and other military glories, seemed to have lost its appeal. A performance of *Das Labyrinth* (the sequel to *The Magic Flute*) in 1803 drew a half-ironic comment from the well-disposed Eipeldauer: ". . . in the midst of many wonderful decorations the elegant audience forgot that our own dear Schikaneder was the opera's daddy, and clapped and applauded as much as if the opera had been an import from Paris."

This is informative theater gossip: Schikaneder the librettist had lost his power to draw an audience. Audiences came because there was something to see, almost as if the opera were "an import from Paris," which of course was the highest praise since French taste was again fashionable even in the Theater an der Wien. Méhul's *Joseph and his Brothers*, Cherubini's *The Water Carriers*, and Grétry's *Richard Lionheart* had taken over from the Italians who had set the tone for over a century. Classicism and its lofty subject matter had won out, and classic works exerted their great influence through elegant productions in Paris—the city that had become Europe's artistic center, shining in the light of Napoleon's rising star.

It is very curious that in the super-reactionary Vienna of Emperor Franz, who could smell out even a lukewarm Jacobin, the so-called "Rescue" or "Horror opera" became established, when in fact it was a child of the "Grande Révolution." The typical subject: a nobleman who is unjustly imprisoned or condemned to death by a tyrant is rescued by a good man (in Cherubini) or by self-sacrificing conjugal love (as in Beethoven's *Fidelio*, which was adapted from a French model). Dozens of works were based on this pattern, revealing an enlightened and humanistic development in taste. Viennese audiences, saturated with theater, wanted more of this—the endlessly churned-out Papageno intermezzi came to be regarded as a nuisance. At any rate, there was no further innocent amusement to be found in tomfoolery. The best of Schikaneder's fantastic creations fell flat, even when he exerted every effort to present them in increasingly colorful settings. Schikaneder's new operas, now lost, which were performed after the opening of the Theater an der Wien—*Tsching! Tsching! Tsching!*, *Die Entlarvten* (The Unmasked),

Die Pfändung oder Der Personalarrest (The Repossession or the Arrest)—in spite of lavish scenery, no longer evoked the audience's sympathy or touched the proverbial "Viennese heart".

The price of opening night tickets was higher than it had been in the Wiedner Theater. Boxes in the parterre and dress circle cost 4 florins, first rows of orchestra and balcony 30 kreuzer, a "Sperrsitz" (a seat that could be locked, reserved for season ticket holders) 48 kreuzer, and the cheapest—hundreds of standing room places high in the fourth balcony—could be had for 9 kreuzer. In spite of the splendor of the new theater, these were cheap prices. We learn from Castelli,[30] that a meal of no less than 12 courses could be had for a florin; that in 1801 a fried fish cost 5 kreuzer and a loaf of bread only one kreuzer; and that he was paid 18 kreuzer a day for private lessons. So it is clear that the Theater an der Wien was very reasonable and truly followed the Volkstheater tradition.

But the house had to be filled, for competition from the Leopoldstadt and the Kärntnertor was far from asleep. Schikaneder's old rule of thumb relative to musical theater no longer worked: he continued to throw money out of the window, but unfortunately it no longer returned through the front door. Even when he forced his luck with new, local, topical plays, it failed.

In 1803 a *Complete Life of Emanuel Schikaneder* in three volumes was bombastically announced, but it was soon cancelled; not a single sentence appeared. Plans for a tour to Amsterdam and Berlin came to nothing, ending in Karlsbad, where in the local summer theater Schikaneder sought to upgrade *The Tyroler Wastel* with new stanzas but only succeeded in embarrassing everyone.

He passed it about that he was planning a third part for *The Magic Flute*, but it was soon evident that this too was pure talk. During his absence Schikaneder's nephew Karl had stood in for him as Wastel at the Theater an der Wien and was well received, arousing the older man's jealousy and ultimately leading to Karl's having to get out of the way by going to Pressburg. By the end of 1802 things had gone so badly that Schikaneder decided to withdraw from the theater altogether, both as director and as actor. An anonymous poet (perhaps it was Schikaneder himself) was quick to celebrate the event in an ode which was added to a book about the new theater: *Der Du geendet ruhmvoll die Laufbahn!* (You who have ended your career so gloriously).

But a cry for help from Zitterbarth, the hapless owner, went out: Schikaneder once more took over "the artistic direction," and in February 1803 he was already appearing in his old roles. He continued to try to interest Beethoven in composing an opera for the Theater an der Wien, but in vain. But he was able to engage Anton Hasenhuth, the popular "Thaddädl" comedian, which was a plus for the local plays, but his own new "Volksstücke," with and without music, that he presented in 1803, no longer pleased the public. *Die Pfändung oder Der Personalarrest* with music by Franz Teyber was a flop. Schikaneder attempted to rehash old subjects in this opera, but they could no longer stand the test of time. Many began to question Schikaneder's mental health. Understandably the endless repetitions of the *Magic Flute* theme produced nothing, and exotic and grandiose operas, in spite of elaborate scenic artistry, could no longer hold their own in the face of the vogue for realistic French rescue opera. But less understandable is the reason the once so successful author of local plays only reaped failure with them now, unless we assume absence of quality and waning inspiration as the simple explanation. Yet the genre of the Viennese "Volksstück" was far from exhausted as proved by Ferdinand Kringsteiner (1775–1810), who appeared in the early years of the century as its newest star. He was to shine for only a brief decade at the Leopoldstadt Theater but upon being engaged as theater dramatist in 1804 he wrote 25 Volksstücke within the short period of six years. The most successful of these were played throughout the whole of Austria, and as adaptations they lived on for a goodly time thereafter.

Kringsteiner was the son of a civil servant, had some practical training, married an officer's daughter and then dedicated himself completely to the theater, although he could scarcely survive on the miserable salary Marinelli paid him- there was no royalty system at the time. He eked out a meager and sickly existence, dying in poverty at the age of 35. The late fame of "the perfecter of the Viennese local play," as Otto Rommel described him, was not really granted, for his popular Volksstücke and parodies suffered the same fate as folk songs: just as these were badly sung to death, Kringsteiner's plays were badly played to death and became almost anonymous raw material for newer adaptations. Only theatrical research restored some honor to the long-forgotten author: his works were better,

Emanuel and Eleonore Schikaneder.
This silhouette is the only surviving likeness
of Schikaneder's wife.

more practical for the theater though his name was little known.

His were all Volksstücke in the Viennese tradition, many with songs and conventional choruses, or parodies on, for example, *Othello* or *Werther*. Kringsteiner learned much from Schikaneder's *Tyroler Wastel*, *Fiaker* and *Die Bürgerlichen Brüder*; he recognized clearly that Laroche's post-Baroque Kasperl comedy had run its course, although he made frequent use of the new comedian Hasenhuth as Thaddädl. He also makes great use of mockery—butts of his jokes are love-crazed old men and petty bourgeois who have gone out of their minds. In the end, of course, everything turns out to be morally proper. "Hör ich nur ein Geigerl, so krieg ich ein' Schneid / Zum tanzen, das ist halt mein' einzige Freud!" (I only have to hear a fiddle to get some pep into me. To dance, that's my only joy) is the excuse of Nanny the coachman's wife who nearly goes off the deep end at the *Black Masked Ball* on the Alsergrund. But the story's dénouement is full of burlesque, as are all Kringsheimer's pieces, based on old patterns but with many new and effective twists and parts. Most of them could have been written by Schikaneder in his best years, so it was not the genre that was exhausted, but rather Schikaneder's inspiration.

Despite 93 performances of works with texts by him in the first half of 1803, it was to be a sad year for Schikaneder, a year calculated to warn a man, up to then spoiled by luck, of the transience of success. He drafted his will, dated probably by pure chance December 17, the evening on which the premiere of another of his comedies *Spass und Ernst* (Fun and Earnest) proved a complete flop. "In consideration of the transitoriness of all that is earthly" and "in perfect health and in full possession of all my faculties" Schikaneder arranged for several legacies, from 12 florins for 12 Holy Masses to the considerable sum of 3000 florins which he bequeathed to his illegitimate son Franz Schikaneder (the child of the serving maid Franziska Ginschlin), while his wife Eleonore was to receive the balance of his estate. He demonstrated his gratitude to a needy and worthy "strolling player," and left the considerable sum of 300 florins to "the famous poet Mr. Wieland in Weimar, author of *Tschinnistan* "or, if the latter should die first, to "Mr. Schiller, our German Schaekspair."

But after all the humiliations and disappointments of 1803, what a satisfaction it must have been that a short while later, in September 1804, he was again asked to be director of his Theater an der Wien, for the third time—chosen, at that, by his fiercest rival, Baron von Braun! Zitterbarth, at the end of his business and financial resources, sold the theater to Braun on February 14, 1803. Braun's decision to engage Schikaneder was clever—without him all joy in acquiring the theater would have been for naught. It also was a good business deal for Braun as he had earlier bought the house adjoining the stage section, so that he realized the enormous sum of 901,500 florins from the sale. Zitterbarth bade the theater a noble farewell, donating over 2000 florins, the takings of the last two performances, to charitable purposes. His was a life which hovered between tragedy and comedy—an obsession for the theater and the never ending friction between him and Schikaneder—and it ended sadly: only two years later and only 49 years old, he died of a chest complaint.

Baron Peter von Braun took over the theater in February 1804. He now appeared to have achieved all the ambitions for which he had striven for decades, often enough ruthlessly playing on the advantages of his noble status. As Imperial and Royal Lord High Steward, as Bohemian and Moravian representative, he was a high-ranking courtier; as court banker and wealthy industrialist he was economically powerful; and now he was also almost undisputed king of the Viennese theater. He had been the leaseholder of both court theaters, near the Burg and at the Kärntnertor, for years, and now he had his own theater as well. He could assign the theatrical members of his empire among his three playhouses at will, and indeed the best of Schikaneder's ensemble were later to go over into service of the court. This company, which had in the main been taken over from the Freihaus Theater by the new Theater an der Wien, was initially made up of only 12 singers and a few more actors (Eleonore Schikaneder only took small parts), but it was gradually enlarged during Schikaneder's first years at the new theater, and proved itself to be a company of more than average ability, led by such efficient Kapellmeisters as Henneberg, Seyfried and Teyber, and under Schikaneder's direction.

By engaging the writer and court official Joseph von Sonnleithner (1766–1835) as his artistic director and main producer, Baron Braun hoped that he could return to better times. The new era certainly promised much, as Braun succeeded in tying Beethoven down and finally seeing to it that he composed an opera for the theater. The fact that Beethoven found Sonnleithner's *Leonore* text worthy of an opera is to Sonnleithner's credit; it was in fact only an adaptation of J. R. Bouilly's *Léonore ou l'amour conjugal* (Leonore or Conjugal Love) on which the Italian *Léonora* opera by Ferdinando Paër which had had such a success in Dresden was also based. In effect, Sonnleithner and Braun harvested what Schikaneder had sown. The former director had been wooing Beethoven for years; had given him a firm opera contract; placed an apartment in the Theater an der Wien at his disposal; and as early as the spring of 1803 had organized the first academy concert, which was dedicated exclusively to Beethoven's works (the oratorio *Christ on the Mount of Olives*, Symphonies 1 and 2, and the Piano Concerto in C minor, Op.37, with the composer as soloist). By November Beethoven had started to set one of Schikaneder's new librettos to music, *Vesta's Feuer* (Vesta's Fire). Two numbers were sketched out; one of them was used in *Fidelio* (as the duet "O namenlose Freude"), whose subject ultimately attracted Beethoven. Incidentally, Schikaneder's keen instinct was also responsible for the temporary recruitment of another famous musical personality to be theater composer: the Abbé Georg Joseph Vogler (1749–1814). He was a brilliant but cranky man, who instructed his pupils—Weber and Meyerbeer among them—in a new method of composition and whose musical battles and depictions of sea storms made him a forerunner of program music. He appeared at the Theater an der Wien in an academy of sacred music and in his own opera. Finally, Schikaneder must also be credited with discovering the singer Anna Milder, the first Leonore in *Fidelio*, who was later to become world famous. He had first given her a part in his opera *Der Spiegel von Arkadien* in 1803.

The hope Braun had taken in his director and producer Sonnleithner was misplaced. The Harlequin pantomimes which the latter introduced were as poorly received as the operas which followed, mostly imports from France (among them Boieldieu's *Caliph of Bagdad*) or the run-of-the mill fare of comedies. Certainly it must have been with a heavy heart that Braun decided to recall his rival Schikaneder to succeed Sonnleithner as director. But Schikaneder's triumph was quickly dimmed as his new comedy *Die*

Hauer in Österreich (The Wine-Growers in Austria)—which received its first performance on September 1, 1804, the day he took up his post again—was another flop and was only repeated once. Schikaneder was trying a little patriotism: in the part of an old vintner Schikaneder endeavored to start a nationalistic campaign, saying that he would not grow any foreign grapes in his German vineyard, and that the young grape-growers should follow his example. Only his most faithful followers in the balcony weakly applauded this appeal; for the most part it was met with icy silence or catcalls. A mere four days later a revival of his opera *Der Stein der Weisen* turned into a similar fiasco. Baron Braun had already tried to win the public's favor with cavalcades and a variety of spectacles depending upon stage machinery, without success—not even the old-time "Schikanederei" any longer proved attractive. But Grétry's opera *Raoul der Blaubart* (Raoul the Bluebeard) did succeed and became a mainstay in the repertoire over the years. And indeed French Singspiel had gradually got the upper hand; every second work during Braun's era was translated from the French.

Schikaneder's return had already met with skepticism and resistance from the critics, particularly those oriented towards literature. But he did not give up, even if all he had to offer were variations on old themes. In the comedy *Licht und Schatten* (Light and Shadow) of March 1805 he repeatedly introduced cutting anti-French remarks, clearly aimed also at French opera. It is a farce about two brothers— the least likeable of the two, who is typically enough a rich landowner, has his children learn French and Italian first, and only later German.

But even the balcony refused its applause for this venture. When Schikaneder appeared before the curtain to take his bow, he was mercilessly booed. He was so shattered that he did something he would never have done before—he apologized for the bad play; he "had been ill" while writing it. At least so the paper *Der Freimütige* reported, but this newspaper was a voice speaking for the new rationalism and was anti-Schikaneder. Whether this report is true or not, the fact that Schikaneder's balance of mind could be questioned is significant.

The opera *Swetards Zaubertal* (Swetard's Magic Valley), first performed in July 1805 with music by A. F. Fischer (since lost), was repeated 41 times by September 1806, therefore a relatively good success for the 1805 season, which had otherwise been a financial catastrophe. As stage director Schikaneder came up with a new gimmick: he created a stage setting, making good use of the deep rear stage, which gave the illusion of a giant telescope through which the astonished public could look. But as librettist Schikaneder had so badly lost his nerve that he dropped his name from the program.

What a decline! The hoped-for savior of the Theater an der Wien had become anonymous. Yet the decline was to continue, although as an actor Schikaneder still trusted his well-tested abilities. At the end of 1804 he did not think it beneath him to play the main part in a trivial "Original Play" entitled *Cornelia d'Oromonte* by a certain Richter. Eipeldauer, ever true to Schikaneder, reports: "Here our merry Mr. Schikaneder wanted to show that he can also play serious roles . . . and he won general applause." In the same way, according to Eipeldauer, he "won general applause" in heroic roles during the year that followed. But other reviewers less supportive of Schikaneder saw the comedian as old-fashioned and lacking in subtlety. (Even *Tyroler Wastel* no longer went down well). Tastes had changed: Even Kasperl-Laroche who had evoked irrepressible laughter for almost a generation was now no longer fashionable.

Nothing seemed to work any more, not even a renewed attempt at grandiose "Schikanederei" staging for the first performance in August 1805 of the opera *Vesta's Fire*, which had been offered to Beethoven but was finally set by Josef Weigl (1766–1846). The latter, Haydn's godfather and a favorite of Gluck, had had immense success with his *Die Schweizerfamilie* (The Swiss Family) and was the highly respected Kapellmeister at the Kärntnertor Theater. As Schikaneder's partner he just rattled off what was conventional, as indeed Schikaneder's libretto had been.

The opera is set as an ancient Roman story of love, jealousy and murder in nine scenic transformations. The Roman Decemvir Romenius pursues the beautiful Volivia, but she has dedicated herself to the goddess Vesta. In the end it seems that brutality triumphs and that the man of power will destroy the temple, but he falls by the hand of an avenger, and Vesta's fire of the title is finally rekindled. Spontini's *La Vestale*, which followed in 1807, took up the same theme anew with spectacular success. Neither the subject nor Schikaneder's text was as absurd and foolish as Schikaneder's belittlers and even Komorzynski would have us believe. Certainly Beethoven's refusal to set it is entirely understandable, in view of the many scenic changes which seemed more important than any humanistic ethos. But anyone taking the trouble to plough through the manuscript, which has been preserved, must conclude that Komorzynski's sweeping judgment, ". . . the text was made up of words and verses without any real sense," was based on ignorance. The opinion expressed in the paper *Der Freimütige*, which had long been critical of Schikaneder (". . . a sorry effort, in which history and poetry, speech and versification have all been insulted in the same way"), seems to have been universally repeated.

In reality *Vesta's Fire* is on the level of Schikaneder's other opera texts after *The Magic Flute*. And in fact, the absence of stereotyped comic characters suggests an effort to achieve something higher, even if we now have to reckon with being "sublimely" bored. Still, the slave Malo is allowed to sing "Komm liebes Täubchen, komm" (Come little dove, come), clearly a true descendant of Monostatos. Every other character, however, pompously strides about in the thick boots of a tragic Athenian actor, a far cry from the humanity of Mozart's *Magic Flute*. But Schikaneder, the poet with hands full of grandiose scenes, here pays reluctant tribute to the fashion of the Opéra Comique. "All the set pieces must be lit so that they look like marble . . . the moon and the stars on the horizon are blood-red; to the left one also sees a sword and a comet . . . the Tiber also turns red"; these are some of the stage instructions by this imaginative man of the theater.

Die Kurgäste am Sauerbrunnen (The Visitors Taking the Waters), produced in April 1806, was a five-act comedy with music by the composer-publisher Diabelli, the strange partner of both Beethoven and Schubert. It was a further attempt to develop new effects from old patterns: there is an honorable peasant, a stupid wife, and a knavish, provincial governor. But all the jokes of the peasant, who feigns drunkenness and madness and was acted by Schikaneder, fell flat. The first performance was to have been a benefit for the director—an old theatrical custom which survived in the provincial theaters of Austria into the 20th century. The beneficiary was given a share of the evening's takings and received presents from his admirers, for which purpose a table was placed on the stage. But Schikaneder was again booed and laughed at after his benefit performance. He collapsed, and the curtain fell on his misery.

This was the sad end to his third and last period as director of the Theater an der Wien. He had not been able to rescue the house, as Baron von Braun had hoped. Braun was at his wits' end. The most significant premiere during his short reign at the Theater an der Wien was Beethoven's *Fidelio* on November 20, 1805, but it could hardly be called a success. The French had occupied Vienna, the imperial court and many of the aristocracy had fled: only a small audience, mostly foreigners, were in the theater, and they failed to understand the work.

Beethoven's radically shortened second version, *Leonore*, was no better received in March of the following year. Braun wanted to close the theater as early as the autumn of 1806, but the Emperor disallowed his petition as a police report had concluded that "the most dangerous hours of the day are the evening hours. They cannot be more harmlessly passed than in the theater." The 77th performance of *The Magic Flute* (altogether there had been 300 repeats by December 23, 1806) took place; it was to be Schikaneder's last appearance in the theater that he had planned and built. In the meantime Baron Braun had located a financially stable successor: a consortium of aristocratic "Cavaliers" which included the Princes Schwarzenberg, Lobkowitz and Esterházy, and the Counts Esterházy, Pálffy von Erdöd, Zichy and Lodron. This artistic elite of the Austrian aristocracy paid not less than 1.2 million florins for the theater, and took charge of the productions.

Thus in the end both Schikaneder and his arch-rival were defeated, but the banker was to survive his farewell from Vienna's most beautiful theater longer and less painfully than the actor.

In evaluating Schikaneder's five and a half years at the Theater an der Wien, we must not let the sad end distort the whole. That as a dramatist he was not able to achieve a second success of the calibre of *The Magic Flute* does not only lie in the fact that he could not find another Mozart as partner. His overtures to Beethoven might not have worked, for they were ideologically worlds apart. Further, Schikaneder's talent as a writer was exhausted, but not so his energy as a director and producer. The activities of the first six months of

The Papageno Gate of the Theater an der Wien reminds us even today of the founder and first director of this playhouse, rich in tradition.

1801 in fact marked his high point: no fewer than 53 new productions in six and a half months![31] Even if one bears in mind that many were simply taken over and adapted from the Freihaus Theater, such a burst of new performances is an almost unthinkable theatrical accomplishment by today's standards. Consider how much the actors had to memorize and with what the stage technicians had to cope! Fifteen works with texts by Schikaneder formed the backbone of the repertoire, which is also something of a record. Only after the backbone of the repertoire had been built up in 1802 out of old and new productions was Schikaneder able to reduce the flood of first nights in the new theater. But with 63 new productions—Mozart's *Don Giovanni*, Georg Benda's monodrama *Pygmalion* and Shakespeare's *Hamlet* were the highlights—the intense activity following the days of the Freihaus was kept up; this is also true of the years that followed: 1803, 64 premieres; 1804, 57; 1805, 46; 1806, 43. Schikaneder's output as an author began to decline sharply toward the end, as is reflected in the raw numbers. Even Braun had to allow nine Schikaneder works to be performed in 1804; in the two years that followed, three and two.

Schikaneder's progressive political-cultural concept, the cultivation of German opera in a popular and varied program, proved sound for a number of years, with many operas composed by the theater's resident staff: Seyfried, Benda, Dittersdorf, and of course, Mozart. But Schikaneder was in the end unable to prevent the vogue of French opera, which he disliked, from setting the tone. Names which today figure mostly in history books—d'Alayrac, Gaveaux, Méhul, Cherubini—were far more popular then, even with Volkstheater audiences, than, for example, Gluck. In spoken drama the German classics, and even Shakespeare, were forced to give way to popular comedies (Kotzebue was becoming an increasingly lucrative box office draw) and to the current tearjerkers and plays about knights. The huge theater had to be filled and so Schikaneder gave way.

The fact that Shakespeare's *Henry IV*, *King Lear* and *Julius Caesar*, Goethe's *Götz*, Schiller's *Räuber*, *Jungfrau von Orléans* and *Wilhelm Tell*; and Kleist's *Kätchen von Heilbronn* were first played at the Theater an der Wien after Schikaneder's departure, but yet in his lifetime, cannot be held against him. Many factors contributed to this outcome: for example, some of these plays were only later approved by the censors. His greatest contribution is found in his concept of popular theater of higher quality, which he first developed in the modest Freihaustheater and then transferred to his new house, and which had a lasting effect in spite of all the vagaries of fashion.

The leap over the narrow Wien river which the Freihaus director had invited his public to take, was to lead him to the height of his career. His decline should not let us overlook his accomplishments, to which the Theater an der Wien, so rich in tradition, still bears witness.[32]

9 Decline and End

"How much more beautiful Vienna has become in the last 20 years! Almost new and beautifully rebuilt squares have been created; a number of splendid buildings can be seen more readily because the shabby structures surrounding them have been removed. It is truly a great and magnificent city!" Such was the enthusiasm of the renowned north German composer Johann Friedrich Reichardt when he visited the capital of the Habsburg monarchy in 1808. Three years previously Francis I had laid aside the Roman and German Imperial crown, content with only that of Austria.

Vienna, including the suburbs, had a population of a good 300,000 (80,000 inhabitants were crowded into the inner city by a 600-foot-wide bastion); after London and Paris it was the third-largest city in Europe. It had at least that rank as a city of the theater.

In their spontaneous enjoyment of the theater, the Viennese may actually have been world champions. There is no reason not to believe the testimony of an expert like Friedrich Ludwig Schröder, who for five years directed the Burgtheater: "This waiting for their favorite, this insisting on silence before an important speech. . . . this loud, long, often repeated outbreak of thunderous applause when at last that which they had waited for has been accomplished . . ." At the time the Viennese were already mad about the theater, particularly the suburban theaters, because they also served as meeting places. "Things were especially merry in the balcony where people noisily devoured their sausages and drank beer, even during the performance. Other forms of pleasure were, without any embarrassment, enjoyed as well: out of consideration for the wishes of the public, the auditorium was not lit, so Viennese roués from all social levels demonstrated their gratitude for such understanding by frequent attendance."[33]) This account of the Leopoldstadt Theater leaves no doubt that audiences were scarcely more prudish in lusty Schikaneder's theater.

Coffee houses had for years been the indispensable meeting places of the Viennese. Later literary cafes, such as the simple Kramer cafe, known as the "coffee cavern", emerged as well. Early in the 19th century the "Neuner" became its rival which was later ennobled, so to say, by Raimund and Grillparzer. In Schikaneder's Vienna, literary productivity lagged far behind that of music and the theater, though modest literary salons began to emerge. Characteristically the first Viennese salon was created by a newcomer from Berlin, Fanny Arnstein, in her banker husband's mansion in the Graben; she was a relative of Mendelssohn. Later Caroline Pichler, the writer whom Mme de Staël on a visit to Vienna ironically called "La Muse du Faubourg," was able to attract both Dorothea Schlegel and Grillparzer to her little literary circle in the Alser suburb.

But what significance can be attached to such elite literary groups when compared with the Viennese passion for dancing? Off and on, for almost 20 years, Austria had been at war with the French. The war, God be praised, was for the most part far away; but the constant conflict led to the emergence of a "third estate" of newly rich— mostly real estate speculators and army suppliers. They, with their hangers-on, were to become a significant element in the social and cultural life of the city. Their full purses stimulated and enlivened every establishment devoted to entertainment. The most luxurious of these were the fashionable dance halls, where the new rich and the socially frustrated worked off steam in like company (often in the old Viennese way, *with* each other).

Although the "Mehllucken," frequented by aristocrats, prostitutes and petty-bourgeois alike, had been in a state of decline since 1800, the "Sperl" and many other like establishments were in good health. The Congress of Vienna was not responsible for the dance craze as is often stated, as "all Vienna" had danced, from archduke to chambermaid, for years. Astonishingly enough, they danced to quite staid music; the waltz which was to set fire to all Europe after Strauss, Sr. and Jr., had not yet appeared: only the stolid German "Ländler". The bandage manufacturer Wolffsohn saw the financial possibilities of the rampant dance madness and in 1808 erected the Apollosaal, which was to provide the most important venue for generations of dancing Viennese and also for the triumph of the Strauss waltzes. With its five large halls and no less than 24 smaller rooms, the Apollosaal was a real monstrosity, and a testimonial to the Viennese craving for pleasure.

At night the Viennese still had to feel their way home through dark and narrow streets, because the gas lights which had been publicly installed beginning in 1803 did not function properly and were not in general use until 14 years later. The theaters must have been equally gloomy, even on the stage. None of the scenic wonders of "Schikanederei" took place in radiant brightness, but rather in dim light that reminds one of the homely parlor. Beginning in 1783 an effort was made to brighten the dim candlelight with so-called "Argand Lamps" which threw their light on the stage from the wings. But by present-day standards we can only marvel at the vivid imagination of Schikaneder's public, which was never able to see its favorites under the "spotlight." It is also astonishing that before the horrifying Ring Theater fire of 1881 there were not often similar catastrophes, what with the flammable scenery and costumes all in close proximity to candles. The cause of that conflagration was a stream of fire, fed from the open rear stage that quickly spread to engulf the audience. Such a holocaust might easily have been sparked off in presenting the so-called "Rosskomödien" (horse comedies) of Schikaneder's successors at the Theater an der Wien. The depth of the stage in this theater was greater than that of any other in Vienna, and was exploited to the full in that the backstage door to the street was left open, enabling steeds and riders to gallop in right up to the footlights. In 1808, while the theater was under the direction of a consortium of highly aristocratic "cavaliers", one of the riding extras galloped right into the orchestra pit.

But neither such accidents as befell his successors at the Theater an der Wien, nor the Viennese half-euphoric, half-frustrated passion for spectacle and dancing which spread like an epidemic after the military defeat at Austerlitz, helped Schikaneder; he was unable to make use of them in his own theater business. Nor did he notice that a new generation of dramatists were beginning to establish themselves. Gleich, Meisl and Bäuerle—who were they, compared to him? But step by step, he was on the way out. Previously unnoticed playwrights, in company with the Leopoldstadt Theater under Hensler's direction, were slowly and steadily gaining a place in the sun. This resident trio of dramatists, whom the historian Otto Rommel called "the great three" before Raimund and Nestroy, were paving the way to the future.

They represented the younger generation of popular theater—an in-between generation. Save for Karl Meisl's (1785–1853) "Mythologische Karikaturen" in which the secularization of illustrious Olympians may be seen to anticipate Offenbach's inspired operettas, or Adolf Bäuerle's (1786–1859) "Kasperl" comedy in which the comic role of "Stabel" was created by Ignaz Schuster, they produced nothing essentially new when compared with Schikaneder. All three were extraordinarily productive: Josef Alois Gleich (1772–1841), the least gifted of the three, produced no fewer than 230 plays and 100 novels. In his case we can discover how at the time playwrights were bled dry by their directors. He was a highly successful author, but his director, Carl, admittedly one of the most businesslike and stingiest in his line, paid him only 100 florins for a play which had over 100 performances and in fact was a hit, while even mediocre actors in the time after Schikaneder could earn 200 florins a month, plus 400 florins a year as a housing allowance. Gleich, and Bäuerle, who as editor of the *Wiener Theater-Zeitung* was able to extend his influence via the published word and who wrote many parts for Raimund, both died in poverty, in spite of their huge output—a new age had overtaken them in their turn, for Nestroy had raised the quality of mass-produced comedies with his incomparable wit.

Schikaneder played no active part in all of this, even in the years before the Congress of Vienna. Immediately after his breakdown at the Theater an der Wien he left the city in which he had spent his best years and had given of the best of his creative talents. He must have been pleased to be asked to take over the direction of the municipal theater in Brünn (Brno) on March 22, 1807, even though it was a step down to move to the provinces. Brünn, surrounded by medieval walls and of middling size, was virtually a German town at the time and could boast a theater culture reaching back to the early 18th century, supported by wealthy German patrician families; but trouble had recently started to brew—no theater leaseholder could hold out for more than two years.

In the end Schikaneder could not either. He had brought a small company with him, including the loyal Perinet and his nephew Karl. Initially the public greeted the famous man jubilantly. Schikaneder tried to live up to his laurels by performing the usual routine repertoire, beginning with old tearjerkers, and when these no longer drew the crowds, with grandiose "Schikanederei." In a newly written play called *Die Schweden vor Brünn. Ein wahres Gemälde voriger Zeiten, worin Vaterlandsliebe und Tapferkeit unserer Vorfahren mit Wahrheit dargestellt werden* (The Swedes at the Gates of Brünn. True Portrait of Earlier Times, in which Our Forefathers, Love of Fatherland and Courage are Truthfully Represented) he flattered both the patriotism and love of spectacle of Brünn's citizenry. Three hundred cavalry and infantry filled the small stage, but that was not enough: he had a vast open-air stage with two rows of boxes erected in a meadow near the neighboring village of Kumrowitz, and there put on *The Swedes Before the Gates of Brünn* with even more extras in uniform and with thundering cannons. He also played his two old hits, *Graf Waltron* and *Grandprofoss*.

What madness it was, to try to transplant the Viennese craving for theatrical extravaganza to the small-town environment of Brünn—it would have been more suited to a Baroque potentate. But quite simply Schikaneder could do nothing else. Clearly he was losing that theatrical judgment which had served him so well, even if he had not lost his mind. As an author he could only think of new versions of old models. He may well have had the Regensburg *Dollinger* success in mind when he staged the patriotic knightly play *Friedegilde, Königin von Mähren* (Friedehilde, Queen of Moravia). His very last work, *Schembera, Herr von Boskowitz* (Schembera, Master of Boskowitz), was "an allegory in four acts suitable for the open air," carelessly written, once again mobilizing all the tried-and-true theatrical ingredients, including magicians, poison, and crowd scenes. But there were not enough paying seat holders in Brünn to make the vast expenditure worthwhile. It was better when Schikaneder transformed the traditional carnival balls at the Redoute in the Krautmarkt into scenes never before dreamed of, with processions on horseback, floating artificial clouds and, as the great sensation, a real air balloon in the middle of the hall. The Berlin journal *Der Freimüthige* reported in 1808, when it announced Schikaneder's departure from Brünn, "the public seems to be very dissatisfied with the administration to date." Whether Schikaneder was financially ruined or not we do not know—but he gave notice himself.

And why not, as he was given yet another opportunity to reconquer Vienna. He was to manage a new Viennese theater, as the little playhouse in the Josefstadt, which had previously played second fiddle to the other suburban theaters, was to be pulled down and rebuilt more generously, and Schikaneder was to be its new director. But this was never to be. Building permission was refused, and thereafter other disasters brought on by the war befell Schikaneder. During the first occupation of Vienna in 1805 the French had been viewed as arrogant but tolerable conquerors, and the Viennese harbored no real hatred of the enemy, but this perception was to be radically changed. The terrible battle of Wagram (1809) left Vienna trembling under the bombardment of heavy artillery. Fear and hatred spread. The French and their allies of the southern German states had occupied Schikaneder's stately little home in Nussdorf and were using it like barbarians. He was forced to sell the devastated and depreciated estate at a great loss, as he was once again in debt. It was of no help to him that Hensler was raking in box office takings at the Leopoldstadt Theater, his former competition, with performances of old Schikaneder plays (*Die Fiaker von Wien*, *Der Tyroler Wastel*, and *Die bürgerlichen Brüder* among others) because author's royalties had not yet come into practice. He may have derived some satisfaction from knowing that "his" Theater an der Wien, directed by the "cavaliers", was rapidly going downhill, whereas *The Magic Flute* was repeatedly given in new productions: Hensler produced it regularly, and in the summer of 1811 the Hoftheater at the Kärntnertor even entered into competition with the Theater an der Wien with a new *Magic Flute* (at the former house, Tamino was played as a "trouser role," sung by the famous Anna Milder!).

The original librettist received nothing out of these revivals and was probably not even aware of them, for his hopes to become the director of the Josefstadt Theater had foundered and his spirit was broken. The infamous bankruptcy law of March 15, 1811, affected hundreds of thousands of other Austrians, and was responsible for Schikaneder's financial ruin. The decree led to the worst inflation of the century: overnight all savings, all official salaries were devalued to the tune of 5 to 1. After the experiences of the 20th century, which in 1922 left Germans juggling in a lunatic fashion with millions and billions, this seems a very mild devaluation. But the Austrians were hit catastrophically. The thought that the decades-long wars with France would have to be paid for sometime must have occurred to anyone of reasonable intelligence, but although Maria Theresia had started to meet the huge war debt by introducing paper money, the Habsburg regime had managed to "muddle through" quite successfully. Prices certainly rose, but gradually, not shockingly. To return to the theater: the Leopoldstadt programs tell us that between 1791 and 1804, the ticket price for a small box only rose from 2 florins 30 kreuzer to 3 florins, and the first orchestra rows from 34 to 36 kreuzer. After losing the battle of Austerlitz Austria had to cede Venice and the Tyrol, which reduced tax revenues and led to a compulsory loan of 75 million florins, following which the value of the currency began to fall.

The devaluation of 1811 hit all who had savings, all civil servants, and the lower aristocracy in government service. A wave of suicides and emigration was the immediate result. Schikaneder might have salvaged some of his fortune from the sale of his little mansion, but that too was gone. His customary energy seemed to flow away; only once did he manage to pull himself together, when the patrician families in the Hungarian city of Pest built a new German theater and offered him the directorship. With his wife he travelled down the Danube to the Hungarian capital, but the opening of the theater in February 1812 took place without him. During the journey the madness which could no longer be hidden by vainglorious talks of future plans finally and openly overtook him. In Pest his speech was confused and he no longer recognized anyone. At least the theater patrons had the grace to give the sick man's wife a small sum of money.

This gift just about covered their journey home—but what then? Eleonore Schikaneder, who had so often been humiliated by her husband, now proved herself to be a loyal and brave companion. There was nothing more for them in Vienna. She tried her best to obtain for him the management of the theater in Steyr in Upper Austria—far away, in "the province." But Schikaneder had become so deranged that he wrecked all her plans, literally-speaking: he ordered the carpenters to destroy the stage scenery with axes. And so after all Vienna, their adopted home, became their last port of call. The couple came to rest in a rented apartment at the Nerbass house, No. 30 in the Alser suburb (today Florianigasse 10). Schikaneder lived for another nine months; his nephew Karl remembered that "his foolishness gave way to quiet madness." Hensler, his former rival who was now the successful director of the Leopoldstadt Theater, was decent enough to come to the aid of this entirely destitute man, giving him the box office takings of a benefit performance of *The Swedes Before the Gates of Brünn*, and the new management of the Theater an der Wien honored the service of its founder with a four percent royalty from performances of *The Magic Flute*—quite unusual at the time, and only done out of charity.

Schikaneder, listless and enfeebled, let everything pass him by. "From morning until evening he sat without moving in his miserable apartment, enveloped in a sheet which covered his head. When a visitor appeared, he stretched his head out of the sheet, stared at the visitor and asked: 'Did you know Maria Theresia and Emperor Joseph?' If the answer was in the affirmative he would utter a few confused words and then disappear under the sheet again, but if the answer to his question was negative, he would vanish in even greater haste, without saying a word."[34]

Emanuel Schikaneder died in his apartment on September 21, 1812, from "nervous collapse," as it was described in the official death certificate. He had formerly been made of money, a Croesus of the theater, but he died as poor as a beggar. The furniture was the property of the landlady, the clothes and books that he left were valued at 71 florins; "of ready cash there was nothing." Singers from the Theater an der Wien paid their last respects by performing Mozart's *Requiem* at his obsequies. There was only enough money for a pauper's funeral and a communal grave in the Währinger Cemetery. His famous *Magic Flute* partner had fared no better. Schikaneder shared with his friend Mozart the same fate: no stone, no cross reveals where he is buried.

The first obituaries written in Vienna dealt with the deceased more as an object of pity than as an artist. This was the case with the publisher and dramatist-colleague Adolf Bäuerle and also Schikaneder's old friend Joseph Richter, who now as "Eipeldauer, Junior" wrote and told his relatives about recent news in the city of Vienna: "Our good Emanuel Schikaneder has played his last part here, as actor and man . . . and has taken his fame with him to the grave. He did not know the first two syllables of his own name: [chicanery—ed.] he was a good fellow."

Eleonore Schikaneder survived her husband by nine years, his brother Urban by five, and his nephew Karl, who had a modest career at the Leopoldstadt Theater and in Prague as a Basso buffo, by 33 years.

Every now and then, apart from *The Magic Flute*, works from Schikaneder's pen which had fallen into such disrepute were performed far into the 19th century. But it took much longer for posterity to realize that although he had aroused pity as "a good fellow" he was also a good dramatist, and a truly great man of the theater.

Notes

1. Jakob Neukäufler. *Aus dem Leben eines deutschen Wanderschauspielers*. Linz, 1930, p. 42 ff.
2. Schikaneder probably only appeared for the second time as stage composer with his own (now lost) Singspiel *Das Urianische Schloss* in Salzburg, 1786. On the occasion of a performance in the Leopoldstadt Theater the composer there at the time, Wenzel Müller, mentioned in his diary of 1787 that both text and music were by Schikaneder.
3. Doubts by the author of this book led to a clarification in 1983: an inquiry in the Theater Collection at the Austrian National Library produced the information that Johann Rautenstrauch was the author of this *Teufel von Wien*.
4. Richard Waldegg, *Sittengeschichte von Wien*. 4th edition, Stuttgart, 1965, p. 189 ff.
5. *Was spielten die Theater? Spielpläne in der Bundesrepublik Deutschland, 1947–1975*. Köln, 1978.
6. Two other members of the Schikaneder family were also involved; Brother Urban sang the First Priest and his daughter Anna, known as Nanny, the First Boy. The opening night playbill does not mention the three boys. Anna Schikaneder, who later had a modest career as a singer and died at the age of 95 in Regensburg, was incorrectly identified as Schikaneder's daughter in Constant von Wurzbach's *Biographisches Lexikon des Kaiserthums Österreich* in 1895.
7. *Monatshefte des Musiktheaters Frankfurt am Main*, 1977/78, p. 32.
8. Hans-Albrecht Koch, "Goethes Fortsetzung der Schikanederschen Zauberflöte." *Jahrbuch des Freien deutschen Hochstiftes*. Tübingen, 1969, p. 124.

9. Erich Neumann, "Archetypische Symbolik des Matriarchalischen und des Patriarchalischen in der Zauberflöte." In: *Wolfgang Amadeus Mozart, Die Zauberflöte*. Reinbek, 1982, p. 235 ff.

10. Egon Komorzynski, *Emanuel Schikaneder*. Vienna, 1951, p. 89 ff.

11. Götz Friedrich, *Die Zauberflöte in Der Inszenierung Walter Felsensteins an der Komischen Oper Berlin 1954*. Berlin, 1958, p. 40.

12. Tomislav Volek, "Die erste Aufführung der Zauberflöte in tschechischer Sprache in Prag *1794*." *Mozart-Jahrbuch*, 1967. Stuttgart, 1968, p. 387 ff.

13. Constant von Wurzbach, *Biographisches Lexikon des Kaiserthums Österreich*. Wien, 1875, p. 300 ff.

14. Quoted from Rainer Riehn, *Musikkonzepte*, Heft 3. München, 1978, p. 67.

15. The garden house, which has been renovated many times, stands today in the garden of the Mozarteum in Salzburg.

16. Otto Rommel, *Das Alt-Wiener Volkstheater*. Wien, 1952, p. 497 ff.

17. After 1945 the melody to Schikaneder's words, "Brüder, reicht die Hand zum Bunde," with a new text by Paula Preradovic, became the national anthem of the Austrian Republic.

18. Friedrich Dieckmann, "Der entlaufene Schneiderssohn oder Wer schrieb die 'Zauberflöte?'" In: *Oper 1981*. Velber, 1981.

19. Julius Cornet, *Die Oper in Deutschland und das Theater der Neuzeit*. Hamburg, 1849.

20. Wolfgang Hildesheimer, *Mozart*. Frankfurt/Main, 1977, p. 335.

21. E. J. Dent, *Mozart's Opera "The Magic Flute."* Cambridge, 1911.

22. Rommel, see note 16, p. 982 ff.

23. Otto Erich Deutsch, "Der rätselhafte Giesecke" in *Musikforschung* V. Kassel, 1952, p. 152 ff.

24. Rommel, see note 16, p. 990.

25. Rommel, see note 16, p. 981.

26. Carl Bär, *Mozart. Krankheit-Tod-Begräbnis*. Salzburg, 1966, p. 119 ff.

27. Egon Komorzynski, see note 10, p. 267.

28. In his list of works, Komorzynski gives the year 1794, but Otto Erich Deutsch, in his more accurate list of new productions at the Wiedner Theater *(Das Freihaus Theater auf der Wieden 1787–1801*. Wien, 1937), does not mention the work at all.

29. Adolf Bäuerle, *Memoiren*. Wien, 1858, volume 1, p. 112 ff.

30. Ignaz von Castelli, *Aus dem Leben eines Wiener Phäaken*. 3rd edition, Stuttgart, 1912, p. 81 ff.

31. Anton Bauer, *150 Jahre Theater an der Wien*. Zürich-Leipzig-Wien, 1952, p. 267 ff.

32. The old house (number 26) was rebuilt in 1901 by the well known firm of theater architects, Fellner and Helmer, into a modern rococo-style apartment house with commercial space. During World War II the

theater was partially destroyed by bombs, but was quickly rebuilt and modernized. Until 1955 it served as a substitute theater for the Staatsoper on the Ring, which had been much more badly damaged. Many notable productions were staged there, particularly Mozart operas. Later it became the principal theater of the festival of Vienna and the home of musicals.

33. Richard Waldegg, see note 4. p. 268.
34. Realis, *Kuriositätenlexikon von Wien.* Wien, 1846, p. 304. Quoted after Constant von Wurzbach, see note 13, p. 300 ff.

List of Works

1. **Librettos for Operas and Singspiele; Plays with Music.** O =
opera, Si = Singspiel, Opt = operetta. Date indicates first performance.

Die Lyranten oder das lustige Elend (The Minstrels or Merry Misery) Opt (3
acts). Music: Emanuel Schikaneder. Innsbruck, 1775.

Der Müllertomerl oder Das Bergmädchen (*Kaspar der Müllertomerl*) (The Miller's
Boy or The Girl from the Mountains). Rustic O. Music: Jakob Josef
Haibel. 1785(?)

Der Luftballon (The Air Balloon). Opt (3). Music: Benedikt Schack.
Kempten, 1786.

Das Urianische Schloss (The Urian Castle). Si. Music: Emanuel Schikaneder
(?) Salzburg, 1786 (?)

Die drei Ringe oder Kaspar, der lächerliche Mundkoch (The Three Rings, or
Kaspar the Ridiculous Cook). Si. Music: B. Schack. Salzburg, 1787.

Lorenz und Suschen (Lorenz and Suschen). Si. Music: B. Schack. Salzburg,
1787(?)

Der Krautschneider (The Cabbage [or Herb] Cutter) Comic Si (4). Music: B.
Schack. Regensburg, 1788.

Der dumme Gärtner aus dem Gebirge oder die zween Anton (The Silly Gardener
from the Hills or The Two Antons). Comic O (2). Music: B. Schack,
Franz Xaver Gerl. Vienna, 1789.

Jakob und Nannerl oder Der angenehme Traum (Jakob and Nannerl or The
Pleasant Dream). Comic O (3). Music: B. Schack. Vienna, 1789.

Die verdeckten Sachen (Hidden Things). Comic O (2). Music: B. Schack,
F. X. Gerl. Vienna, 1789.

Was macht der Anton im Winter? (What Does Anton Do in Winter?) Comic O
(2). Music: B. Schack, F. X. Gerl. Vienna, 1790.

Die schöne Isländerin oder Der Mufti von Samarkanda (The Beautiful Lady from Iceland or The Mufti from Samarkand). Magic comedy with songs. Music:? Vienna, 1790.

Der Fall ist noch weit seltner oder Die geplagten Ehemänner (The Case is Much Stranger, or Pestered Husbands). Sequel to Martin y Soler's *Una cosa rara*. O (2). Music: B. Schack. Vienna, 1790.

Der Frühling oder der Anton ist noch nicht tot (Spring, or Anton Is Not Yet Dead). Comic O. Music: B. Schack, F. X. Gerl and others (?). Vienna, 1790.

Der Stein der Weisen oder die Zauberinsel (The Wisemen's Stone or The Magic Isle). Heroic-comic O (2). Music: B.Schack, F. X. Gerl. Vienna, 1790.

Anton bei Hofe oder Das Namensfest (Anton at Court or The Nameday Celebration). Comic O (2). Music: B. Schack. Vienna, 1791.

Die Zauberflöte (The Magic Flute). Grand O (2). Music: Mozart. Vienna, 1791.

Der redliche Landmann (The Honest Countryman). Rustic family play with music. Music: Johann Baptist Henneberg. Vienna, 1792.

Johanna von Weimar (Johanna of Weimar). Knight play with music. (8) Music: J. B. Henneberg. Vienna, 1792.

Der Renegat oder Anton in der Türkei (The Renegade or Anton in Turkey). Comic O (2). Music: B. Schack. Vienna, 1792.

Die Kriegsgesetze oder Die deutsche Griechin (Rules of War or the German Greek Lady). Military scenes with songs (3). Music:? Vienna, 1792.

Die Eisen-Königin (The Iron Queen). Magic O. (3). Music: J. B. Henneberg. Vienna, 1793.

Der Zauberpfeil oder Das Kabinett der Wahrheit (The Magic Arrow or The Cabinet of Truth). Grand O (2). Music: Johann Georg Lickl. Vienna, 1793.

Der wohltätige Derwisch oder Die Schellenkappe ("Die Zaubertrommel") (The Charitable Dervish or The Cap and Bells—The Magic Drum). Magic O (3). Music: B. Schack, J. B. Henneberg (F. X. Gerl?). Vienna, 1793.

Die Waldmänner (The Woodmen). Comic O (3). Music: J. B. Henneberg. Vienna, 1793.

Die Hirten am Rhein (Shepherds on the Rhine). Magic O (2). Music:? Vienna, 1794.

Der Spiegel von Arkadien (The Mirror of Arcady). Grand heroic-comic O (2). Music: Franz Xaver Süssmayr. Vienna, 1794.

Das Häuschen im Walde oder Antons Reise nach seinem Geburtsort (The Hut in the Woods or Anton's Journey to His Birthplace). Comic O (2). Music: B. Schack. Vienna, 1795.

Der Scherenschleifer (The Scissor Sharpener). Carnival O (2). Music: J. B. Henneberg. Vienna, 1795.

Der Königssohn aus Ithaka (The King's Son from Ithaca). Grand heroic-comic O (2). Music: Franz Anton Hoffmeister. Vienna, 1795.

Der Höllenberg oder Prüfung und Lohn (The Mountain of Hell or Trial and Reward). Heroic-comic O (2). Music: Josef Wölfl. Vienna, 1795.

Der Tyroler Wastel (Wastel the Tyrolean). O (3). Music: Jakob Josef Haibel. Vienna, 1796.

Österrreichs treue Brüder oder die Scharfschützen von Tyrol (Austria's Faithful Brothers or The Sharpshooters from Tyrol). Patriotic Si (2). Music: J. J. Haibel. Vienna, 1796.

Das medizinische Konsilium (The Medical Council). Comic O (2). Music: J. J. Haibel. Vienna, 1797.

Der Löwenbrunn (The Lion's Well). Heroic-comic O (2). Music: Ignaz von Seyfried. Vienna, 1797.

Babylons Pyramiden (Babylon's Pyramids). Grand heroic-comic O (2). Music: Johann Gallus-Mederitsch, Peter von Winter. Vienna, 1797.

Das Labyrinth oder Der Kampf mit den Elementen (The Labyrinth or The Struggle with the Elements) (Sequel to *The Magic Flute*). Heroic-comic O (2). Music: P. v. Winter. Vienna, 1798.

Die Ostindier vom Spittelberg (The East Indians from the Spittelberg), *Die Rückkehr aus Ostindien* (The Return from East India). Comic Si (2). Music: I. v. Seyfried, Matthäus Stegmayer and others. Vienna, 1799.

Konrad Langbart von Friedburg oder Der Berggeist (Konrad Langbart from Friedburg or The Mountain Ghost). Knightly drama with songs (3). Music: J. B. Henneberg. Vienna, 1799.

Mina und Peru oder die Königspflicht (Mina and Peru or The King's Duty). Heroic-comic Si (2). Music: J. B. Henneberg, I. v. Seyfried. Vienna, 1799.

Der Papagey und die Gans oder Die zisalpinischen Perücken (The Parrot and the Goose or The Wigs from this Side of the Alps). Rustic-comic family portrait with songs (3). Music: J. J. Haibel. Vienna, 1799.

Der Wundermann am Rheinfall (The Miracle Man at the Rheinfall). Grand comic O (2). Music: I. v. Seyfried. Vienna, 1799.

Die Spinnerin am Gatterhölzl oder der Stock-im-Eisen-Platz (The Woman Spinner in Gatterhölzl or Stock-im-Eisen Square). Austrian folk legend with songs (3). Music:? Vienna, 1800.

Amors Schiffchen in der Brigittenaue (Amor's Little Ship in the Brigittenaue). Comic O (1). Music: I. v. Seyfried. Vienna, 1800.

Proteus und Arabiens Söhne (Proteus and Arabia's Sons). Magic Si (3). Music: I. v. Seyfried, M. Stegmayer. Vienna, 1801.

Thespis. Epilogue (1). Music: A. F. Fischer. Vienna, 1801.

Thespis' Traum (Thespis's Dream) Prologue (1). Music: A. F. Fischer. Vienna, 1801.

Alexander. Grand heroic O (2). Music: Franz Teyber. Vienna, 1801.

Tsching! Tsching!. Si (3). Music: J. J. Haibel. Vienna, 1802.

Die Entlarvten (The Unmasked Ones). Si. (3) Music: A. F. Fischer. Vienna, 1803.

Die Pfändung oder Der Personalarrest (The Seizure or The Arrest). Comic O (2). Music: F.Teyber. Vienna, 1803.

Swetards Zaubertal (Swetard's Magic Valley). Grand O (2). Music: A. F. Fischer. Vienna, 1805.

Vestas Feuer (Vesta's Fire). Grand heroic O (2). Music: Joseph Weigl. Vienna, 1805.

Die Kurgäste am Sauerbrunnen (Guests Taking the Waters at Sauerbrunnen). Opt (5). Music: Anton Diabelli. Vienna, 1806.

Das Zaubermädchen in Schreywald (The Magic Girl in Schreywald). O (libretto examined by the censors Brünn, 1809).

Das Fest der Götter (The Feast of the Gods). Satyrical O (libretto censored Brünn, 1809).

2. **Spoken Plays** Dr= drama, C=comedy, Tr=tragedy.

Der junge Siegwart (Young Siegwart). Dr (5). Nürnberg, 1779.

Das Regensburger Schiff (The Regensburg Ship). C (3). Salzburg, 1780.

Die Raubvögel (Birds of Prey). Dr (5). First performance unknown. Printed Salzburg, 1783.

Das Laster kömmt am Tage (Vice Is Revealed). Dr (4). First performance unknown. Printed Salzburg, 1783.

Philippine Welserin, die schöne Herzogin von Tyrol (Philippine Welser, the Beautiful Duchess from Tyrol). Dr (5). Augsburg(?), 1780.

Herzog Ludwig von Steyermark oder Sarmäts Feuerbär (Duke Ludwig of Steyermark or Sarmät's Fire Bear). Dr (4). City unknown, 1781.

Der Bucentaurus oder Die Vermählung mit dem Meere in Venedig (The Bucentaurus or The Marriage with the Sea in Venice). "*Dolmaros Nachtgespenst* (Dolmaros Night Ghost). Dr Pressburg(?), 1784.

Eltern, reizet eure Kinder, und Kinder, reizet eure Eltern nicht (Parents, Do Not Provoke Your Children; Children, Do Not Provoke Your Parents). Tr. Pressburg, 1784.

Vogelkomödie (Bird Comedy). Pressburg, 1784.

Der Grandprofoss (The Grand Provost). Tr. (4) ? (before 1785), printed 1787.

König Attila oder die Hexe von Augsburg (King Attila or The Witch from Augsburg). Historical Dr (4). 1783–1787(?)

Die getreuen Untertanen oder Der ehrliche Bandit (The Faithful Subjects or The Honest Bandit). C (3). First performance unknown. Printed 1792.

Die Postknechte oder die Hochzeit ohne Braut (The Postmen or The Wedding Without a Bride). C (5). First performance unknown. Printed 1792.

Die Schneckenpost (Snail's Pace Mail). Carnival play (3). 1783–1787(?).

Der Hauspummer. 1783–1787(?)

Der Hauszins oder Der Schneider als Protecteur (The Rent or The Tailor as Protector). C (4). 1783–1787(?)

Hanns Dollinger oder Das heimliche Blutgericht (Hans Dollinger or The Secret Blood Feud). Dr (3). Regensburg, 1788.

Das Schwert der Gerechtigkeit (The Sword of Justice). A scene from antiquity (4). Vienna, 1790.

Das Schokolade-Mädchen (The Chocolate Girl). C (2). Vienna, 1792.

Das abgebrannte Haus (The Burnt-Down House). C (1). Vienna, 1792.

Die Fiaker in Wien (The Coachmen in Vienna). C (5). Vienna, 1792.

Die Fiaker in Wien (The Coachmen in Vienna) Pt II. C (5). Vienna, 1793.

Die Fiaker in Baden (The Coachmen in Baden). C (4). Vienna, 1793.

Die Schneckenhändler aus Schwaben (The Snail Dealers from Swabia). C (2). Vienna, 1794.

Die Verwirrung im Gasthofe (Confusion at the Inn). C (1). Vienna, 1794.

Der Fleischhauer von Ödenburg (The Butcher from Ödenburg). C. Vienna, 1794(?)

Die Fürstenmutter (The Prince's Mother). C (4). Vienna, 1794.

Lumpen und Fetzen (Rags and Tatters). C. Vienna, 1794.

Der Hausfrieden (Peace at Home) (Part II of *Das abgebrannte Haus*). C (3). Vienna, 1795.

Die Kaufmannsbude (The Merchant's Booth). C (4). Vienna, 1796.

Die bürgerlichen Brüder oder Die Frau aus Krems (The Bourgeois Brothers or The Woman from Krems). Bourgeois family portrait (5). Vienna, 1797.

Der Teufel in Wien (The Devil in Vienna). C (3). Vienna, 1799.

Die Reise nach Steiermark (The Journey to Styria) (Part II of *Der Teufel in Wien*). Rustic C (5). Vienna, 1799.

Mutter und Tochter als Nebenbuhlerinnen (Mother and Daughter as Rivals). C (3). Vienna, 1800.

Die Mittag-und Abendtafel im Prater (The Midday and Evening Meal in the Prater). C (1). Vienna, 1800.

Das Medaillon (The Medallion). C (1). Vienna, 1800.

Der Goldmacher (The Gold Maker). C. Vienna, 1801.

Spass und Ernst (In Jest and in Earnest). C. Vienna, 1803.

Die Hauer in Österreich (The Winegrowers in Austria). C (4). Vienna, 1804.

Licht und Schatten (Light and Shadow). C (4). Vienna, 1805.

Die Schweden vor Brünn (The Swedes Before the Gates of Brünn). D. Brünn, 1807.

Schembera, Herr von Boskowitz (Schembera, Master of Boskowitz). Allegorical D (4). Brünn, 1808.

Das letzte Gericht (The Last Judgment). Brünn, 1808(?)

Schemberas Geist (Schembera's Ghost). Brünn, 1808.

Friedegilde, Königin von Mähren (Friedegilde, Queen of Moravia). Brünn, 1808.

Bibliography

Abert, Hermann. *W. A. Mozart.* 5th ed. of O. Jahn's *Mozart.* Leipzig, 1921.

Bär, Carl. *Mozart. Krankheit—Tod—Begräbnis.* Salzburg, 1966.

Bauer, Anton. *150 Jahre Theater a.d. Wien.* Wien, 1952.

Bauer, Anton. *Opern und Operetten in Wien.* Graz, Köln, 1955.

Bäuerle, Adolf *Memoiren.* Wien, 1858.

Blümml, Emil K. *Aus Mozarts Freundeskreis.* Wien, Prag, Leipzig, 1923.

Brukner, Fritz. *Die Zauberflöte.* Wien, 1934.

Castelli, Ignaz von. *Memoiren meines Lebens.* Vol I. Wien, 1913.

Castelli, Ignaz von. *Aus dem Leben eines Wiener Phäaken.* Stuttgart, 1912.

Chailley, Jacques. "Die Symbolik in der Zauberflöte." *Mozart Jahrbuch.* Salzburg, 1968.

Chailley, Jacques. *La flûte enchantée, opéra maçonique.* Paris, 1975 (English transl. New York, 1982).

Cornet, Julius. *Die Oper in Deutschland und das Theater der Neuzeit.* Hamburg, 1849.

Dent, Edward J. *Mozart's Opera The Magic Flute.* Cambridge, 1911.

Dent, Edward J. *Mozarts Opern.* Berlin, 1922 (Originally published in English, London, 1913, rev. 1947).

Deutsch, Otto Erich. *Das Freihaustheater auf der Wieden, 1787–1801.* Wien, 1937.

Deutsch, Otto Erich. "Der rätselhafte Giesecke." *Musikforschung* V, 1952.

Deutsch, Otto Erich. "Schikaneders Testament" *Österreichische Musikzeitschrift* 18, 1963.

Dieckmann, Friedrich. "Der entlaufene Schneidersohn oder Wer schrieb die Zauberflöte?" *Oper, 1981.* Velber, 1981.

d'Elvert, Christian Ritter. *Geschichte des Theaters in Mähren und österreichisch Schlesien.* Brünn, 1852.

Endrös, Hermann. "Emanuel Schikaneder und das Augsburger Theater." *Augsburger Mozartbuch*, 1942/43.

Friedel, Johann. *Kleine und ungedruckte Schriften.* N.p., 1784.

Friedrich, Goetz. "Der Theatermann Schikaneder." *Theater der Zeit*, 11, Heft 9,10. Berlin, 1956.

Friedrich, Goetz. *Die Zauberflöte in der Inszenierung Walter Felsensteins an der Kom. Oper Berlin.* Berlin, 1958.

Gugitz, Gustav. *Alt-Wiener Thespiskarren.* Wien, 1925.

Gugitz, Gustav. "Johann Friedel." *Jahrbuch der Grillparzer Gesellschaft*, vol. 15. Wien, n.d.

Jahn, Otto. *W. A. Mozart.* Leipzig, 1865–1869.

Junk, Viktor. "Goethe und die Zauberflöte." *Wiener Figaro*, 10, October–November 1939.

Keim, Josef. *Woher stammt Schikaneder?* Augsburg, 1962.

Kierkegaard, Sören. *Entweder-Oder.* Köln, 1967.

Koch, Hans Albrecht. "Goethes Fortsetzung der Schikanederschen Zauberflöte." *Jahrbuch des Freien deutschen Hochstiftes.* Tübingen, 1969.

Komorzynski, Egon. *Emanuel Schikaneder.* Berlin, 1901.

Komorzynski, Egon. "Der Streit um den Text der Zauberflöte" *Alt-Wiener Kalender*, Wien, 1922.

Komorzynski, Egon. *Der Vater der Zauberflöte.* Wien, 1948.

Komorzynski, Egon. *Emanuel Schikaneder.* Wien, Wiesbaden, 1951.

Mettenleitner, Dominikus. *Musikgeschichte der Stadt Regensburg.* Regensburg, 1866.

Nettl, Paul. *Musik und Freimaurerei.* Esslingen, 1956.

Neukäufler, Jakob. *Aus dem Leben eines Wanderschauspielers.* Linz, 1930.

Neumann, Erich. "Archetypische Symbolik des Matriarchalischen und Patriarchalischen in der Zauberflöte." In: *W. A. Mozart, Die Zauberflöte.* Reinbek, 1982.

Perinet, Joachim. *Theatralischer Guckkasten.* Wien, 1807.

Perinet, Joachim. *Wiener Theater-Almanach.* Wien, 1803, 1804.

Pichler, Karoline. *Denkwürdigkeiten.* Wien, 1914.

Philipp, Hugo Wolfgang. *Die Urform der Zauberflöte.* Wiesbaden, 1949.

Realis (Coeckelberge von Dutzele, Gerhard). *Kuriositäten-Lexikon von Wien.* Wien, 1846.

Reichardt, Johann Friedrich. "Vertraute Briefe 1808–1809." *Denkwürdigkeiten aus Alt-Österreich* XV,XVI. München, 1915.

Richter, Josef. *Briefe eines Eipeldauers.* München, 1970.

Riehn, Rainer. "Die Zauberflöte." In: *Ist die Zauberflöte ein Machwerk?* München, 1978.

Rille, A. *Geschichte des Brünner Stadttheaters 1743 bis 1884.* Brünn, 1885.

Rommel, Otto. "Barock-Tradition auf dem Österreichisch-bayrischen Volkstheater." *Sammlung Deutscher Literatur*, vols I–VI. Leipzig, 1931.

Rommel, Otto. *Das parodistische Zauberspiel.* Leipzig, 1937.

Rommel, Otto. *Die Alt-Wiener Volkskomödie*. Wien, 1952.

Rosenberg, Alfons. *Die Zauberflöte*. München, 1964.

Schacherl, Lili. *Der Komödie-Karren*.

Schikaneder, Johann Karl. "Emanuel Schikaneder." *Der Gesellschafter* XVIII. Nos. 71–74. Berlin, 1843.

Schuh, Willi. "Il flauto magico. *Festschrift für F. Blume*. Kassel, 1963.

Schuh, Willi. "Gieseckes Handexemplar des Zauberflöte-Librettos." *Neue Zürcher Zeitung*, 28.4.1978, Foreign edition.

Senn, Walter. "Schikaneders Weg zum Theater." *Acta Mozartiana*. Vol. 9, Heft 3, 1962.

Skalicki, Wolfram. "Das Bühnenbild der Zauberflöte." *Maske und Kothurn* 2, Heft 1,2. Graz, Köln, 1956.

Spiel, Hilde. *Wien*. München, 1971.

Stieger. *Opernlexikon*. Tutzing, 1981.

Tietze, H. *Wien*. Wien, Leipzig, 1931.

Voll, Matthäus. *Chronol. Verzeichnis aller Schauspiele, Opern, Pantomimen. . . . , welche seit April 1794 bis 1807 i.d.k.k. Hoftheatern als auch in den k.k. priv. Schauspielhäusern aufgeführt wurden*. Wien, 1807.

Waldegg, Richard. *Sittengeschichte von Wien*. Stuttgart, 1965.

Weilen, Alexander von. *Geschichte des Wiener Theaterwesens. Das Theater Wiens*. Wien, 1899.

Wurzbach. Constant von. *Biogr. Lexikon des Kaiserthums Österreich*. Wien, 1875.

List of Illustrations, with Sources

Index of Persons